A COLLECTION OF

UNIDENTIFIED FLYING OBJECT PHENOMENA

A COLLECTION OF
UNIDENTIFIED FLYING OBJECT PHENOMENA

CLINTON LAIRD

Author Reputation Press LLC
45 Dan Road Suite 5
Canton MA 02021
www.authorreputationpress.com
Hotline: 1(800) 220-7660
Fax: 1(855) 752-6001

Ordering Information:
Quantity sales. Special discounts are available on quantity purchases by corporations, associations, and others. For details, contact the publisher at the address above.

Printed in the United States of America.

ISBN-13:   Softcover   978-1-64961-776-7
              eBook   978-1-64961-777-4
              Hardcover   978-1-64961-778-1

Library of Congress Control Number: 2021917548

Disclaimer

This book is based on a collection of articles from known and unknown authors for educational purposes. Any profit made from the sale of this book will go to charity or educational institutions. An effort to eliminate all information from articles proven to be false has been made however certain articles cannot be substantiated and the information is given for the reader can make their own decision.

Table of Contents

Preface

I have always had an interest in Unidentified Flying Objects (UFOs) starting when I was four years old. I remember hearing on the radio that a private pilot, Kenneth Arnold sighted nine UFOs flying near Mount Rainier in the State of Washington. I was visiting my older cousin in Seattle at that time, and I asked her what a UFO is? She replied "A flying object that is not an airplane, believed to be from outer Space". I then asked her, "What is Outer Space"? She replied, "Places in the universe that are far away from Earth".

When I was fifteen, I attended Riverside Military Academy in Gainesville, Georgia. On the second day of school, I was eating lunch in the school cafeteria when a teacher sat next to me at the head of the table, which was customary at a Military School. He was a rather good looking white male, about 30 years old, five feet 10 inches tall, well built, with light brown colored hair and blue eyes. He introduced himself as Charles Huntley. We started talking, and in the course of conversation, I mentioned that I was born in Hollywood, California, but raised in Carmel. He replied that he was very familiar with the city, and started talking about some of the town's features. I asked him where he was from, and he casually replied, "The Pleiades". I asked him if that was some town near our school here in Georgia. He said no, it was approximately 450 light years away from Earth! I said, "You mean that you were not born on this planet"? He replied, "Yes, I am not of this World". Being somewhat confused, I decided that it was time to leave for my classes It is not every day that you run into a person that claims that they are not of this World.!

I did not see Captain Huntley again for about a week or two until I received a promotion in rank at the school, and was assigned to Captain Huntley's hall. By this time, he was quite a conversation piece around the school campus. Not only did the students talk about him, but also the school faculty. In the afternoons, he was seen staring at the Sun with a pair of binoculars, giving him the name "Sun God" by the students. He also apparently demonstrated his ability of Extra Sensory Perception (ESP) to the students and faculty, but I had never witnessed it. Cadets said that he glowed in the dark. Some even said that they walked by his room and saw him lying in bed with objects levitating around his room at his dictation. To me these were all exaggerations, a kind of induced group hyperbole. I never saw any of these things the entire time I lived on his hall. He was very nice to me, though strange, but always very interesting. Nevertheless, none of us on his floor were going to walk down the hall after taps to use the bathroom, fearful of weird goings-on.

My physics instructor, Mr. Smith, was told that the school's founder and president, General Beaver had invited Captain Huntley to his house. Beaver told Huntley that he would have to prove his Psychic abilities once and for all. He said that he hid a $5 bill bearing his own signature somewhere in his mansion, and if he could not find it in a few minutes, that he would have to terminate the Captain's employment with the Academy. Captain Huntley walked directly into the library, reached for a book, and opened it to a specific page that contained the five dollar bill with General Beaver's signature.

Being assigned to his dorm floor for about a month or so, we had occasional conversations. He was a very spiritual man, and explained that the thing that people rarely spoke of UFOs, intuition, telepathy, psychometry, clairvoyance, precognition, etc., and had little knowledge of Egyptology. After 60 or so years, I do not remember most of these conversations. I do clearly remember that he told me that we had another Sun in our solar system, and that a pyramid in Arctic or Antarctica would soon be discovered along with secret chambers in Egypt's Great Pyramid of Giza. He said that if a person fasted, drinking only water for a few days, then went alone into the King's Chamber saying aloud, "Glory to Allah! There is no other God but God; Mohammed is His prophet, and I am one of his friends", that the spirts within the pyramid would reveal themselves.

October 5, 1959 was my 16th birthday. Captain Huntley said that he would be leaving the school for good the next day, traveling on a UFO. Sure enough, the next day he was gone. A few months later, I received a letter from him saying the he was now teaching at the Army and Navy Military

School in Carlsbad, California. His letter went into great detail about how the biblical Book of Genesis was misinterpreted. He claimed it was the history of the World. The names Cain, Abel, Noah, Abram, Sara, Isaac, Rebecca, Esau, Jacob, Ishmael, etc. was actually referring to Countries and not actual people. He used the biblical phase, "One day to God is one thousand years" in order to adjust the timelines, and somehow, he concluded that Genesis contained the history of the World. I never heard from the Sun God again. Looking back, he probably was dismissed from Riverside Military Academy because he became too much of a distraction. I personally feel that Captain Huntley was a guy suffering from some sort of mental disorder, but if he was an extraterrestrial, you could not find a better being. To this day in my imagination he is somewhere out there amid the stars, seeking the meaning and truths of life.

Chapter 1

Early History of UFOs

Early Egyptian and African Myths

Most of our information regarding early Egyptian creation myths comes from a collection of ancient Egyptian religious texts from the time of the Old Kingdom (2780 – 2250 B.C.E) known as the "Pyramid Texts". They are the oldest known religious texts in the world. Written in the old-style Egyptian, the Pyramid Texts were carved on the walls and sarcophagi of the pyramids at Saqqara during the 5th and 6th Dynasties.

Other important information regarding early Egypt comes from The Turin Papyrus, also called Turin Papyrus of Kings or the Turin Canon. These are hieratic manuscripts of the 19th dynasty (1292–1190 B.C.E.) which lists all the Pharaohs who ruled over Ancient Egypt from earliest times to the reign of Ramses II (1279–13 B.C.E.). Not only does this list include all of the 'official' historic Pharaohs of Ancient Egypt, but it also includes the deities or "Gods" who came from above and reigned over the lands of Egypt before the first mortal Pharaoh of Egypt, whose lineage spread over 13,000 years.

The Egyptian High Priest, Manetho (approximately 285–246 B.C.E), who had access to unlimited ancient texts from the Library of Alexandria, wrote for the Pharaoh the history of Ancient Egypt in 30 volumes. Manetho makes reference to the divine beings that ruled during Pre-Pharaonic Egypt.

According to Egyptian mythology, Akhenaten, a Pharaoh of the Eighteenth dynasty, ruled for 17 years and was the father of Tutankhamun. He was said to have descended from the gods who arrived on Earth at the time of Zep Tepi from the neighboring star, Sirius, and established the original Syrian-Egyptian civilization. According to the Pyramid Texts, "Zep Tepi" was a time of emergence from the earthly chaos, and the gods took control and ruled the earth. Many researchers believe that the ancient Egyptian civilization originated in the year 36.900 B.C.E, when gods came from the heavens, and ruled over the land of the Pharaohs.

Ancient Stele make reference to the Egyptian god Horus, suggesting that he was a physical ruler of the Egypt thousands of years ago. Another Egyptian god, Thoth, is said to have reigned over the lands of Egypt from 8670 to 7100 B.C.E.

Mainstream scholars consider these ancient texts as pure myth, and the reason why most details of the texts have been overlooked and omitted from the history books. However, Is there any physical evidence that Aliens, considered as gods from the star Sirius (the "Dog Star" in the constellation Canis Major), ruled Egypt and had offspring with humans?

There is one physical trait that appears in all the members of the Egyptian royals during the Armana epoch (latter half of the Eighteenth Dynasty 1550 BCE to 1292 BCE.). This royalty includes: King Tut (Tutankhamun); his father King Atkenaton; his mother Queen Nefertiti and their six female children; Rameses II and his (suspected) first son Amun-her-Khepeshef; and Tutankhamun's great-great-great-grandfather, Thutmosis III. All of these people had evidence of elongated skulls. Whether or not this was a genetic trait, or one forced on the royal members at birth is unknown. While the cranium appears extended at the rear, they do not show any evidence of artificial deformation, as with other ancient cultures from China, and Meso- and South America, where it was considered a look of beauty. Perhaps it is relevant that in the 1st Century, Egyptian priest-scribes, then keepers of the world's oldest known records, claimed that the earliest rulers of Egypt were non-humans.

In Ancient Egypt, Sirius was regarded as the most important star in the sky. In fact, it was astronomically the foundation of the Egyptians' entire religious system. It was revered as Sothis and was associated with Isis, the mother goddess of Egyptian mythology. Isis is the female aspect of the trinity formed by herself, Osiris and their son Horus.

Ancient Egyptians held Sirius in such a high regard that most of their deities were associated, in some way or another, with the star. Anubis, the dog-headed god of death, had an obvious connection with Sirius, the Dog Star. Toth-Hermes, the god who was the great teacher of humanity, was also connected with Sirius.

The Egyptian calendar system was based on the heliacal rising of Sirius that occurred just before the annual flooding of the Nile during summer. The star's celestial movement was also observed and revered by ancient Greeks, Sumerians, Babylonians and countless other civilizations, and notably, the Dogon tribe of West Africa, who are discussed later in this chapter.

The star was therefore considered sacred, and its apparition in the sky was accompanied with feasts and celebrations. The Dog Star heralded the coming of the hot and dry days of July and August, hence the popular term "the dog days of summer".

Several occult researchers have claimed that the Great Pyramid of Giza was built in perfect alignment with the stars, especially Sirius. The light from these stars was said to be used in ancient Egyptian ceremonies.

Paracas Skulls

Paracas is a desert peninsula located within the Pisco Province on the south coast of Peru. It is here were Peruvian archaeologist, Julio Tello, made an amazing discovery in 1928 – a massive and elaborate graveyard containing Incan tombs filled with the remains of individuals with the largest elongated skulls found anywhere in the world. These have come to be known as the ' Paracas skulls '. In total, Tello found more than 300 of these elongated skulls, which are believed to be over 3,000 years old.

DNA samples were taken from three of the elongated skulls for DNA testing. The samples consisted of hair and bone powder, which was extracted by drilling deeply into the foramen magnum. This process was used to reduce the risk of contamination. In addition, full protective clothing was worn. The samples were then sent to three separate labs for testing – one in Canada, and two in the United States. The geneticists were only told that the samples came from an ancient mummy, so as not to create any preconceived ideas.

From the samples, only the mitochondrial DNA (DNA from the mother's side) could be extracted. Out of four hair samples, one of them couldn't be sequenced. The remaining three hair samples all showed a Haplogroup H2A, a genetic population group which is found most frequently in Eastern Europe around the Caspian Sea, and at a lower frequency in Western Europe. The bone sample from the most elongated skull resulted in Haplogroup T2B, a group who originated in Mesopotamia, now Syria, and known as the original Syrian-Egyptian civilization. The results are also consistent with the fact that many of the Paracas skulls still contain traces of red hair, a color that is not natively found in South America, but originates in the Middle East and Europe.

Permission was obtained from the Peruvian government to do a second round of genetic testing on some of the skulls, working together with archaeologist, Ruben Soto. A total of 18 skulls, approximately 2,000 to 3,000 years old were sent. The DNA results from 12 of these came back from two separate labs, at Canada's Lakehead University and at UCLA in the U.S.

The DNA from four of the elongated skulls is from Haplogroup B, Native American ancestry, but the other eight were mostly from Haplogroup H, H1A, H2 and U2E. Mitochondrial Haplogroup H is predominantly found in Europe. Subclade H1 are found on the Iberian Peninsula and among the Tuareg Berbers of Libya. U2E is considered a European-specific Subclade of U2, which is an old lineage that emerged from the Caucasus Mountains region more than 50,000 years ago.

The mitochondrial DNA also, showed mutations that were unknown to any man, primate or animal found on planet Earth. The mutations present in the samples of the Paracas skulls suggest that researchers were dealing with a completely new 'human-like being,' very different from Homo sapiens, Neanderthals or Denisovans. The DNA testing programs can only compare sample DNA with those that are known, and those are held in a huge database culled from the Human Genome Project (2003), residing at Genentech in the U.S.

The DNA results show that Europe and the Middle East migrated to the Americas long before it is conventionally believed. The results also suggest that there might be a linkage with the elongated skulls of the ancient Egyptian royal family who are claimed to have been non-human, or a hybrid of alien/human breeding.

In the Bible, Genesis 6:1–4 talks about the Nephilim, who, are the offspring of the Fallen Angels and the women of earth, resulting in a hybrid entity, said to be based in the area of the Levant, the same place that the Paracas DNA traces to.

Dogon mythology

Other physical evidence that Aliens had arrived on Earth from Sirius can be found in Dogon creation mythology. Deeply-rooted traditions of the Dogon people of western Africa speak of the Nommos who visited from a companion star to Sirius. The Nommos are known as advanced beings that have also appeared in numerous related myths found in Sumerian and other Mesopotamian cultures.

Dogon mythology tells that the Nommos, a race of amphibious aliens, visited them on a very large star ship on several occasions. They are said to have "descended from the sky in a vessel accompanied by fire and thunder," and imparted profound knowledge to humans. They tell us the Nommos shared knowledge of Sirius with them and left behind several artifacts. They tell of a companion star in the Sirius star system which has a 50 year elliptical orbit, and is not visible to the naked eye. Modern astronomers did not know the companion star even existed until 1862.

One artifact depicting Sirius carbon dates to 400 years ago, a little over 230 years before astronomers suspected the existence of the companion white dwarf Known as Sirius B. The Dogon say this this star is composed of the heaviest metal in the Universe. The Dogon tribe further describes the existence of a third star in this binary star system, which has not yet been discovered by modern astronomers, and would be referred to as Sirius C. The Dogon say that this third star in the system has an orbiting planet that is the home of the Nommos. Every 50 years, the Dogon people celebrate the cycle of Sirius A and B. These ancient tribes, without the use of telescopes, have crafted artifacts that describe the Sirius star system more than 200 years before modern astronomers discovered Sirius B.

Amazingly, the Dogon people also knew of Saturn's rings, and the many moons of Jupiter.

Sirius, also known as the Dog Star, is found in the constellation α Canis Majoris (Alpha Canis Majoris), or Canicula. It is the single brightest star in the night sky, having an apparent magnitude of -1.44. In contrast, our Sun star has an apparent magnitude of -26.7. It is a binary star system composed of Sirius A and Sirius B, at a distance of 8.60 light years from Earth. Sirius is not the brightest star because it is more luminous than other visible stars, but because it is located so close to the solar system. It is the fifth closest star system to Earth and contains two of the eight nearest stars to Earth. Mainstream science does not consider the planets orbiting the Sirius star system to be a prime candidate for life.

Carl Sagan, the populist astronomer, concluded that the Dogon could not have acquired their knowledge without contact with an advanced technological civilization. He suggests that that civilization was terrestrial rather than extraterrestrial, however, and that this part of Western Africa has had many visitors from technological societies who passed through on the trade routes.

Although it is unclear, it cannot be dismissed that alien life from the vicinity of Sirius may have had contact with human life. As unreal as it sounds, we cannot dispute that ancient Egyptian and Dogon mythology firmly testify that god-like beings have been involved with humans here on Earth.

Aliens and Religion

The Bible was written over 2,000 years ago with the King James Version translation into English by the Church of England in 1011 CE. It is a collection of sacred scripture of both Judaism and Christianity. Christian Bibles include the books of the Hebrew Bible, but arranged in a different order: Jewish Scripture ends with the people of Israel restored to Jerusalem and the temple and the Christian arrangement ends with the book of the prophet Malachi. The Jewish Tanakh divides the Hebrew Bible into 24 books, while the same texts are usually arranged as 39 books in Christian Old Testaments. Complete Christian Bibles range from the 66 books of the Protestant Bible to the 81 books in the Ethiopian Orthodox Bible.

The Qur'an (Koran) is the religious text of Islam. All three religions worship the same God, Lord of the universe. The Qur'an assumes familiarity with major narratives recounted in Jewish and Christian scriptures, summarizing some, dwelling at length on others, and, in some cases, presenting alternative accounts and interpretations of events. Muslims believe that the Qur'an was repeatedly revealed from Allah to Muhammad verbally through the angel Jibrīl (Gabriel) over a period of approximately twenty-three years, beginning in 610 CE, when he was forty, and concluding in 632 CE, the year of his death. A lot has happened since the writing of the Qur'an or Bible. We now have automobiles; airplanes, televisions, radios, electricity, light bulbs and we can communicate with cell phones. A person trying to describe these items over 1,000 years ago in the Qur'an or Bible would explain them in terms of things of their known world and experience.

"Heaven" in both the Old and New Testaments of the Bible is mentioned 730 times. It is translated from Hebrew and Greek words that mean "the sky", or directly related to the sky. This is a different meaning than the Heaven that we often think of as an otherworldly realm in which people who have died continue to exist in an afterlife.

Clouds don't stop and hover for days, weeks, and months as in the Bible. To a person trying to describe, in Bible times, what we consider today a flying machine would use terms that they are familiar with like flying in a thick cloud. Thick clouds, swift clouds, bright clouds, dark clouds, white clouds, low clouds, great clouds, and fiery clouds are all referenced in the Bible, and quite possibly, all refer to a flying vehicle. The word pillar is translated from "ammuwd" meaning a column or base of column in other words a platform. Therefore, pillar of a cloud would mean a vehicle platform, or sky vehicle. The Hebrew word for "chariot" is "rekeb" of which one of the meanings is millstone, a thick disc-shaped object used in grinding grain. Platforms, vessels, whirling chariots of fire, sky thrones, fiery horses, cherubim, thick darkness, great fire, whirlwinds, fiery wheels, pavilions, dark waters, storms, sky dwellings, rolls, and sanctuaries refer to vehicles in the sky.

There are many reports of UFO in the Bible such as the Star of Bethlehem that guided the Wise men. Exodus tells the story of Moses leading the Jews from Egypt. God appears to Moses as a "burning bush" (Exodus 3). Later, during the exodus, Moses and the Jews are led by a "pillar of cloud" by day and a "pillar of fire" by night And while the Bible interprets this as God speaking to Moses leading the Jews, some theorists feel that the Biblical descriptions of fire and clouds are similar to some modern UFO descriptions. The pillars of clouds and fire shows up in subsequent books of the Old Testament as well, including in Exodus 40, Numbers 14:14, Deuteronomy 1:33, and Nehemiah 9:12 and 9:19

Other descriptions in the Book of Exodus tell of Moses being carried to a mountain in a cloud (24:18), and of God descending in a cloud (34:5), which some interpret as the appearance of an Alien with a UFO. Many other references to clouds behaving in oddly specific manners (such as guiding people, carrying people, arising from the sea, bringing messengers from God, and more) also exist throughout the Old Testament that are very different from how one might observe the patterns of clouds today.

Exodus 13:21 states, "And the Lord went before them by day in a pillar of a cloud, to lead them the way; and by night in a pillar of fire, to give them light; to go by day and night." In all cases, the literal translation from Hebrew for the pillar of cloud and the pillar of fire remains the same. The word for pillar is ammuwd "aw-mood" meaning a solid, cylindrical object. The word for cloud is anan, "aw-nawn", and it means cloud. It has been documented that cigar-shaped UFOs often surround themselves with a cloud. The word for fire is "'esh", or "aysh", which means flaming, or in this case, a glowing object. This is how it would have been reported today: "The Cigar-Shaped UFO Was a Dark Cloud by Day and a Glowing Object by Night."

Exodus 13:22 says, "He took not away the pillar of the cloud by day, nor the pillar of fire by night, from before the people."

Exodus 14:19, "And the angel of God, which went before the camp of Israel, removed and went behind them; and the pillar of the cloud went from before their face, and stood behind them.

What is significant about this passage of the Old Testament is that it indicates that the "Angel of God" was operating this mysterious object. This particular angel was given a formal name In the Hebrew text, He was called Malak, ("mal-awk"). This means a messenger specifically sent by God, who was dispatched to protect the Israelites.

Exodus 14:24 "And it came to pass, that in the morning watch the Lord looked unto the host of the Egyptians through the pillar of fire and of the cloud, and troubled the host of the Egyptians."

Exodus 33:9 "And it came to pass, as Moses entered into the tabernacle, the cloudy pillar descended, and stood at the door of the tabernacle, and the Lord talked with Moses."

Exodus 34:5 "And the Lord descended in the cloud, and stood with him there, and proclaimed the name of the Lord."

Numbers 12:5 "And the Lord came down in the pillar of the cloud, and stood in the door of the tabernacle, and called Aaron and Miriam and they both came forth."

Who was Moses?

The Bible and the Koran speak of Moses being born in Egypt, brought up in the pharaonic royal palace, and leading the Israelites in their flight to Canaan. In historical terms, when did Moses live, and who was the "Pharaoh of Oppression"? These questions have bewildered scholars for centuries. An analysis of historical events will show that King Tut's father Egyptian King Akhenaten and Biblical Moses could be the same person.

While little is known about Moses and the Egyptian pharaoh Akhenaten background knowledge of both men is helpful to our understanding. Moses is said to have been born about 1400 BCE which closely matches Akhenaten's birth in 1427 BCE. The Bible was written by man inspired by God. The orthodox evangelicals believe that every word in the Bible is God's words, and that Moses was Akhenaten's adoptive son (King Tut's adoptive brother). Non-religious people would say that Moses never existed at all, and the whole story is a fictitious tale.

Modern scholars believe that the story of the Exodus has some historical core, but the Bible was never intended primarily as a historical document, and contains little that is accurate or reliable. In the following article below, Mr. Ahmed Osman takes the middle view that the Bible tales were given to man through a dream, and like all dreams, might contain inaccurate details, while remaining true to the historical influences. This makes Moses the Egyptian pharaoh Akhenaten. His Biblical father Amram was pharaoh Amenhotep III, Biblical mother Jochebed was the Egyptian Tiye, and Biblical brother Aaron the Egyptian Crown Prince Thutmosis. Akhenaten's only brother, Thutmosis, was older and traditionally, heir to the throne. Moses had only one brother Aaron, who was older. The Bible says Moses was raised as a brother to the heir of the throne. Prince Thutmosis served as a priest. The Bibles says that Moses brother Aaron was also a priest. Both Moses and Akhenaten were born in the same region with similar birth dates.

Being sympathetic to the plight of the slave workers, Crown Prince Thutmosis was expelled from the pharaoh's court and disappeared. Nothing further is known about him, but it is believed that he had been kidnapped and assassinated by the Amun priests. His sarcophagus was never used. Most of what we know about Prince Thutmosis comes from the inscriptions on the limestone sarcophagus of his cat, Ta-miu (she-cat), now on display at the Cairo Museum. Many scholars believe that the Egyptian Crown Prince Thutmosis was, in fact, the biblical Moses.

There is physical evidence that Moses' brother Aaron is the same person as Akhenaten's brother Thutmosis. Upon Aaron's death, his body was buried at Petra in Jordan, according to the Bible. Some believe he was buried atop Aaron's Mountain (Jabaal Harun) in Petra, but this is only a possible grave site, and is not accepted by many religious scholars. In the early 1800s, two British explorers in Petra discovered an Egyptian staff (walking stick) was found at another possible grave site in a cave at Petra. This grave was empty, but it is believed to have contained the body of a person in very high social standing. The staff was purchased by a British collector, and later acquired by the Birmingham Museum where it is now on display in the Egyptian gallery. The staff had the inscription, written in ancient Egyptian, "Thutmosis a person High in the Pharaohs Court" which could only be Akhenaten's brother, Thutmosis. If this is the actual grave site of Moses' brother Aaron, it would prove that Aaron and Thutmosis are one in the same.

The following article comes from "Moses and Akhenaten: The Secret History of Egypt at the Time of the Exodus" by Ahmed Osman, October 1, 2002:

"Akhenaten was born in Year 12 of his father Amenhotep III's rule, 1394 BCE, in the summer royal palace in the border city of Zarw in northern

Sinai. Zarw, modern Kantara East, was the center of the land of Goshen where the Israelites dwelt, and in the same location where Moses was born. Contrary to the biblical account, Moses was born inside the royal palace. His mother Queen Tiye had an elder son, Thutmosis, who died a short time before Akhenaten's birth. Thutmosis had been educated and trained at the royal residence in Memphis, before he mysteriously disappeared, believed to have been kidnapped and assassinated by the Amun priests. Fearing for his safety, his mother Tiye sent Akhenaten by water to the safekeeping of her father's Israelite family outside the walls of Zarw, which was the origin of the baby-in-the-bulrushes story.

The reason for the priests' hostility to the young prince was the fact that Tiye, his mother, was not the legitimate heiress to the throne. She couldn't therefore be accepted as a consort for the state god Amun. If Tiye's son acceded to the throne, this would be regarded as forming a new dynasty of non-Amunite kings over Egypt. During his early years, his mother kept Akhenaten away from both royal residences at Memphis and Thebes. He spent his childhood at the border city of Zarw, nursed by the wife of the queen's younger brother General Aye. Later, Akhenaten was moved to Heliopolis, north of Cairo, to receive his education under the supervision of Anen the priest of Ra, who was the elder brother of Queen Tiye.

Young Akhenaten appeared at the capital city Thebes, for the first time, when he reached the age of sixteen. There he met with Nefertiti, his half sister daughter of Sitamun, for the first time and fell in love with her. Tiye, his mother, encouraged this relationship realizing that his marriage to Nefertiti, the heiress, is the only way he can gain the right to follow his father on the throne.

Following his marriage to Nefertiti, Amenhotep decided to make Akhenaten his co-regent, which upset the priests of Amun. The conflict between Amenhotep and the priests had started sixteen years earlier, as a result of his marriage to Tiye, daughter of Yuya and Tuya. On his accession to the throne as co-regent, Akhenaten took the name of Amenhotep IV. At Thebes, during the early years of his co-regency, Nefertiti was active in supporting her husband and became more prominent than Akhenaten in official occasions, as well as on all monuments.

However, the climate of hostility that surrounded Akhenaten at the time of his birth surfaced again after his appointment as co-regent. The Amun priesthood opposed this appointment, and openly challenged Amenhotep III's decision.

When the Amun priests objected to his appointment, Akhenaten responded by building temples to his new God, Aten. He built three temples for Aten, one at the back end of the Carnac complex, the other at Luxor near the Nile bank, and the third at Memphis. Akhenaten snubbed the Amun priests by not inviting them to any of the festivities. In the early part of his co-regency, and in his fourth year when he celebrated his sed festival jubilee, he banned all deities but his own God from the occasion. Twelve months later he made a further break with tradition by changing his name to Akhenaten in honor of his new deity. To the resentful Egyptian establishment Aten was seen as a challenger who would replace the powerful state god Amun and not come under his domination. In the tense climate that prevailed, Tiye arranged a compromise by persuading her son to leave Thebes and establish a new capital at Armana.

The situation calmed down, following Akhenaten's departure, while Amenhotep ruled alone in Thebes. For building his new city at Amarna, Akhenaten chose a land that belonged to no god or goddess. The building started in his Year 4 and ended in Year 8. He and his family moved from Thebes to Amarna in Year 6. Here Akhenaten built his new capital where he and his followers could be free to worship their God. Akhenaten conceived of a single controlling intelligence, above all beings including the gods. The king and queen were the major figures in the cult of Aten, whose festivals they celebrated with the local people with music, chanting, offering of fruits and flowers, and rituals in the open air.

Following the death of his father, Amenhotep III, he organized a great celebration at Amarna in his Year 12, for foreign princes bearing tribute because of his assumption of sole rule.. It was then that the king decided to abolish the worship of all gods in Egypt, except Aten. Akhenaten gave orders to his troops instructing them to close all the temples, confiscate its estates, and sack the priests, leaving only Aten's temples throughout the country. Units were dispatched to excise the names of the ancient gods wherever they were found written or engraved, a course that can only have created mounting opposition to his already rejected authority. This persecution entailed the closing of the temples, confiscating property, and the dispatch of artisans who entered everywhere to hack out the names of the deities from inscriptions. The excommunication of Amun's name was supervised by the army. Each time a squad of workmen entered a temple or tomb to destroy the name of Amun, it was supported by a squad of soldiers who came to see that the royal decree was carried out to the fullest.

The military garrison at Amarna had detachments of Sinai Bedouins and foreign auxiliaries, in addition to Egyptian units. The loyalty of the army to Akhenaten was assured by its commander, Aye, his uncle, who held posts among the highest in the military.

The persecution of the old gods, however, proved to be hateful to the majority of Egyptians, including members of the army. Ultimately the harshness of the persecution had a certain reaction upon the soldiers who, themselves, had been raised in the old beliefs. After all, the officers and soldiers themselves believed in the same gods whose images the king ordered them to destroy. They worshipped in the very temples which they were ordered to close. A conflict arose between the king and his army. Akhenaten's belief in one God, however, was too deep for him to allow any compromise with the priests. Horemheb, Pa-Ramses and Seti, planned a military coup against the king, and ordered their troops from the north and south to move towards Amarna. Aye, who received news of the troops' movements, brought his chariots to guard Amarna. When the army and chariots came face to face at Amarna's borders, Aye advised the king to abdicate the throne to his son Tutankhaten, in order to save the dynasty. Akhenaten agreed to abdicate and left Amarna with Pa-Nehesy, the high priest of Aten, and few of his followers to live in exile in area of Sarabit El-Khadem in southern Sinai.

On hearing about Horemheb's death, Akhenaten decided to leave his exile in Sinai and come back to Egypt, in order to reclaim his throne. Since his abdication, he had been living in exile in southern Sinai, with few of his followers, for about twenty five years, during the reigns of Tutankhamun, Aye, and Horemheb. Here, Akhenaten lived among the Shasu (Midianites Bedouins with whom he formed an alliance.

In his rough Bedouin cloths, Akhenaten arrived at Pa-Ramses' residence in the border city of Zarw, his birthplace that had been turned into a prison for his followers. General Pa-Ramses, by now an old man, was making arrangements for his coronation, and getting ready to become the first ruler of a new 19th Ramesside dynasty, when he was informed of

Akhenaten's arrival. Akhenaten challenged Pa-Ramses' right to the throne. The general, taken by surprise, decided to call a meeting of the wise men of Egypt to decide between them. At the gathering Akhenaten produced his scepter of royal power, which he had taken with him to exile, and performed some secret rituals, which only the king had the knowledge of. Once they saw the scepter of royal authority and Akhenaten's performance of the rituals, the wise men fell down in adoration in front of him, and declared him to be the legitimate king of Egypt. Ramses, however, who was in control of the army, refused to accept the wise men's verdict and decided to establish his rule by force.

When Akhenaten realized that his life was threatened by Rameses, he escaped from Zarw with some of his followers during the night, and rejoined his Shasu allies in Sinai. However, he refused to accept defeat and decided to carry on challenging Ramses' right to rule Egypt. Akhenaten gathered his Shasu allies in Sinai, and decided to cross the borders of Egypt into Canaan (a region approximating present-day Israel), where he could establish his rule in foreign parts of the Egyptian empire, in order to prepare an army to allow him to return and challenge Ramses. When Ramses got knowledge of Akhenaten's plan, he decided to go out at the head of his army and crush the Bedouin power before they crosses the borders to Canaan. Rameses, however, died at this moment and was followed by his son Seti I.

Seti left the body of his father for the priests to mummify, and went out to chase Akhenaten and his Shasu followers in northern Sinai. After setting out on the route between the fortified city of Zarw and Gaza and passing the fortified water stations, pushing along the road in the Negev, the king scattered the Shasu who from time to time gathered in sufficient numbers to meet him. A military confrontation took place in the very first days of Seti I, on the route between Zarw and Gaza in Canaan. Just across the Egyptian border he arrived at the fortified town of Pe-Kanan, (Gaza), and stopped the Shasu entering it

Ezekiel's Wheel within Wheel

Ezekiel a priest about the year 600 BCE would be emboldened by the story of Moses and the Tabernacle. Scholars not having lived in the time period do not know all the Bible's meanings. There is no original manuscript of the Bible. As Hebrew and Greek were the original languages of the Bible, like all languages, some idioms and concepts were not easily translated.

To Ezekiel in referring to the orientation of an object like left, right, front, or back, he most likely would use the Biblical terms that he was most familiar with, such as from the Tabernacle. According to rabbinical tradition about 1,350 BCE Hebrew tribes were driven out of Egypt. They based themselves at Mount Sinai, where Moses received the Ten Commandments. A portable dwelling was built to specifications of God known as the Tabernacle. The twelve Hebrew Tribes were told by God to camp around the Tabernacle holding the banners of their family known as the Camps. To the east there was Judah with the banner of a lion in gold with a bright orange-tinged red color backdrop. To the South there was Reuben with a banner of a man against the background of gold. To the west there was Ephraim with the banner of an ox in black over a backdrop of gold. To the north there was Dan with the banner of an eagle of gold against a Blue backdrop. Thus to the right side referred to a lion, to the back side referred man, to the left side referred to ox, and to the front side referred eagle. These symbols were used similar to how we use the orientation of a ship port side, starboard side, bow, and Stern. Note that this refers to the craft and not the Cardinal Points of a compass (North, East, South or West) or the direction a person is facing. The Bible was written and translated by people that were not familiar with the modern machines of today, including airplanes. The Biblical Prophet, Ezekiel, presumed "Living Creatures" were alive since they could fly through the air and do things only living creatures were capable of doing in his time period. Therefore, "Living Creatures" might be referring to a UFO controlled by a living creature, a pilot. Presuming that he considered that a UFO was alive, he might be describing the undercarriage of a landing system which includes a landing strut (a structural platform that is pivoted on one side) in which he calls a wing, landing gear doors, and bracing. A "face" has many definitions of which one is a "surface".

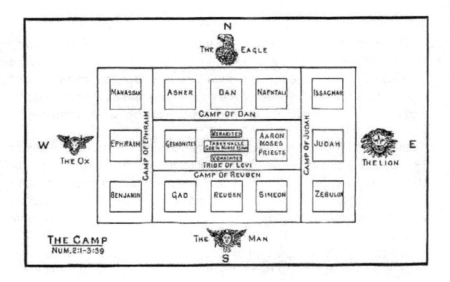

With all the above in mind, the Bible gives us a good description of what one of these flying vehicles looks like in the Book of Ezekiel where Ezekiel describes four Living Creatures called "Cherubim.

Paraphrasing, this is my interpretation of the Bible's Ezekiel 1:4 to 1:26:

1:4 And I looked, and, a whirlwind came out of the north, a great cloud, and a fire enfolding itself, and a brightness was about it, and out of the midst thereof as the color of orange-yellow, out of the midst of the fire.

1-5 Also out of the midst thereof came the look of four flying machines. And this was their appearance; the pilots had the look of a man.

1-6 And every flying vehicle had four cowling surfaces, and every vehicle had four landing gears.

1-7 And their end of landing gear legs were straight legs; and the bottom of the foot was like a round footpad: and they glow like the color of polished brass.

1- 8 And the flying machines had struts under their four landing gear on each side; and the flying machines each had the cowling surfaces and their four landing gears.

1-9 Their four landing gears were pulled up; the flying machines did not turn when they flew; the flying machines all flew straight forward.

1-10 As for the look of the surfaces, the four flying machines each the stern side on one surface, and the starboard side on one surface, on the right side: and the four flying machines each had port side on the surface on the left side; the four flying machines each also had the stern side on the surface.

1-11 Thus were the cowlings surfaces: and the flying vehicles four landing gears were extended upward retracted into the flying vehicle; a landing gear of each flying vehicle were joined one to another or adjacent to each other (Note: This would be on the right side under the cowlings with the image of a man and lion), and two landing gears covered the flying vehicles bodies (This would be under the cowling on the left side with an image of an ox and the under the cowling with the image of an eagle.)

1-12 And all the flying vehicles flew straight forward: as directed by the pilot (spirit), the flying vehicles flew; and the flying vehicles did not turn when the flying vehicles flew.

1-13 As for the looks of the flying vehicles, their appearance was dark grey with a bright red aura, and like the appearance of lamps: the red aura went up and down among the flying machines; and the aura was bright, and out of the aura came lightning.

1-14 And the flying machines maneuvered as the appearance of a flash of lightning.

1-15 Now as I observe the flying machines, I observe one flying machine landed by the flying machines, with cowlings in flying position.

1-16 The appearance of the flying machines and their performance was white lacking color: and the four flying machines had one look: and their appearance and performance was as the flying machines were a wheel in the middle of a wheel.

1-17 When the flying machines flew through the air, they flew through the air tilted on their sides: and the flying machines did not turn when they flew through the air.

1-18 As for the flying machines rings, they were so overhead that they were frightful; and their rings were full of portholes which surround the circumference of the four flying machines.

1-19 And in the departure of the flying machines, the flying machines go in formation, and in the flying machines ascend from off the ground, ascended are the flying machines.

1-20 To whatever place the pilot was to go, the flying machines flew, to that place the flying machine pilot was to go; and the wheels ascended alongside everyone: for the pilot of the flying machine was in the flying machines.

1-21 When that flew, this flew; and when that landed, this landed; and when that ascended from the earth, the flying machines ascended alongside everyone: for the pilot of the flying machine was in the flying machines.

1-22 And the look of the dome on the upper surfaces of the flying machines was frightening transparent, extended on over above the flying machines upper surface.

1-23 And under the transparent dome the flying machines inside hinged structural platforms were extended out straight, one toward another; and each flying machine had two hinged structural platforms covering its physical structure.

1-24 And when the flying vehicles flew, I heard the noise of their vehicles, like the noise of a lot of water, as the sound of the all-powerful, the sound of conversation, as the clutter of multitude people: when the flying machines landed, the flying machines let down their landing gear.

1-25 And there was a voice from the second story that was over the vehicles retractable floor upper surfaces, when the flying machines landed, and had let down the landing gear.

1-26 And above the second story that was over the vehicles retractable floor upper surfaces was the look of a pilot's seat, as the look of a brilliant blue color: and on the look of a pilot's seat was the look as the form of a man sitting on it.

The fact that the Bible describes the objects as in the sky and how they fly reinforces the physical nature of these vehicles. They descend and land on the ground, they ascend and takeoff from the ground, they hover above the ground, and that they travel swiftly in flight shows that they are aerial vehicles. These flight traits also show that these vehicles are under control while in flight and not actual clouds, whirlwinds, or storms. Since a being speak out of the object it implies that the vehicle is a controlled by a being or pilot. Therefore a person could conclude with a fare degree of certainty that flying machines in the Bible called "Cherubim" are the same thing that we refer to as UFOs today.

The Bible gives many examples of angels appearing in flying vehicles or on solid ground. Using hundreds of verses as evidence, we can determine the following: The Gods and divine beings of the Bible travel in rapidly flying, glowing, flashing, spinning, metallic objects, which appear dark and solid, like low clouds in daylight, while brightly lit, with projected beams of light at night. These objects descend to the ground, ascend into the sky, and hover above the ground for long periods. Sounds are broadcast from them, and they exhibit advanced knowledge that appear to alter the natural laws of science. Humans and other beings are described as ascending up into and descending down from these objects and perception of time is altered. In many of the world's ancient writings those beings called gods commonly fly in objects with very similar descriptions to those in the Bible.

An angel is "an ethereal being found in many religions, whose duties are to assist and serve God". Angels are the deputies and messengers of God. They are the most physically present of the spiritual beings in the eternal world of the God. They are protectors of the God and mankind. They are not gods. The images that we know today as angels were based on the imagination of painters and sculptors of long ago. They are depicted as having bird-like wings, soft and beautiful features, perfect blonde hair, and lily-white skin, gentle in nature, crowned with a halo, strumming a harp, and standing on a cloud, or flying amongst the clouds. Such descriptions are nowhere to be found in scripture. With centuries of conditioning, the image of what angels "should" look like is firmly ingrained in the human mind. What is important to consider is that the image of angels was determined by artists and the nature of angels was taken from tradition, not scripture.

The Bible refers to flying machines as "Living Creatures" and "Cherubim". Seraphim and Beasts are described in a manner that indicates they may also be devices or machines. The beings flying of these vehicles are God, angels and perhaps modern day men. Does Satan or the devils also fly in these machines? The 12th chapter of Revelation contains the description of a woman giving birth to a child, who Satan attempts to kill. He fails, is engaged in battle by the forces of the Archangel Michael and is defeated, and "cast" to the Earth with his angels. (Revelation 12:7) "And there was war in heaven: Michael and his angels fought against the dragon; and the dragon fought and his angels prevailed not; neither was their place found any more in heaven. And the great dragon was cast out, that old serpent, called the Devil, and Satan, which deceiveth the whole world: he was cast out into the earth, and his angels were cast out with him." Therefore the Bible tells us that Satan, the Devil and his angles have not been flying around in our modern skies since the birth of Christ. In verse 8, the phrase "neither was their place found any more in heaven" show that this condition is permanent.

For almost 2000 years after the last book of the Bible was written, there were no forms of artificial light. The only lights known were the sun, the moon, stars, fire, lightning, and reflections from those sources. It is not surprising that these sources are what the authors used to describe the illumination appearing from these vehicles and the beings associated with them. In Exodus 13:21 "And the Lord went before them by day in a pillar of a cloud, to lead them the way; and by night in a pillar of fire, to give them light; to go by day and night".

Translates "The Lord 'Yahweh' lead the nation of Israel out of Egypt by day in a UFO and by night by a brightly luminous red or orange UFO, for they could travel day and night."

The fact that the authors wrote about the flight routine of these objects is evidence that they have a distinct physical presence. Also, note the fact that UFOs do not appear without The Lord "Yahweh" himself or his ambassadors clearly described as directing these flying objects.

The same characteristics described in the Bible and many other ancient writings are used to describe UFO sightings throughout our history, right up to our modern era. In our skies today, we see the same incredible high tech flying craft, with the same flight characteristics, and the same advanced technology. The only difference is that in the Bible and in other ancient writings they were clearly identified as the flying vehicles that the gods used for transportation. In our modern age they are called "unidentified flying objects", presumably piloted by aliens. Modern UFOs are the same flying vehicles controlled by the same beings that flew in ancient times. Gods and angels that were associated with the ancient record are the same beings reported in our modern age. Now they are called aliens or extraterrestrials. The difference is in name only.

For thousands of years people, all over the world, have reported direct contact with occupants of high-tech flying objects. Only in recent times has there been any consideration that they are a threat to mankind. Fear that UFOs might enslave the world and steal the Earth's resources or even worst use people as fuel and eat them. Fears of the unknown not because UFOs have become more aggressive or that they have interfered with the flow of human conduct caused this. UFO abductions are sometimes used to prove evil intent, yet, less than 1% of all reported UFOs involve communication or direct contact with occupants. Only a few of these claim to be an actual abduction or being taken aboard. No one has ever been able to prove conclusively that they were victims of an obtrusive or violent encounter.

Where is Heaven

To maintain a fleet of UFOs or Cherubim requires many personnel and a base of operations. You need to be able to manufacture the vehicles, mechanics for repair and service, and fuel to operate them. Food is essential for everyone involved in such operations.

If you take the Bible at its word, UFOs (or Cherubim) supplied the food to feed the people of Israel for forty years when they fled from Egypt in the time of Moses. All of this requires a large base, with many people to operate from, but no base can be found. So you have to take the words from God through the reading of the Bible.

A fleet of flying vehicles, described as the army or Hosts of God (Yahweh), appears several times in the Bible. Psalms 68:17 "The chariots of God are twenty thousand, even thousands of angels: the Lord is among them." Hebrew for chariot is "Merkabah" meaning The Heavenly Throne. The

Hebrew dictionary defines Merkabah as "the conception of Yahweh riding upon cherubim."

The Bible describes this personnel in military terms, such as encampment (Gen.32:1-2), command structure (Ps.91:11-12; Matt.13:41; Rev.7:2), and combat (Jdg.5:20; Job 19:12; Rev.12:7). Its specific hierarchy differs slightly from the Hierarchy of Angels as it surrounds more military services, whereas the Hierarchy of angels is a division of angels into non-military services to God. These fleet and personnel claim that they come from heaven but where is heaven? The Bible distinguishes at least three uses of the word "heaven". The first can be found in Genesis 1:8 and 20, and refers to the atmosphere over the earth in which birds fly. The second, mentioned in Genesis 1:14, is the setting for the celestial lights, later identified (Genesis 1:16) as the sun, moon and stars. And the third heaven is where God is (2 Corinthians 12:1-5). So:

First heaven is the earth's atmosphere or the air.

Second heaven is in space, the universe.

Third heaven is Paradise and being where God is.

Where is the third heaven or paradise located? Our universe is a rather complicated place, and we don't know for sure where (or if) heaven is located. The Bible is very explicit that heaven is a real place. It is the place where God dwells in the sense of manifesting himself, appearing to the angels and apparently to those who have died trusting in the Lord and have gone to be with him (our great retirement home in the sky). It is not the same thing as our atmosphere heaven or the outer space heaven. It is once called the "third heaven," apparently to distinguish it from these other two. So let us look at the possible places of where the third heaven or paradise can be located.

Sky Model

Basically the idea is that the sky is some kind of a roof over our heads, and that angels come down through holes, either flying down to Earth's surface, or lowering a ladder or something of that sort. I don't think there is too much question that people have maintained that view, and it certainly is common today to find theologians saying that's what the Bible teaches.

Dimensional Model

To understand this model we have to go into the world of theoretical physicists Stephen Hawking and Edward Witte to examine particle physics, an attempt to reconcile quantum mechanics and general relativity. This is known as the theory of everything, and describes the interaction with one another of fundamental forces or interactive forces and matter in a mathematically complete system.

The fundamental forces are the simplest particles in the universe and the basic building blocks from which all other particles are made. They have no substructure. The four known fundamental interactions, all of which are a force applied to an object by another body that is not in direct contact with it. They are: electromagnetism (the force that causes the interaction between electrically charged particles); strong interaction (the force that binds protons and neutrons together to form the nucleus of an atom); weak interaction (the force that holds the neutron together and causes radioactive beta-decay); and gravitation (the mutual force of attraction between all particles or bodies that have mass).

The atom, long believed to be the smallest building block of matter, consists of even smaller components called protons, neutrons and electrons. Protons and neutrons are themselves made up of even smaller particles called quarks. Quantum theory is the set of rules that describes the interactions of these particles. All these particles, and all of the forms of energy in the universe, could be constructed by hypothetical one-dimensional, infinitely small building-blocks that have only the dimension of length, but not height or width. In theoretical physics, these building blocks are thought to be "1-dimensional slices of a 2-dimensional membrane vibrating in 11-dimensional space". These building blocks are thought to vibrate in multiple dimensions, and depending on how they vibrate they might be seen in 3-dimensional space as matter, light, or the effect of gravity. It is the vibration of the building blocks which determines whether it appears to be matter or energy, and every form of matter or energy is the result of the vibration of these building blocks.

We are familiar with height, width, and length as three dimensional space and time gives a total of four observable dimensions. However, the universe is made up of multiple dimensions. These building blocks of matter supported the possibility of 11 dimensions based on various observations of the fundamental forces or interactive forces, and matter.

What does an 11 dimensional universe look like? To us it can look as confusing, chaotic, or nonexistent, etc. This is because we cannot see or even know it is there. An example is your "being" or "soul". For all practical reasoning, and within the rules of accepted science, your soul does not exist. Your logic about your soul's existence is totally confusing, chaotic, and only points to the fact that your soul or being does not exist, but you reason that this logic is wrong because you do exist. This is an example of just one of these dimensions. The other dimensions, according theoretical physics, support a "multiverse" or many universes, in addition to our known universe. Here, each universe takes the form of a D-brane (Dirichlet membrane), which is the notion that "Strings" can attach and loosen, as String Theory prescribes. Objects in each universe are essentially confined to the D-brane of their universe, but may be able to interact with other universes via gravity, a force which is not restricted to D-branes."

Having multiple dimensions, the universes could quite literally occupy the same space, but because the rules, constants, and variables of nature may be different, we cannot see it or interact with it. Nevertheless, it is there, and it would occupy and make up the same space that we exist in. That could mean that you might be sitting here reading this article, and in this other universe, a motorcycle rider might be driving right through your same space, but you wouldn't hear or feel a thing!

One of these universes could be the Third Heaven. It is all around us, but has a different set of forces that don't interact with our known forces, and at least no with any of our sensory apparatus. If a person wanted to go from one universe to another, that person would need to have some sort of switch, some way of turning the interaction between our world and the other on and off, so they can become visible or invisible to us. This "switch" is dimensional, one that we cannot see or even know it is there. To us it may not even exist, except within the limitations of our brain.

Moving in and out of the three-dimensional space makes an object first visible, and then invisible, to beings who are confined in that space. Moving out and then back into the three-dimensional space makes a traveler able, and then unable to see the larger dimensional space outside. This model has invisibility built in. There is always this dimension into which we cannot see, move, or visualize. UFOs, as well as people, have been reported to move in and out of our three-dimensional space. This has not only been reported in the Bible, but by testimony from people throughout history. This model offers a possible way as to how this is achieved.

Another questionable facet of accepted Biblical doctrine is the Holy Spirit as an individual member of a supreme triad. Is the Holy Spirit or Holy Ghost, a being, a spiritual force, or perhaps the vibrations in 11-dimensional space that Dr. Kaku refers to as, "The mind of God".

Deep Space Model

In this view, heaven is beyond the stars, beyond the galaxies, perhaps beyond the universe, millions or billions of light years away. As man has gone out into space, inching farther into the void, and has not seen any obvious evidence of God, angels, or UFOs. It appears that UFOs or Cherubim obey the laws of nature and are restricted to the maximum speed of light. The nearest solar system to our earth is about 6 light years away. This would mean that it would take a minimum of 12 years to fly round trip to Earth if UFOs or Cherubim could fly at the speed of light, which is unlikely. This way-out model therefore has what we might call a transport problem. From the biblical accounts in general, it appears that the contact between heaven and earth is quite rapid. It doesn't seem to be something that takes a long time -- "today, you will be with me in Paradise." We could say, "Oh, well, God has no problem with instantaneous transport.

In Albert Einstein's theory of space and time, the two combine as a single entity called "space-time." We treat space-time as a smooth fabric which is distorted by the presence of energy. What's happening is simply that the distance between any two points in the Universe is changing according to a particular set of rules in the context of General Relativity. If you were able to reduce the distance between any two points by some force, an object traveling between the two points would appear to be traveling greater than the speed of light The more force you were able to apply to the distance between the two points would decrease to almost nothing.

Using this concept of a nuclear strong force gravity modifier (see Chapter 3), if enough force was applied, a space craft could travel from one point in our Universe to any other point in our universe, instantaneously. This force is produced by creating antimatter in order to release the strong force that holds element 115 together. All this happens on the microscopic level. In other words, at a small distance ahead of the craft in the direction of travel, the distance of travel would be reduced causing the craft to move forward, similar to being sucked by a vacuum. Once the craft moves forward, the process would repeat itself.

There is one type of extraterrestrial being that fits all the criteria of the Biblical angels, and they are the "Nordics". They are named so, because they look like Norse Gods - blonde with brilliant blue eyes, fair complexion, and having the bodies of tall, finely-toned athletes.

The "Greys", on the other hand, are extraterrestrial beings who get a lot of attention when it comes to alien sightings. Their appearance is short of stature, wrinkled gray skin, and having the iconic large black eyes, which is the main feature of their face.

The Nordics are a species that come into contact with humans almost as much as the Greys, but they are more interested in the well-being of the human race and religion than the Greys. Some eyewitness reports claim to have seen Nordics in the same alien craft as Greys. A possible explanation for this is that those Greys were slaves or servants to the Nordics. If the Nordic ETs are in fact the biblical angels, and Heaven is where they come from, then Biblical Heaven is located in Pleiades Star cluster.

Chapter 2

Brief UFO History

UFO History to 1947

UFOs have been seen from Earth as long as there have been people to record them. While there is no written record of prehistoric UFOs, there are plenty of pictographs, petroglyphs, and other forms of art left behind going back as far as 45,000 BCE. In the Hunan Province of China, there are clear depictions in rock carvings of round UFO-like symbols that are thousands of years old. Texts and manuscripts going back more than 3000 years are found in China that tell of "Sons from the sky", descending to Earth on a star which was in the shape of what we now refer to as a saucer.

In Egypt at The Palace of Pharaoh Thutmosis III around 1500 BCE, manuscripts recorded "Circles of fire [that] hovered over the palace". In 329 BCE Alexander the Great recorded two great silver shields in the sky, spitting fire around the rims, that dived repeatedly at his army as they were attempting a river crossing. The action so panicked his elephants, horses, and men that they had to abandon the river crossing until the following day. In the year 776 CE, as the Saxons were laying siege to Charlemagne's Sigiburg castle in France, "Flying Shields", reddish in color, appeared in the sky and rained down fire on the attacking army and protected the French.

The first official investigation of a UFO sighting occurred in Japan in the year 1235. During the night while General Yoritsume and his army were encamped, mysterious lights were observed in the heavens. The general ordered a "full-scale scientific investigation" of these strange events. Later in Japan, in 1271, the famous priest Nichiren was about to be beheaded at Tatsunokuchi, Kamakura, when there appeared in the sky an object like a full moon, shiny and bright. The officials panicked and the execution was not carried out.

On Christopher Columbus' voyage in 1492, while on the deck of the Santa Maria, Columbus and Pedro Gutierrez observed, "a light glimmering at a great distance." It vanished and reappeared several times during the night, moving up and down, "in sudden and passing gleams." It was sighted 4 hours before land was sighted, and taken by Columbus as a sign they would soon come to land.

The astronomer Edmond Halley, discoverer of his namesake comet, recalls an experience in 1716 in which he saw an object that hovered for more than two hours. In England, 1882, a number of eminent scientists, including the Greenwich astronomer Dr. E. Walter Maunder, English scientist J. Rand Capron, and noted Dutch astronomers Audemans and Zeeman, along with several others, witnessed a saucer-shaped object during the night.

In Portugal in 1917, an assembled crowd of people, having been told by three little girls that the Virgin Mary would appear on a certain date and at a certain location, witnessed what they described as "the Sun" moving out of its position, coming close to the Earth, wobbling, moving to and fro, and then retreating back to its original position. Known as the "Miracle of Fatima," researchers, religious historians, and the Catholic Church have not been able to adequately explain the events of that day.

The Aurora UFO Crash of 1897

On April 17, 1897, a UFO crashed on a farm near Aurora, Texas, United States. The incident, similar to the more famous Roswell UFO incident 50 years later, is claimed to have resulted in a fatality of the occupant. The being was "not of this world." The UFO is said to have hit a windmill on the property of Judge J.S. Proctor two days earlier, at around 6 a.m. local (Central) time, which resulted in the crash. The alien did not survive the crash. According to a report by an officer named T.J. Weems of the Army Signal Service, it was a "Martian". The alien was buried at the nearby Aurora Cemetery with Christian rites" by a traveling pastor named William Russell Taybor. The cemetery contained a Texas Historical Commission marker mentioning the incident, but it has since been removed.

Reportedly, wreckage from the crash site was dumped into a nearby well located under the damaged windmill. Adding to the mystery was the story of Mr. Brawley Oates who purchased Judge Proctor's property around 1935. Oates cleaned out the debris from the well in order to use it as a water source, but later developed an extremely severe case of arthritis, which he claimed to be the result of contaminated water from the wreckage that had been dumped into the well. As a result, Oates sealed the well with a concrete slab, and placed an outbuilding atop the slab. According to writing on the slab, this was done in 1945.

In December, 2005, the television show UFO Files first aired an episode related to the Aurora incident, titled "Texas' Roswell." It featured a 1973 investigation led by Bill Case, an aviation writer for the Dallas Times Herald, and Director of the Texas Mutual UFO Network (MUFON).

MUFON uncovered two new eyewitnesses to the crash. Mary Evans, who was 15 at the time, told of how her parents went to the crash site and the discovery of the alien body. Charlie Stephens, who was age 10, told how he saw the airship trailing smoke as it headed north toward Aurora. He wanted to see what happened, but his father made him finish his chores; later, he told how his father went to town the next day and saw wreckage from the crash.

MUFON then investigated the Aurora Cemetery and uncovered a grave marker that appeared to show a flying saucer of some sort, as well as readings from its metal detector. MUFON asked for permission to exhume the site, but the cemetery association declined permission. After the MUFON investigation, the marker mysteriously disappeared from the cemetery and a three-inch pipe was placed into the ground; MUFON's metal detector no longer picked up metal readings from the grave, thus it was presumed that the metal was removed from the grave.

MUFON's report eventually stated that the evidence was inconclusive, but did not rule out the possibility of a hoax. The episode featured an interview with Mayor Brammer who discussed the town's intriguing history.

On November 19, 2008, the television broadcast, UFO Hunters aired a documentary regarding the Aurora incident, titled, "First Contact". The documentary featured one notable change from the UFO Files story – Tim Oates, grandson of Brawley Oates and the now-owner of the property with the sealed well where the UFO wreckage was purportedly buried, allowed the investigators to unseal the well, in order to examine it for possible debris. Water was taken from the well which tested normal except for large amounts of aluminum present; the well had no significant debris contents. It was stated in the episode that large pieces of metal had been removed from the well by a past owner of the property. Further, the remains of a windmill base were found near the well site.

UFO Files re-examined the Aurora Cemetery for any further evidence. Although the cemetery association still did not permit exhumation, UFO Files used ground-penetrating radar (GPR) and photos from prior visits, and an unmarked grave was found in the area near other 1890s graves. The condition of the grave, however, was badly deteriorated, and the GPR could not conclusively prove what type of remains had previously existed. The land owner gave them pieces of metal that contained mostly aluminum and an unknown element.

The Battle of Los Angeles

On February 23, 1942 an aerial barrage over Los Angles was initiated thinking UFOs were an attacking force from Japan, It became known as The Battle of Los Angeles, also known as the Great Los Angeles Air Raid.

In the months following the Imperial Japanese Navy's attack on Pearl Harbor in Hawaii on December 7, 1941, and the United States' entry into World War II the next day, public outrage and paranoia intensified across the country and especially on the West Coast, where fears of a Japanese attack on or invasion of the mainland were acknowledged as realistic possibilities. As the U.S. began mobilizing for the war, anti-aircraft guns were installed, bunkers were built, and air raid precautions were drilled into the populace all over the country. Contributing to the paranoia was the fact that many American merchant ships were indeed attacked by Japanese submarines in waters off the West Coast.

On February 23, 1942, at 7:15 pm, during one of President Franklin D. Roosevelt's Fireside Chats, Japanese submarine I-17 surfaced near Santa Barbara, California, and shelled Ellwood Oil field in Goleta. Although damage was minimal with no injuries, the attack had a profound effect on the public imagination. West Coast residents came to believe that the Japanese could storm their beaches at any moment.

The next day, the Office of Naval Intelligence issued a warning that an attack on mainland California could be expected within the next ten hours. That evening, many flares and blinking lights were reported from the vicinity of defense plants. An alert was called at 7:18 pm, and was lifted at 10:23 pm. Renewed activity began early in the morning of 25 February. US Navy radar had picked up an unidentified object 120 miles to the west of the city, and had been tracking it since shortly after midnight. By 2:15 am, anti-aircraft stations were put on standby alert. Air raid sirens sounded at 2:25 a.m. throughout Los Angeles County. A total blackout was ordered, and thousands of air raid wardens were summoned to their positions. Citizens of Culver City and Santa Monica would be the first to witness the surreal sight of a giant unknown object hovering over the suburban areas of Los Angeles. The U.S. Army's 37th Coast Artillery Brigade swung into action, lighting up the clear, black skies with their massive spotlights.

Katie was a young and highly-successful interior decorator and artist. She lived on the west side of Los Angeles, not far from Santa Monica. Katie volunteered to become an Air Raid Warden as did 12,000 other residents in the sprawling city of Los Angeles and surrounding communities. In the early morning hours of February 25th, Katie's phone rang. It was the Air Raid supervisor in her district notifying her of an alert and asking if she had seen the object in the sky very close to her home. She immediately walked to a window and looked up. "It was huge! It was just enormous! And it was practically right over my house. I had never seen anything like it in my life!" she said. "It was just hovering there in the sky and hardly moving at all." With the city blacked out, Katie, and hundreds of thousands of others, were able to see the eerie visitor with spectacular clarity. "It was a lovely pale orange and about the most beautiful thing you've ever seen. I could see it perfectly because it was very close. It was big! They sent fighter planes up (the Army denied any of its fighters were in action) and I watched them in groups approach it and then turn away. They were shooting at it, but it didn't seem to matter. Katie is insistent about the use of planes in the attack on the object. The planes were apparently called off after several minutes and then at 3:16 am, the 37th Coast Artillery Brigade began firing .50-caliber machine guns and 12.8-pound anti-aircraft shells into the air at the reported aircraft. "It was like the Fourth of July, but much louder. They were firing like crazy, but they couldn't touch it." The attack on the object lasted over half an hour. Many eyewitnesses talked of numerous "direct hits" on the big craft but no damage at all was visible. In fact, it would appear as though the huge shells simply fell to the ground at the last moment. "I'll never forget what a magnificent sight it was, just marvelous. And what a gorgeous color!" said Katie.

Retired anthropology professor, Scott Littleton, who was only a young boy at the time, and whose father was also an air raid warden, had an almost perfect view of the incident. He described the object as, "like a lozenge". Artillery shells were exploding "all around it". Also, like Katie, he claimed the very real presence of American fighter aircraft. Eyewitness accounts described the object as, "a surreal, hanging, magic lantern." The object was especially visible as it hovered over the MGM studios in Culver City. The object eventually made its way over Long Beach before it silently disappeared from view. The artillery fire continued sporadically until 4:14 am. The "all clear" was sounded and the blackout order was lifted at 7:21 a.m. Over 1,440 shells of anti-aircraft ammunition were eventually fired. Several buildings and vehicles were damaged by shell fragments, and five civilians died as an indirect result of the anti-aircraft fire. Three were killed in car accidents in the ensuing chaos and two of heart attacks attributed to the stress of the hour-long action.

Within hours after the air raid, Secretary of the Navy Frank Knox held a press conference, saying the entire incident had been a false alarm due to anxiety and "war nerves". The Fourth Air Force had indicated its belief that there were no planes over Los Angeles. But the Army did not publish these initial conclusions. Instead, it waited a day, until after a thorough examination of witnesses had been concluded. On the basis of these hearings, local commanders altered their stance, and indicated a belief that from one to five "unidentified airplanes" had been over Los Angeles. Some contemporary press outlets suspected a cover-up of the truth. An editorial in the Long Beach Independent wrote, "There is a mysterious reticence about the whole affair and it appears that some form of censorship is trying to halt discussion on the matter."

The first well documented reports in the United States started on June 24, 1947 when private pilot Kenneth Arnold spotted nine disk-shaped objects in the air near Mt. Rainier, Washington. Mr. Arnold described that these objects moved like a rock skipping over water. Newspapers coined them with the phrase, "flying saucers". This started a wave of UFO sightings. In the months of June and July of 1947, 853 sightings occurred. California had the most sightings with 107 cases while Washington was second with 84 sightings. Oregon was third with 52 sightings and Idaho fourth with 43 sightings.

Maury Island Incident, 1947

In 1947, a common hazard in the waters of Puget Sound was the logs that floated on its surface. They escaped from "jams" waiting to be turned into lumber at nearby mills on the shore. Several men worked as an informal harbor patrol, snagging these logs and taking them to the mills for a salvage fee. Harold Dahl worked on one of these boats, and his supervisor on shore was Fred Crisman.

Dahl reported that on June 21, 1947 he was on his patrol boat with two men, his son, and their dog. Around two in the afternoon, Dahl's boat approached the east shore of Maury Island. Maury Island is now attached to Vashon Island by a causeway road, and is about six miles west of Des Moines, Washington. Dahl looked in the sky and saw six objects floating about two thousand feet above his boat. The objects were made of some reflective metal, doughnut shaped, and about one hundred feet in diameter. The center holes were about twenty-five feet in diameter. Dahl said he also saw round portholes and what he thought was an observation window. Five of the craft circled over the sixth, which dropped slowly. It stopped and hovered about five hundred feet above the water.

Dahl put to shore because he was afraid that the center aircraft was going to crash into his boat. Once ashore, Dahl took several pictures with his camera. The lower ship stayed in position for about five minutes, with the others still circling above. One of the craft left the formation and moved down, touching one of the lower ones. The two kept contact for several minutes, until Dahl said he heard a thud. Suddenly, thousands of pieces of what he thought were newspapers dropped from the inside of the center vehicle. Most of the debris landed in the bay, though some hit the beach. Dahl recovered a few pieces, finding it was a white, lightweight metal. Along with the white metal, the UFO dropped about twenty tons of a dark metal material, which he said looked like lava rock. When the lava rock hit the water, it was so hot that steam erupted. They took cover after several pieces landed on his boat. Some debris hit his son on the arm, burning him, and another piece killed his dog.

After the rain of metal, all six craft rose into the air and headed west out to sea. Dahl went to his boat and tried to radio for help, but it did not work. They sailed back toward their dock, dropping the dog over the side as a burial at sea. Dahl took his son to the hospital for treatment and then told his boss, Fred Crisman, what had happened. Dahl gave Crisman the camera, and when the prints were developed, they showed the strange air ships. However, the negatives had spots on them, which he compared to film damaged by exposure to radiation. Crisman said he did not believe Dahl's story, so he went back to Maury Island and gathered some rock samples. He said that while he was gathering the rocks, one of the airships appeared overhead, as if it was watching him.

Dahl told investigators that the next morning, a man wearing a dark suit visited him, and suggested they go to breakfast together. Dahl drove his own car, following the stranger's late model black Buick to a local eatery. While they ate, the stranger asked no questions; instead he gave a detailed account of what had happened to Dahl the day before. The man in black warned Dahl that bad things would happen to him and his family if he told anyone about the incident. This was the first case that a witness claimed that a "man in black" intimidated him into silence.

Dahl and Crisman sent a package containing a box of metal fragments and statements about the strange happenings on the 21st and 22nd of July to publisher Ray Palmer, a magazine editor in Chicago. As the fragments were being sent to Chicago, the now famous UFO sighting by Kenneth Arnold took place at Mount Rainier in Washington State. Palmer contacted Arnold and asked him to detail the incident for the story he was writing for one of

Palmer's publications. Palmer inaugurated the first issue of Fate magazine in January 1948 with a cover featuring flying discs, along with Arnold's intriguing first-hand account.

Arnold arrived in Tacoma in late July with airline pilot E.J. Smith. The two of them met with Dahl and Crisman, examined Dahl's boat, and conducted extensive interviews. Dahl and Crisman did not produce the pictures, however. Dahl also told Arnold that his son had disappeared. Dahl said later that his son was found waiting tables in Montana, but he could not remember how he got there. On the afternoon of July 31, Captain Lee Davidson and First Lieutenant Frank Brown of the U.S. Army Air Force flew to Tacoma from Hamilton Field, California.

In addition to being pilots, the two men were intelligence specialists. They met with Arnold, Smith, and Crisman for several hours. One of the officers said that he thought there might have been "something" to the story, but they had to leave around midnight. They were in a hurry to be at Hamilton Field on August 1, the day when the Air Force was to split from the Army. The two officers flew out of McChord Air Field around two o'clock in the morning on a B-25 bomber, with a crew of two other men. About twenty minutes later, the airplane crashed near Centralia, Washington. The two enlisted men managed to parachute to safety, but Davidson and Brown were killed, making them the U.S. Air Force's first casualties.

Dahl and Crisman said that the Air Force officers took some of the strange metal onboard. People thought they heard anti-aircraft guns shoot the plane down. The local newspapers and FBI received phone calls stating that the plane was shot down in order to cover up the information Brown and Davidson had found. Because of the loss of life, the Air Force broadened its investigation and the FBI launched their own. The Air Force investigators determined that the crash had been a terrible accident. One of the engines caught fire and the men to begin bailing out. Before Brown and Davidson could jump out, a wing broke and struck the tail section, which also broke off. The plane went into a spin, trapping the men inside.

Another Air Force investigator spoke with Dahl and Crisman and visited their boat. He stated that the damage he saw did not match the damage the two boatmen had described. There were no piles of metal on Maury Island, and the existing samples looked like slag from a metal smelter. His conclusion matched that of the FBI investigator: that Dahl and Crisman had faked the incident to gain publicity for a magazine article. The FBI warned Dahl and Crisman that their hoax had not succeeded, and that if they dropped the matter, the government would not prosecute the two men for the fraud which had resulted in the deaths of the two officers. At first Dahl and Crisman went along. They made statements that the story was a fake and simply refused to give interviews on the matter. But a few years later in the January 1950 issue of Fate magazine, Crisman stated that the incident had happened. Some investigators recently visited the crash site, hoping to find some of the strange rocks to prove things one way or another, but so far, no answers have been found. Dahl's alleged photographs were also nowhere to be found.

Kenneth Arnold 1947 UFO Sighting

Kenneth Arnold was a 32-year-old businessman and pilot who at the time were searching for a downed transport plane. He initially thought the flying objects were jet aircraft, but was unable to discern any tails at the ends of what he had assumed were airplane fuselages. Looking more closely, he noted that all but one of the objects looked like flat discs. The story of Arnold's sighting was reported in newspaper articles almost immediately and the term "flying saucers" was first coined in the news headlines for this story.

On Tuesday, June 24, 1947, Arnold told reporters from the East Oregonian publication that during a flight in his own plane, between Chehalis and Yakima, a chain of nine peculiar-looking aircraft, each about the size of a C-54, was seen in the region from Mount Rainier to Mount Adams. "They flew close to the mountaintops, in a diagonal chainlike line," he said later. "It was as if they were linked together." The discs appeared to be twenty to twenty-five miles away and moving at fantastic speed, which Arnold estimated was twelve hundred miles per hour. "I watched them [for] about three minutes," he said. "They were swerving in and out around the high mountain peaks. They looked like a pie pan, and so shiny, they reflected the sun like a mirror. I never saw anything so flat. Their fronts were circular, and their backs were triangular—but one of them looked crescent- shaped."

The Flying Saucer as I Saw it... by Kenneth Arnold

Arnold guessed that they were traveling at least twice the speed of sound. In the last days of June 1947, breaking the sound barrier had yet to be attained, and was the subject of much speculation and discussion among pilots. Arnold's first thought was that they were some kind of new secret jets or guided missiles. But there was also another possibility that came to his mind after a moment - Soviet aircraft, as 1947 was a threshold year in the developing Cold War.

At Yakima, he told his story to pilots who remarked that the craft were bound to have been guided missiles from Moses Lake, Washington. Arnold recalled that "I felt satisfied that that's probably what they were. However, I had never heard of a missile base at Moses Lake." When he landed at Pendleton, Oregon, Arnold learned that his story had arrived ahead of him. The Yakima pilots had telephoned Pendleton to notify them of Arnold's arrival and had related his adventure. No news reporters were present. After discussing this with the folks at Pendleton, and reaching the conclusion that these missiles were something out of the ordinary, Arnold, prepared with his maps and calculations so as to give "the best description I could" set off to the local FBI office. He found the office closed. Not having any luck with the FBI, Arnold decided to look up the journalists from the East Oregonian. One consideration in particular seems to have pushed him. As he explained to them, he had met, probably at the Hotel Pendleton where he was staying, a man from Ukiah, Oregon, who had said that he had seen a similar formation of craft there. Before leaving Pendleton, he went to the offices of the East Oregonian. He told Nolan Skiff and Bill Bequette about his adventure. Arnold described the discs as moving "like a saucer if you skipped it across the water." Skeptical, Skiff and Bequette were won over by Arnold's honesty. Bequette later submitted the story to the Associated Press.

As soon as Arnold's story became widely known, sightings of flying discs proliferated. Starting from June 26 and over the days following, there were hundreds, even thousands, of newspaper articles devoted to flying discs. Most of the time saucers were explained away by scientists and military experts who asserted that "the observers just imagined they saw something, or there is some meteorological explanation for the phenomena." Statements quoted in these stories are filled with expressions like, "mass hypnosis" and, "foolish things." Saucers were compared to the Loch Ness Monster. The saucer craze created such a turmoil that the U.S. Air Force began an investigation in the early days of July. At the request of the Air Materiel Command, Arnold produced a written report detailing his sighting, which he had sent to Wright Field in Dayton, Ohio.

In 1948 Arnold's report landed on J. Allen Hynek's desk. Hynek was a civilian astronomer whom the Air Force had asked to study the reports, avoiding any possible confusion with natural astronomical phenomena. Hynek's conclusion was that Arnold had seen some kind of aircraft. Arnold heard nothing about the eventual whereabouts of his report. He reasoned that he had to try other strategies in order to find a solution to his unusual sighting.

He accepted an invitation from the Chicago publisher, Ray Palmer, to go to Tacoma, Washington, and investigate another sighting. Palmer was the editor of the science fiction magazine called, Amazing Stories. The case Arnold investigated turned out to be a crude hoax, at least from the point of view of the FBI investigators. Arnold called in the two military investigators who had interviewed him earlier, along with Harold Dahl and Fred Crisman from the Maury Island UFO incident. Sadly, Brown and Davidson died in the airplane crash, returning to Hamilton Field, California with artifacts from that event. From then on, the "saucer" story followed different paths.

In January 1948 the recently formed U.S. Air Force launched PROJECT SIGN in order to investigate the overwhelming number of UFO sightings. This project, located in the Technical Intelligence Division at Wright-Patterson Air Force Base, was classified as Secret, and the public had access only to that which the press was allowed to report.

In the valleys around Mount Adams, Washington there are an incredible number of UFO sightings and other paranormal phenomena seen in the forests around the area. A few TV went to this area, and had some strange experiences, especially at night.

James Gilliland's ranch sits in an area that is a prime viewing spot for all of these unusual occurrences. He "hosts" visitors to his ranch and promotes them to experience the nightly events. He established "Enlightened Contact with Extra Terrestrial Intelligence," which sounds more like a cult, than an investigation into peculiar phenomena.

Popular Mechanics magazine did a country-wide study, issuing a report of its findings in December 2009 in an article called, "U.S. Map of the Top UFO Hotspots and How to Report a Sighting." Yakima County, Washington ranked 4th in the nation for the most UFOs spotted in a "Less Populated County", according to the magazine. From 1947 to current day, something out of the ordinary has been going on in that area for a long time.

Roswell UFO Crash

The Roswell UFO crash is the most famous UFO incident in history. It involved two UFOs. One exploded in the air near Corona, New Mexico spreading debris over a large area and the other UFO impacted the ground on the Plains of San Agustin New Mexico. Hundreds of people were interviewed by various researchers, only a few of these people claimed to have seen debris or aliens. Of these 300-plus individuals reportedly interviewed for UFO Crash at Roswell, only 41 can be "considered genuine first -hand witnesses" and only 23 can be "reasonably thought to have seen physical evidence, debris". Of these, only seven have asserted anything suggestive of otherworldly origins for the debris. However these 41 witnesses include doctors, nurses, military personnel, and pilots flying the Roswell debris to Wright-Patterson Air Force Base in Ohio.

No case has received more worldwide attention. Not only did the alleged crash of a flying saucer create mass coverage, but remains today an often discussed case. The Roswell saga actually began in Germany with the end of World War II. Russian and American intelligence teams began to track down scientific booty of the advanced German technology. The US War Department decided that the US must not only control this technology, but also the scientists who had helped develop it. It was believed by the United States that we were alarmingly backward in many fields of research. That if we do not take this opportunity to seize this advanced German technology and the brains that developed it, that the United States will remain several years behind in fields already exploited. A top secret project later termed `Operation Paperclip' was initiated to bring this technology and its scientists to the United States. There was however, one slight problem: It was illegal, for US law explicitly prohibited Nazi officials from immigrating to America, and as many as three-quarters of the scientists in question were allegedly committed passionate Nazis.

President Truman, however, decided that the national interest was paramount and that America needed the German scientists to work on America's behalf. Operation Paperclip was carried out by the Joint Intelligence Objectives Agency (JIOA) and had two aims: Firstly, to exploit German Scientists for American research by rounding up Nazi scientists and taking them to America; and, secondly, to deny these intellectual resources to the Soviet Union. The name `Operation Paperclip' was derived from the fact that those individuals selected to go to the United States were distinguished by paperclips on their files joining their scientific papers with regular immigration forms. At least 1600 scientists and their dependents were taken to America under Operation Paperclip and its successor projects.

One of these scientists was Dr. Wernher von Braun. Von Braun was leader of what has been called the "Rocket Team", which developed the V–2 ballistic missile for the Nazis during World War II. Von Braun engineered the surrender of 500 of his top rocket scientists, along with plans and test vehicles, to the Americans. He and his Rocket Team were sent to Fort Bliss, Texas. There they worked on rockets for the U.S. Army, launching them at White Sands Proving Ground, New Mexico. White Sands Proving Grounds was established in July 1945 where Robert Goddard had begun experimentation with liquid fuel rocket engines. Dr. von Braun and his Rocket Team used Goddard's work as a starting point in a quest to build a rocket powerful enough to escape Earth's gravity.

On June 25 in Silver City, New Mexico, a dentist by the name of Dr. R. F. Sensenbaugher reported seeing a saucer-shaped UFO fly over the area. It was about one-half the size of the full moon. Two days later, in Pope, New Mexico, W. C. Dobbs reported a white, glowing object flying overhead, not too far from the White Sands missile range. On the same day, Captain E. B. Detchmendy reported to his commanding officer that he saw a white, glowing UFO pass over the missile range. Two days later, on June 29, rocket expert C. J. Zohn and three of his technicians, who were stationed at White Sands, watched a giant silver disc moving northward over the desert. Air Force security officials at White Sands theorized that the von Braun rocket program or the Trinity nuclear testing site might be the object of surveillance by UFOs, which they believed were a spacecraft from another world.

Air Force Lt. Col. Richard French, an Air Force pilot and Military Intelligence officer who was in Alamogordo, N.M., was being tested in an altitude chamber, an annual requirement for rated officers. In an exclusive interview, he told The Huffington Post that a UFO was "shot down by an experimental U.S. airplane that was flying out of White Sands, N.M. The pilot used an electronic pulse-type weapon that disabled and took away all the controls of the UFO, and that's why it crashed" on July 2, 1947. "When they hit it with that electromagnetic pulse — bingo! — there goes all their electronics and, consequently, the UFO was uncontrollable."

The UFO was joined by a second UFO believed to be an attempt to assist or rescue the disabled UFO. The UFOs were tracked at three separate installations; Alamogordo, White Sands, and Roswell. In Roswell, on the same day, Mr. and Mrs. Dan Wilmot reported that two inverted saucers faced mouth to mouth, moving at a high rate of speed over their house. On the evening of July 2 during a severe thunderstorm in the area of Roswell,

New Mexico with lots of lightning, William W. "Mac" Brazel, a foreman at a sheep ranch on the Foster homestead heard what sounded to him as a loud explosion over the thunder.

The Corona Site

The next morning, Mr. Brazel rode out as usual to check on his sheep, along with his old neighbor's seven year old boy, William D. "Dee" Proctor. They came upon an area about a quarter of a mile long and several hundred feet wide that was strewn with debris, shiny bits and pieces unlike anything Mac had ever seen. He picked up some of the material and carried it with him back to the ranch headquarters, where he put it in a shed. Later that day, Brazel put a small piece of the debris in his pocket when he drove Dee Proctor to his home about ten miles away. He showed the debris to Dee's parents, William and Loretta Proctor, and wanted them to go back and look at the debris field with him.

The next night, Brazel went into the town of Corona, where he told his uncle, Hollis Wilson, about the debris. Wilson and another man who was present told Mac about the "flying saucers" that were being reported around the area and advised him to report his find to the authorities. So, on July 6, when Mac was going into Roswell to see about trading for a new pick-up truck, he took some of the debris with him and stopped off at the office of Chaves County Sheriff George Wilcox. At first, Wilcox paid little attention, but when Mac showed him a piece of the debris, he realized that this might be important, so Wilcox called Roswell Army Air Force Base, which was an elite facility, and home to the only atomic bomb group in existence at the time. He spoke with Major Jesse A. Marcel, the base intelligence officer for the 509th Bomb Wing. Marcel told Wilcox he would come into Roswell and talk to Brazel.

Meanwhile, Frank Joyce of radio station KGFL called Sheriff Wilcox looking for news, and was told about Mac Brazel's discovery. Joyce phoned and interviewed Mac over the phone. Major Marcel later arrived at the Sheriff's office to question Mac and see the debris. Then Major Marcel went back to the base to make his report. He reported the incident to Colonel William H. Blanchard, the base commander, and was told to return to the site for further investigation. Marcel took his Buick, and an Army Counter Intelligence Corps officer named Sheridan Cavitt drove a Jeep, and they followed Mac Brazel back to the ranch.

By the time they got to the ranch it was too late in the evening to go to the site, so they spent the night in an old house on the ranch. The next morning, Mac saddled two horses, and he and Cavitt rode out to the site while Marcel followed in the Jeep. After showing them the debris field and watching for a few minutes, Mac left them to their task and went back to finish his chores.

Marcel and Cavitt were amazed to see the vast amount of area the wreckage covered. It was scattered over three quarters of a mile long and several hundred feet wide. They said "It was definitely not a weather or tracking device, nor was it any sort of plane or missile." Marcel said, "I don't know what it was, but it certainly wasn't anything built by us, and it most certainly wasn't any weather balloon....small beams about three eighths or a half inch square with some sort of hieroglyphics on them that nobody could decipher. These looked something like balsa wood, and about the same weight, except that they were not wood at all. They were very hard, although flexible, and would not burn at all. There was a great deal of an unusual parchment-like substance which was brown in color and extremely strong, and a great number of small pieces of a metal like tinfoil, except that it wasn't tinfoil.

"I was interested in electronics and kept looking for something that resembled instruments or electronic equipment, but I didn't find anything." He did find a black, metallic looking box several inches square. As there was no apparent way to open this, and since it didn't appear to be an instrument package of any sort, they threw it in the back of the Jeep with the rest of the stuff. Marcel said "It had little numbers with symbols that we had to call hieroglyphics because I could not understand them. They were pink and purple. They looked like they were painted on. I even took my cigarette lighter and tried to burn the material we found that resembled parchment and balsa, but it would not burn - wouldn't even smoke....the pieces of metal that we brought back were so thin, just like the tinfoil in a pack of cigarettes....you could not tear or cut it either. We even tried making a dent in it with a sixteen-pound sledgehammer, and there was still no dent in it."

Marcel and Cavitt filled the Jeep up with debris, and then Marcel sent Cavitt back to the base with it. Marcel then took his Buick out to the sight and filled it with debris as well. He later said that even the two vehicles full was just a minor portion of the debris. Marcel headed back to base, but on the way, he stopped off at his home to show the debris to his wife and son, Jesse Jr.

On July 8, 1947, Roswell Army Air Field public information office issued a press release stating that personnel from the field's 509th Bomb Group had recovered a crashed "flying disc" from a ranch near Roswell, sparking intense media interest. When Marcel got back to the base, Colonel Blanchard ordered him to load the debris onto a B-29 and fly with it to Wright Field in Ohio, stopping at Carswell Army Air Force Base in Fort Worth, Texas on the way. Marcel did so, but as soon as he landed at Carswell, Brigadier General Roger Ramey, Commander of the 8th Air Force, took over. The debris was taken to Ramey's office and spread out on brown paper. Marcel said later that one photo was taken of him with the real debris, then Ramey took him into another room, and when he came back, a weather balloon had been substituted for the debris. A weather officer, Warrant Officer Irving Newton was brought in, and he immediately identified the material he saw as a weather balloon and a Rawin-type radar target. A Rawin radar target was a reflector made of metal foil and balsa wood sticks that was attached to a weather balloon so that it could be tracked on radar. Ramey announced to the press that the "flying saucer" was only a weather balloon. After more photographs with the weather balloon, Ramey ordered Marcel back to Roswell with a strong hint to keep quiet about the incident. When Marcel got back to Roswell, he found that he had been made to look rather foolish for not recognizing the debris as a "weather balloon."

Frank Joyce of KGFL radio had told his boss, Walt Whitmore Sr. about Mac Brazel's find. Whitmore then drove out to the ranch to talk to Mac about the incident. Whitmore then went back to his own home in Roswell, where Mac spent the night. Next morning, they went down to KGFL and called the base. The military came out and picked Mac up and carried him back to the base, where he was kept under guard in the "guest house" for several days.

On July 8, Mac was escorted by the military to the offices of the Roswell Daily Record, where he gave a press interview. The story he told them was a bit different from what he had told before, however. Now he said that he and his son had originally discovered the debris on June 14, but that he was in such a hurry that he ignored it. Then, on July 4, he and his wife and two of his children rode out to the site and picked up some of the debris, which consisted of smoky gray rubber strips, tinfoil, heavy paper, and some small sticks. He said that he had twice before found weather balloons on the ranch but that this material in no way resembled what he had found before.

Mac's military escorts led him out to a car and drove him to KGFL. People who saw him leave the newspaper office said he kept his head down and pretended not to see any of his friends. At KGFL, he was allowed to go in alone while his escorts waited outside. He went in and began telling Frank Joyce the same story he had told at the Record. Joyce interrupted him and asked why he was telling a different story than he had told earlier. Mac became agitated. At the end of the interview, Mac went back out to where his military escort was waiting, and they took him back to the base

When released by the military, Mac refused to say anything other than that he had found a weather balloon. He privately complained of his treatment by the military, who he said wouldn't even let him call his wife. He told his children that he had taken an oath not to talk about the incident. Within a year, he moved off the ranch and into Tularosa. There he opened a refrigerated meat locker rental establishment where people could rent lockers to keep their meat, as there were few home freezers in those days. Mac Brazel passed away in 1963.

San Agustin Site
A second crash site was found by Grady L. "Barney" Barnett while working in the Plains of San Agustin near Magdalena, New Mexico on July 3, 1947, when he had come upon a crashed disc-shaped object. This flying disc had alien bodies strewn about it. There were aliens inside and outside of the craft. Gerald Anderson and his family were also in the area, rock hunting on that same day, when they came upon the crashed saucer-shaped craft. The craft had four dead aliens inside. Though Gerald was only six years old at the time the extraordinary sighting was one he would never forget. Archaeologist, Dr. Buskirk, and five of his students also came upon the crash scene. Steve MacKenzie saw four bodies around the crashed UFO. He said that another one was out of sight.

Commander Major Edwin Easley of the Military Police cordoned off the crash site. Sergeant Thomas Gonzales, a guard with the 509th at the crash site, saw bodies he called "little men." Frank Kaufman a member of the Army team witnessed a "strange looking craft embedded in a cliff." Other members of his detachment were ordered to put debris into crates which were sent to Roswell AAFB and stored under heavy military guard.

Herbert Ellis, a painting contractor at Roswell Army Airfield Base saw an alien "walking" into the Roswell Army hospital. Ray Danzer, a plumbing contractor, was standing outside of the emergency room, when he saw alien bodies being brought into the base hospital on stretchers. Dumbfounded by the event, he was shaken back to reality by military police who warned him to leave, and forget what he saw. Joseph Montoya, Lt. Governor of New Mexico, saw "four little men" in Hangar P-3, today known as building 84. One of them was still alive. He described the beings as wearing what he described as a "flight suit, silver in color, and tight fitting." He recalled that "the aliens had four fingers on each hand. Their fingers were long and thin. They had oversized heads, with big eyes. Their mouth was small, like a cut across a piece of wood. "I tell you they're not from this world."

Mary Bush, who was secretary to the base hospital administrator, was called on to assist two doctors in a hospital room where three "alien" bodies were being examined. Though suffocated by an overwhelming odor from the bodies, she clearly recalled that the aliens had four fingers, and no thumbs. They were "a creature from another world."

Glenn Dennis was a mortician working for the Ballard Funeral Home in Roswell, which had a contract to provide mortuary services for the Roswell Army Air Field. Mr. Dennis received a call from the base mortuary officer, asking him how to prepare bodies that had been lying out on the desert for a period of time. Being curious, he decided to go to Roswell base infirmary to see what was going on. When he arrived, the infirmary door was open and he entered. Inside he saw some wreckage. There were several pieces which looked like the bottom of a canoe, about three feet in length. It resembled stainless steel with a purple hue, as if it had been exposed to high temperature. There was some strange looking writing on the material, which he described as resembling Egyptian hieroglyphics.

There were two Military Police officers nearby, standing guard. He recognized his friend, Naomi Marie Self, a nurse for 23 years, coming out of one of the examining rooms with a cloth over her mouth. She said, "My gosh, get out of here or you're going to be in a lot of trouble." Then two MPs approached him. A Captain asked who he was, and what he was doing here. The Captain then told him, "You did not see anything. There was no crash here, and if you say anything about this at all, you could get into a lot of trouble." The MPs quickly escorted him out of the infirmary. They said that they had orders to follow him back to the Ballard Funeral Home.

Later that day, flight engineer Sgt. Robert Porter loaded debris into a B-29, and along with Major Marcel, flew from Roswell Air Force Base to General Ramey's office in Ft Worth, Texas. Marcel was to show some recovered material to Gen. Roger Ramey before proceeding on to Wright Field, Ohio. Shortly afterwards a second plane, a C-54 flown by Captain Oliver Wendell "Pappy" Henderson, a senior pilot at the Roswell air base flew from Roswell to Wright Air Fiel, Ohio, transporting the wreckage and alien bodies. "Pappy", who had a Top-Secret security clearance, described the alien beings as smaller than a normal man, about four feet, pale, with slanted eyes and overly large heads for their size. They were humanoid-looking, but different from us, looking yellowish, and a bit Asian-looking. They looked nice, almost as though they would be friendly if they were alive. The aliens where wearing suits made from a material that was different from anything he had ever seen. The bodies had been packed in dry ice in order to preserve them, and placed in a 7 x 7 foot crate. Sgt. Robert Smith of Roswell 1st Air Transport Unit was taken to the hangar to load the crates. He said that he loaded crates on two or three C-54 aircraft, and that one of the crates took up the entire plane. "It wasn't that heavy, but it was a large volume."

When the planes arrived at Wright Air Field, the wreckage debris was taken to Hangar-18, along with the dead aliens who were put into a refrigeration unit in the hanger. Two members of a film unit stationed at Wright-Patterson were summoned by an officer to get their 16 mm movie cameras and follow him. The two workers were led by the officer to a heavily guarded airplane hangar, Hangar-18. Inside, they saw a badly damaged, circular craft of unknown origin. There was debris from the UFO wreckage scattered over a large area, which was placed on a huge canvas tarp. The officer instructed the two cameramen to take film of anything and everything in sight.

Upon finishing this assignment, they were taken to the very rear of the hanger to a refrigeration unit. There, they saw two storage bins which held the bodies of two, small alien creatures! The beings were very thin, gray in color, with large eyes, but no eyelids. One of these beings had obviously suffered bodily damage, showing signs of being burned, while the other showed no apparent signs of injury. They were about 3 1/2 foot tall, of thin build, and had grayish skin. They had large, black eyes, only a slit for a mouth, small, flat noses, and small ears. They recalled that the beings had extra-long arms with less than five digits on the hands, which were like animal claws. The feet had three stubby, webbed toes, and a ridge on the bottom of their feet. They were clad in jump suits, with zippers up the front. Their suits had an emblem resembling a bird. The photojournalists were sworn to secrecy, with the threat of the loss of their pensions and a fast discharge from the Army if they told anyone about what they saw.

Lt. Col. Marion "Black Mac" Magruder, along with a specialized team of scientists, were flown to Wright-Patterson on a "matter of utmost urgency." They were taken into a room, and briefed on the extraterrestrial spacecraft that had crashed two weeks before near the town of Roswell, New Mexico. While in this room, they were given the opportunity to examine some of the crash debris from the alien ship. Then, they were taken into another room, where they saw an alien being still alive! Magruder's description of the alien is very similar to other reports from those who were allowed to see the beings: small, spindly, large eyes, and oversized heads. It is most often reported that the Roswell crash yielded four alien beings, three dead and one alive. Leon B. Visse, who researched cellular genetic material, was given access to a secret room where he examined two of the alien bodies.

The live alien became known as "EBE1", and was taken to the military base in Los Alamos, where he was kept in captivity until his death in 1952. He was a very intelligent being who picked up English very quickly from the guards and military personal around him. EBE1 never got upset or angry with his captivity, and helped many officials with their studies and their questions. The typical lifespan of EBE's civilization is between 350 and 400 Earth years. It is thought that the conditions here on Earth, and the trauma of the crash contributed to EBE's passing. He claimed to have come from the planet "Serpo" in the Zeta Reticuli binary star system, which has two suns providing energy to the local planets.

In 1947, Brigadier General Thomas J. Dubose was Gen. Ramey's Chief of Staff. In recorded interviews, Dubose said the whole Roswell matter was conducted in the strictest secrecy and even involved the White House. In July, 1947, then-Director of the FBI, J. Edgar Hoover demanded that the

US military give the FBI access to the "crashed discs." Hoover "insisted on full access to [the] discs recovered." He said, "The Army grabbed it, and would not let us have it for cursory examination." In 1964, Air Force officer Brigadier General Arthur Exon was named the base commander. General Exon continued to deny Hoover's FBI access to the hidden, secret facilities of the base.

Senator Barry M. Goldwater of Arizona, a former Major General in the US Army Air Corp, now a senior member of the US Senate Select Committee on Intelligence, requested entry into a special storage area at Wright-Patterson Air Force Base. Goldwater was told by General Curtis LeMay, Chairman of the Military Joint Chiefs of Staff at the Pentagon, that he had no need to know, and was denied passage. This awakened Goldwater to the fact that the UFO situation is at the highest level of national secrecy, much higher than that of the H-Bomb, and more than anything else that is known within the Pentagon, FBI, CIA, DIA, NSA, et al. That is, nothing has a higher security protocol than alien beings visiting and interacting with our planet. The United States Air Force knows the truth, but will it ever be revealed?

The U.S. Military, as well as top officials from other countries, fear that the acknowledgement of UFOs and aliens from other worlds, might start a panic similar to H. G. Wells' famous radio broadcast, "The War of the Worlds." Broadcast on October 30, 1938 by the Columbia Broadcasting System (CBS), the first two thirds of the 60-minute "special newscast" was presented as a series of "news bulletins", which suggested to the six million listeners that an actual alien invasion by Martians was currently in progress. Millions believed it to be true, and 1.2 million were, "genuinely frightened." Some listeners fainted, while others grabbed their families and headed into the mountains. While UFOs actually did not provide a threat to National Security, how would the Military explain foreigners from other worlds flying UFOs freely over towns, military bases, etc. without the military being able to stop them?

There was also fear that such acknowledgement of aliens and UFOs would have a pronounced effect on the religions of the World. How could religions explain otherworldly beings, particularly perhaps, with the notion that Man is made in the image of God? The known aliens were humanoid, but clearly, far different from Homo Sapiens. What panic or backlash to the Military might result?

What excited the Military most was the fact that by examining the wreckage and communicating with the aliens, reverse engineering was possible. The Military might advance science by thousands of years, and produce highly effective weaponry, aircraft, and who-knows-what, that the military could not even imagine. For these reasons, it was determined that all information regarding UFOs and otherworldly aliens should be denied by the United States. Special departments were set up in order to disclaim all accounts, and even deride the many people that had reported such things. Intimidation was the name of the game, threatening those who came forward with their claims, and making them out to be crazy and mentally unstable. Any and all photos and evidence that they might have were confiscated, never to be spoken of again. False reports were issued in order to confuse the general public.

Such was the case of the "Roswell Incident", which was explained as a crashed weather balloon by the military. The case was quickly "closed", and almost completely ignored for more than 30 years thereafter.

In 1978, physicist Stanton T. Friedman interviewed Major Jesse Marcel, who was involved with the original recovery of the debris in 1947. Marcel expressed his belief that the military had covered up the retrieval of the alien spacecraft. His story spread throughout the nation, bringing worldwide attention to the "Roswell incident". People have to ask themselves if the "Roswell incident", with its associated aliens and UFOs, are just imaginary or real. Consider that over 500 eyewitnesses who had been involved in the "Roswell Incident" have provided documentation of their experiences. Many have come forward and spoken on the matter just before their death, or toward the end of their lives, when Government threats were no longer effective. These include the witnesses at both crash sites, the first responders to the incident, military people in charge, scientists including Joseph Montoyathen-Lt. Governor of New Mexico. Military Police at Roswell, nurses involved with the examination of the aliens, people transferring the UFO/alien debris to the planes in Roswell and Wright Air Field, the film crew at Wright Air Field, and so on. Cover-ups by the military on the "Roswell Incident", as well as all other UFO and aliens, continue to this day.

FBI Director J. Edgar Hoover UFO Memo's

The following documents were released through the 1977 Freedom of Information Act and can be viewed on the FBI Vault – online searchable document retrieval for researchers and media.

FBI Special Agent Percy Wyly Telex to J. Edgar Hoover July 8, 1947

On July 8 1947, FBI Special Agent Percy Wyly sent a Telex message marked "Urgent. " to J. Edgar Hoover and to the Special Agent in Charge in Cincinnati. In summary, Hoover is informed that the "disc and balloon" were "being transported by special plane for examination" to Wright Field. The debris was reported to have resembled "a high altitude weather balloon with a radar reflector – but that "telephonic conversation had not borne out that belief." The teletype indicates that the results of the study of the Roswell crash debris would be forwarded to the FBI's Cincinnati office and to Director Hoover. But, no documents have ever surfaced to indicate that this ever happened.

Agent Wyly was conveying information that had been provided to him by Major Edwin M. Kirton of the Army Air Force Intelligence of the 8th Army Air Force at Ft. Worth, Texas. Kirton was one of General Roger Ramey's key officers. Publicly Kirton debunked the incident, telling the Dallas Morning News that the Roswell crash was of a weather balloon while telling Wyly that it was not.

FBI Agent D.M. Ladd memo to J. Edgar Hoover July 10, 1947

FBI Agent D.M. Ladd indicated to Hoover that on July 9 1947, Brigadier General George Schulgen of Pentagon Intelligence personally discussed with a Special Agent of the FBI the possibility of assistance from the FBI in investigating the flying disc phenomena. Ladd indicates to Hoover that he did not believe that the Bureau should offer such assistance because the majority of "alleged discs reported found have been pranks."

Clyde Tolson, Associate Director of the FBI, received Ladd's memo, read and considered it, and annotated on it his disagreement with Ladd, saying: "I think we should do this" – meaning that he believes that the Bureau should consider investigating with the Pentagon. Hoover qualifies his agreement with Tolson, but cautions him in a handwritten notation:

"I would do it but before agreeing to it we must insist upon full access to discs recovered. For instance in the La case the Army grabbed it and would not let us have it for cursory examination."

The "La" is presumed signifying Louisiana referring to a Shreveport Louisiana incident occurring on July 7 that turned out to be a hoax.

Tolson and Hoover no doubt continued their dialog privately on the crashed saucer matter: Should they pursue this investigation on their own – or should they cooperate with the Pentagon? The two ultimately decided not to move forward in working with the military on the matter.

Hoover Memo to General McDonald, Sept 27 1947

On September 27 1947, Hoover wrote to the Pentagon a letter informing them that he was discontinuing any FBI agent investigation of crashed discs. He characterized such crashes as those of "ash cans, toilet seats and what not." He would defer any such investigations of that type to the Air Force. His attitude in his rebuking reply to the military is almost smarmy. It is as if he knew that they were trying to "play" him and that they have not given him "full access."

Hoover simply did not trust the military and did not wish to work with them. He knew that he had not been given the "real deal" on the crash at Roswell. His agent Percy Wyly relayed that Hoover would be getting the crash debris results. But there appears Hoover never received anything back from the Air Force. Hover was left to rely only on press reports of the crash and on his agent Wyly's precious few bits of information that were obtained from Ramey's, Major Kirton. Hoover did in fact maintain interest in the crashed disc matters despite what he told the Pentagon. And his closest agents were informing him on crashed saucer stories.

FBI Agent Guy Hottel memo to Hoover, March 22 1950

FBI Agent Guy Hottel explains to Hoover that "an Air Force investigator" source had informed him that three flying discs had prior been recovered in New Mexico. The source indicates that this may have been due to the effect of radar on the craft. Each disc had three occupants that were three feet tall. Seeking the Director's guidance, Hottel indicates that he has not taken any further action on the matter.

The three disks mentioned recovered in New Mexico were probably the two from the Roswell crash sites Corona, San Agustin, and the Aztec 1948 UFO crash site.

Hoover had told the military back in September of 1947 that he did not want to participate with the Pentagon in investigating such crash cases. But here we are three years on and we see that Hoover is receiving details on just such events. Hoover had lied to the Pentagon. Though he had told the Pentagon that he wanted no part of it – what Hoover had really meant was that he did not want any part of working with the military on such UFO crash matters. He did not trust them. He wanted to work only with people that he could trust on this, his own people

Hoover trusted on such investigations his long-time friends and co-workers Special Agent Guy Hottel and FBI Associate Director Clyde Tolson:

Tolson (who had agreed with Hoover that they should investigate crashed discs) was Hoover's #2 for decades, and the person with whom he shared living quarters.

Guy Hottel (the author of the 1950 crashed disc memo) was one of Hoover's favored agents and acted as Hoover's personal bodyguard. Hoover had entrusted Guy to perform some of the most discreet investigations the agency had ever conducted. This is because as early as the 1930s the three of them – Hottel, Hoover and Tolson – would do things such as going to Miami and staying together at hotels to gamble and socialize. Tolson and Hottel had even roomed together in the 1920s at college.

Chapter 3

The UFO Conspiracy

The Extraterrestrial Accord

UFO conspiracy theories argue that various governments and politicians globally, most especially the officials of Washington, D.C., are suppressing evidence of extraterrestrial unidentified flying objects and alien visitors. Such conspiracy theories commonly argue that Earth governments, especially the Government of the United States, are in communication or cooperation with extraterrestrials despite public claims to the contrary, and further, that some governments are explicitly allowing alien abduction. In the aftermath of the 1938 War of the Worlds broadcast, the Government was afraid of the potential public reaction to confirmed evidence of UFOs.

The UFO conspiracy theories began when a group had established communication with the aliens in 1952. In an exhibition of force, a series of unidentified flying objects flew over the U.S. Capital in Washington D.C. on July 12 to July 29, 1952. President Harry S. Truman passed the office of The President of the United States onto Dwight. D. Eisenhower on January 19, 1953. Truman gave Eisenhower a hefty file concerning top-secret, top classified files about a project called "Majestic 12." A meeting with the aliens was proposed by the military, knowing that in the event of a conflict, whoever controlled the air would win, but our aircraft was no match to the aliens' UFOs. The U.S. wanted to know what the aliens were up to. Eisenhower rejected a face-to-face meeting with the aliens at first, but a year of ultra-secret negotiations with government officials ensued, and he learned that the aliens, "came in peace". A meeting between the aliens and Eisenhower was scheduled on February 21, 1954 at Edwards Air Force Base in California.

Eisenhower felt that if the public knew of the meeting, it might produce fear and unrest. He decided to spend several days in Palm Springs on Vacation. Then on Saturday afternoon, he disappeared, going to Edwards Air Force Base for the day. His White House Press Secretary, James Haggert informed the media that Eisenhower had chipped a tooth while eating fried chicken, and that the president had visited a dentist for repair. Eisenhower returned to Palm Springs the following morning.

According to William Cooper, a Naval Intelligence briefing team member with total access to classified documents, Eisenhower had arrived at Edwards Air Force Base to the bewilderment, and panic among the officials present. They were met by two humanoid aliens that came from the Pleiades star cluster, and resembled Nordic "Scandinavians." The ETs were about six feet tall with long blonde hair, blue eyes, and fair skin. They became known as the "Pleiadian Aliens". With the assistance and permission of the Pleiadians, Air Force officials were allowed to study and handle five separate and distinct types of aircraft. Discussions were held between the ETs and Eisenhower in a polite manner, but no agreements were reached. The Aliens supposedly wanted humans to stop nuclear testing, but Eisenhower didn't want to give it up. There was uncertainty about how to respond to the aliens, and to fears that due to the Cold War, the aliens could turn to the Soviets if the Americans spurned them.

Seven different types of aliens were known. The most common type is known as the" Greys". There are two different types of Greys. The first seem to be the leaders and the more intelligent of the two. They are approximately 5 to 8 feet tall, with large heads, large dark eyes, long skinny fingers arms and legs, have a small mouth, small ear holes, and have been reported to have 2 small nostrils. They are hairless and seem to communicate through some kind of telepathy with each other as well as humans. The second are worker Greys. They are much smaller than the other Greys at around 3½ to 4½ feet tall, stubbier fingers arms and legs, but are similar to the larger Greys, same shaped head, eyes, ear holes, and small holes for nostrils. They don't seem to be as intelligent as the taller Greys.

The Air Force and Majestic Twelve a secret committee of scientists, military leaders, and government officials, formed in 1947 by an executive order by U.S. President Harry S. Truman to facilitate recovery and investigation of alien spacecraft. were more familiar with the Greys in that Seventy-three percent of all reported alien encounters in the United States describe Grey aliens, The Greys come from the Zeta Reticuli binary star system, which is visible in the Southern Hemisphere, and approximately 38 light years away from Earth. They were the occupants of the 1947 Roswell UFO crash.

An autopsy of one of the Roswell crash victims was performed. In 1995, filmmaker Ray Santilli claimed to have obtained 22 reels of 16 mm film that depicted the autopsy of a Roswell Grey. However, in 2006 Santilli announced that the film was not the original, but was instead a "reconstruction" created after the original film was found to have degraded. Film emulsions in those days were highly toxic and posed a fire hazard. He maintained that the footage released to the public contained only a small percentage of the original footage.

Upon examination, it was determined that Greys have a genetic disorder in their digestive system, where it is atrophied and dysfunctional There is an indication that they suffer from unknown doses of nuclear radiation that had damaged the genetic makeup of their DNA. They sustain themselves by using an enzyme or hormonal secretion obtained from the tongues and throats of cows or humans. The secretion, extracted from cow's blood, is mixed with other substances that are applied directly onto Grey skin, which absorbs the mixture, then excretes the waste back out from the epidermal.

The Greys are probably the most known alien species because of the publicity from the Roswell crash of 1947 and their abductions of humans. Such were the cases of Barney and Betty Hill in 1961, and with the Travis Walton abduction in 1975. Greys abduct humans in order to perform experiments with the human body. Many abductees have reported having male sperm taken from them as well as eggs from women. The smaller Greys don't seem to be as intelligent as the taller Greys and do much of the grunt work during probing, while the taller Greys perform more detailed science in areas like collecting sperm and egg samples, and genetic materials. After the experiments, they release and return the people back to where they were abducted. It is believed that the Greys are trying to fill the gaps of their damaged DNA with healthy human DNA.

Negotiations continued with the aliens for about a year after the Edwards Air Force Base meeting of February 21, 1954. The Greys took advantage of the failure of the first meeting by offering more favorable terms. The Pleiadian aliens claimed that the Grey aliens were not trustworthy, but President Eisenhower did not want to stop nuclear testing and desired to obtain alien technology for military purposes. Eisenhower decided to have a secret second meeting with the aliens, to be held at Holloman AFB in New Mexico in February of 1955, located some 120 miles from the famous Roswell alien crash, but this time with the Grey aliens, not the Pleiadian aliens.

Eisenhower's Lockheed Constellation landed at Holloman AFB with about twenty people on board, including secret service men and a small crew. The presidential airplane taxied and stopped at about a half mile away from the base tower. The civilians and military personnel on the base had been told that while the president was here, this would be a "business as usual" day. Right after the plane landed, the radar officers were given instructions to shut off all radar equipment. Minutes later, a ground patrol reported two unidentified flying objects approaching. The tower received another report, a third UFO spotted behind the first two. The UFOs approached the president's plane, sitting alone on the runway. The first two flying saucers hovered about 300 feet over Eisenhower's plane, and one descended on the far side of the airplane and touched down about 200 feet in front of it. The other object hovered over buildings with a good vantage point of anything that might come towards the plane and the other ship. The disc on the ground opened a hatch, and a small ramp was extended. Eisenhower descended the staircase of his plane and walked in the direction of the object on the ground. He paused for a short moment at the bottom of the ramp. It appeared that he was shaking hands with another individual, but the distance from observers would not allow a description. The president entered the spacecraft. One can imagine the tension that the Officials, Secret Service, and base personnel felt. President Eisenhower emerged from the spacecraft after about 45 minutes and returned to his Lockheed Constellation.

According to witnesses and researchers, they discussed the Greada Treaty, which was signed by the both the President and the alien race known as Greys. Later, other races got together on the Greada Treaty, Tall Whites, Reptilians, and the Anunnaki. In the 1954 alleged Greada Treaty, the Eisenhower administration bypassed the U.S. Constitution, and formed a pact with the aliens. At first, the aliens apparently wanted the public to be told the truth about their existence. In the final treaty, they seemingly had changed their minds and wanted to remain secret.

The 1954 Greada Treaty states:

1) We would not be involved in their affairs and they would not become involved in ours.
2) They would help us with developing our technology.
3) They would not make a treaty with any other nation on Earth.
4) The aliens could abduct humans and livestock on a limited basis for medical examination and monitoring; The people subjected to these experiences would not be harmed, and would be returned to their point of abduction with no recollection of the event. They had to provide the names of all those they had abducted to Earth's Majestic 12 committee.
5) The public would not be informed about the existence of aliens.
6) The U.S. could also do medical examinations and genetic experimentation on the aliens, and they would share information with us.
7) The aliens would be granted secret facilities for their accommodations and experiments.

On March 5, 2013, an unnamed CIA agent known as "Agent Kewper" gave a deathbed confession in which he states that he worked on "Project Bluebook", investigations that could not be explained or rebuked by the CIA. These agents may have been what is now referred to as the "Men in

Black". In 1958, Kewper's boss, the Director of CIA Operations for Eastern United States, told him he had a new assignment, and wanted the agent to accompany him to the White house, as they were requested by President Dwight D. Eisenhower. In the presence of Vice President Richard Nixon, President Eisenhower said that he was at odds with the Majestic-12, who hadn't reported back to him on the aliens that were housed at Area 51, the ultra-secret facility east of the Nevada Test Site. Eisenhower said that he had phoned the people from Majestic-12, meeting at S4 in Area 51, and was told that they Government had no jurisdiction over their activities.

He told the two CIA agents to go the S4, and tell them that they had one week in which to report back to Eisenhower on what they were doing. If they refused to provide information, Eisenhower would invade the base using elements of the First Army who were stationed in Colorado, and take over the facility. He did not care what type of classified material they had.

The two agents went to Area 51 where they were taken to S4. They said that they were shown multiple UFOs, each kept in a unit which had a garage door on it. The first door was opened to reveal the Roswell crash wreckage. It was badly damaged and looked as if it was heavy aluminum foil but weighed about 150 to 300 pounds and was easy to rock back and forth. They were told that all aliens from Roswell crash were dead except for two. Later, they were shown an autopsy film of one of the aliens. After the film, they were taken into a room where they saw a live "Grey Alien", and the Director was allowed a partial interview the alien. The Alien looked a little like an "Oriental." It did not look human because of his skin tone and the shape and size of his head. His brain was big, his nose small, ears like holes, and the mouth was very small.

The two CIA agents returned to Washington D. C. and met with President Eisenhower, Vice President Nixon, and the FBI Director Hoover. They met on the second floor of the Office of Strategic Services (OSS) warehouse building. The agents told the group about their findings, about the black projects, and the interview with the live alien. President Eisenhower, not aware of the live alien at Area 51, was very concerned.

Through the years, there have been more reports of UFO landings at Holloman Air Force base. On April 24, 1964, three UFOs flew into Holloman. They were tracked on radar and actually captured on film. One of the craft seemed to wobble, and eventually landed. Three humanoids with blue-gray complexions, and dressed in tight-fitting flight suits, were met by the base commander and four other officers. The aliens stayed for several days while their aircraft was being repaired. What was discussed in the meetings is still a mystery. It is also a mystery as to why so many people were involved in the meetings and, to date, so few people have broken their silence.

In 1973, Robert Emenegger and Alan Sandler, two well-connected Los Angeles businessmen, were invited to Norton Air Force Base in California to discuss a possible documentary film on advanced research projects. Two military officials, one the base's head of the Air Force Office of Special Investigations, the other, audio-visual director Paul Shartle, discussed a film on UFOs. Emenegger and Sandler were told of a 16 mm film taken at Holloman AFB, New Mexico, on May 1971, showing "three disc-shaped craft." One of the craft landed, and two of them went away.

A door opened on the landed vehicle and three beings emerged, Shartle said. They were human-size, had an odd grayish complexion, and a pronounced nose. They wore tight fitting jump suits, and thin headdresses that appeared to be communication devices, and in their hands they held a 'translator'. The Holloman base commander and other Air Force officers went out to meet them. Emenegger was led to believe he would be given the film for use in his documentary. He was even shown the landing site and the building in which the spaceship had been stored, and there were others (Buildings 383 and 1382). Meetings between Air Force personnel and the aliens had been conducted over the next several days.

MAY 1971...HOLLOMAN AFB NEW MEXICO

Actual Photo frame from Holloman Film

According to sources, the landing had taken place at 6 a.m. The extraterrestrials were "doctors and professional types." Their eyes had vertical slits like a cat's, and their mouths were thin and slit-like, with no chins." Emenegger was told that he would be given 3200 feet of film taken of the landing. At the last minute, however, permission was withdrawn, although Emenegger and Sandler were encouraged to describe the Holloman episode as something hypothetical, something that could happen or might happen in the future. A documentary narrated by the legendary Rod Serling, "UFOs: Past, Present and Future," was produced in 1974. It has a segment on UFO landings at Holloman AFB and the 1955 meeting with Eisenhower. The documentary was nominated for a Golden Globe award as the best documentary of the year. A later documentary, released in 1976, "UFOS: It Has Begun," also referenced Holloman AFB and the landings that have occurred there.

Majestic-12 and Special Projects

In July, 1947, General George C. Marshall formed a group to study the Roswell-Magdalena UFO crash recovery and debris. They had complete control of the "Flying Saucer Program" and were able to hide all physical evidence from the event. Within 6 months of the Roswell crash, on July 2, 1947, and the retrieval of another crashed UFO at San Augustine Flats near Magdalena, New Mexico on July 3, 1947, a great deal of reorganization of agencies took place. The reason for this was to analyze, and attempt the duplication of the UFO technologies.

The 1747 activities consisted of the following groups: The Research and Development Board; Air Force Research and Development; the Office of Naval Research; the CIA Office of Scientific Intelligence; and Office of Scientific Intelligence. No single one of these groups knew the whole story, only the parts that they were allowed to know ("Compartmentalized Security"). In July 26, 1947 Congress approved the National Security Act of 1947 and President Harry S. Truman signed it, thereby authorizing the CIA and its first Director, Rear Admiral Roscoe Hillenkoetter.

On September 24, 1947 President Truman authorized secretary of Defense James Forrestal to form the Top Secret operation known as the Majestic-12 (MJ-12). The purpose of the group was to determine how to handle the implications of the Roswell incident, and the existence of extraterrestrial beings. It was responsible for every aspect of the interface with the alien life forms, including security and intelligence, as well as disseminating disinformation to the general public and foreign entities in regard to the alien presence.

MJ-12 consisted of 12 scholars chosen from a group of 32 members known as the Jason Society. The actual cost of funding the project was very high, and the money mostly came from the world's illegal drug trade. This was done to hide the funding sources, and thus keep the secret from Congress, the people of the United States, and later even the U.S. President.

The MJ-12 group was located in Maryland, on land donated by the Rockefeller family, and is only accessible by air. It is code named "The Country Club". Its original members were:

- Dr. Lloyd V. Berkener - Explorer and scientist, he headed a group that later became the Weapons Systems Evaluation Group. He was also a member of a CIA panel that determined that UFOs did not constitute a threat to U.S. national security. Berkener was the executive director at Carnegie Institute, and was a member of the Joint Research and Development Board in 1946.
- Dr. Detlev Bronk - Physiologist, aviation expert, and prominent member of the National Academy of Science, he served as president of both Johns Hopkins and Rockefeller Universities. He was chairman of the Nuclear Research Committee and the medical advisor for the Atomic Energy Commission. Bronk also served on the Scientific Advisory Committee of Brookhaven National Laboratory where he worked with Dr. Edward Condon (who completed a major UFO study for the Air Force).
- Dr. Vannevar Bush - A leader in research and development at Massachusetts Institute of Technology and Carnegie Institute, he was at one time the head of each of the following: Office of Scientific Research and Development, the Joint Research and Development Board, and the National Advisory Committee on Aeronautics. The Office of Scientific Research and Development was responsible for the development of the atomic bomb. Bush also put together the National Defense Research Council in 1941.
- James Forrestal - Forrestal was undersecretary of the Navy, then secretary of the Navy. He became the first secretary of Defense in 1947, during the time of the Roswell crash. He died in 1949, under very mysterious circumstances. More about this later in the chapter.
- Gordon Gray - Secretary of the Army, he later held several high security positions under Presidents Truman and Eisenhower. He was also a consultant on UFOs and reported directly to CIA Director Walter B. Smith.

- Admiral Roscoe Hillenkoetter - He was the first director of the Central Intelligence Agency (CIA). Later he was chosen a member of the National Investigations Committee on Aerial Phenomena (NICAP). He publicly stated that "UFOs are [a] real concern, but through official secrecy and ridicule, many citizens are led to believe the unknown flying objects are nonsense." He charged that, "To hide the facts, the Air Force has silenced its personnel" through the issuance of stiff regulations.
- Dr. Jerome Hunsaker - Head of the National Advisory Committee on Aeronautics; chairman of the Departments of Mechanical and Aeronautical Engineering at MIT.
- Dr. Donald Menzel - Director of the Harvard College Observatory and an expert in cryptanalysis, the science of breaking codes and deciphering unknown languages and symbols. Menzel was involved in very high-level intelligence operations during and after World War II.
- General Robert M. Montegue - Head of the Armed Forces Special Weapons Center, he was also an Army general at Fort Bliss and as such had control over the White Sands Nuclear Research facility and the Sandia Atomic Energy Commission facility at Albuquerque, New Mexico during the time of the saucer crash at Roswell.
- Admiral Sidney Souers - Souers was the first Director of Central Intelligence, the precursor to the Central Intelligence Agency. He was also a member of the National Security Council and a special consultant for military intelligence operations.
- General Nathan Twining - Chairman of the Joint Chiefs of Staff, Chief of Staff of the U.S. Air Force, Twining was also the commander of the Air Materiel Command based at Wright-Patterson Air base, where the debris and bodies from the Roswell crash were taken. Twining was known to have cancelled a scheduled trip on July 8, 1947, just days after the crash at Roswell and the same day Roswell Army Air Base sent out a press release stating that a flying saucer had been recovered. In a now-famous memo, Twining stated that UFOs were very real.
- General Hoyt Vandenberg - Chief of Staff of the U.S. Air Force and former Director of Central Intelligence, he was allegedly in charge of security for the MJ-12 group. Vandenberg Air Force base in California, which has become a major rocket launch site, is named for him.

In 1954 President Eisenhower, by Secret Executive Order, "Order Number 54-12changed the MJ-12 Committee (operating under the National Security Council) was renamed the "54-12 Committee" with the President of The United States having responsibility to approve all covert projects. Today it is known as the "40 Committee" which has access to advanced technology and to teams conducting cover-up operations. In the past, this committee was headed by Dr. Henry Kissinger, using the code name "The Overseer".

OPERATION MAJORITY is the name of the operation responsible for every aspect, project, and all consequences of alien presence on Earth. MAJESTY was listed as the code name for the President of the United States for communications concerning this information.

In 1947, PROJECT SIGN was created to acquire as much information as possible about UFOs, their performance characteristics and their purposes. In order to preserve security, liaison between SIGN and MJ-12 was limited to two individuals within the intelligence division of the Air Materiel Command, whose role was to pass along certain types of information through proper channels. SIGN evolved into PROJECT GRUDGE in December of 1948. GRUDGE had an overt civilian counterpart named PROJECT BLUE BOOK. Only "Safe" reports were passed to BLUE BOOK.

GRUDGE was funded by the CIA using funding from confidential, non-appropriated sources, in addition to money from the illicit drug trade. The purpose of GRUDGE was to collect all scientific, technological, medical and intelligence information from UFO and Identified alien craft sightings, as well as contact with alien life forms. This information was saved in 16 volumes of files, and has been used to advance the United States Air Force Space Program.

BLUE BOOK was a U.S. Air Force collection and disinformation project relating to UFOs and alien intelligence. This project was terminated, and its collected information and duties were absorbed by PROJECT AQUARIUS. A classified report named "Grudge/Blue Book, Report Number 13" is the only significant information derived from the project and is unavailable to the public.

PROJECT POUNCE was formed to recover all crashed UFOs and alien beings. POUNCE provided cover stories and operations to mask the true endeavor, whenever necessary. Cover stories which have been used, were: crashed experimental aircraft, construction, mining, etc. This project has been successful and is ongoing today.

The National Reconnaissance Office (NRO) function is to manage the development and operation of the nation's reconnaissance satellite and overhead platforms, and provides security for all Majority Agency for Joint Intelligence (MAJI) projects. It consists of a security team and task force especially trained to provide alien-tasked projects. MAJI, also known as the "Men in Black" (MIB, are men who dress in dark suits, wearing sunglasses, who claim to be government agents. They typically harass or threaten UFO witnesses in order to silence them about what they have experienced. They are usually men of short stature with deeply tanned complexions, driving large late model cars, but also use unmarked black helicopters. MIB always have detailed information on the persons they contact. They will claim to be from an agency collecting information on the unexplained phenomenon their subjects had encountered. Men in Black will claim to be from the U.S. Air Force or the CIA and flash convincing-looking badges and demand that the witness recant their story or hand over photographs or physical evidence of a UFO. If the witness refuses or questions their credentials, they will subtly or overtly threaten the witness or their family with bodily harm or other hardships. If a person tries to verify their badges or credentials they will find either they do not exist or have been dead for some time. This is an ongoing project that operates today.

All information, disinformation, and intelligence is gathered and evaluated through MAJI. It operates in conjunction with the CIA, NSA, DIA, and the Office of Naval Intelligence. This is a very powerful organization, and all U.S. alien projects are under its control. MAJI is responsible only to the 40 Committee.

While all the above is well documented, the official response from the United States Government is that the documents are counterfeit and that there is no "E.O. 54-12" or alien UFO projects. If this is the case, it would only make sense because of the plethora of "Roswell Incident" documentation with the assertion that alien and UFOs do exist.

Extraterrestrial Recovery and Disposal Manual

The following passage from an 'alleged official document' leaked to UFO researchers describes the official secrecy policy adopted in April 1954.

Any encounter with entities known to be of extraterrestrial origin is to be considered to be a matter of national security and therefore classified TOP SECRET. Under no circumstances is the general public or the public press to learn of the existence of these entities. The official government policy is that such creatures do not exist, and that no agency of the federal government is now engaged in any study of extraterrestrials or their artifacts. Any deviation from this stated policy is absolutely forbidden.

In December 1953, the Joint Chiefs of Staff issued Army-Navy-Air Force publication 146 that made the unauthorized release of information concerning UFOs a crime under the Espionage Act, punishable by up to 10 years in prison and a $10,000 fine.

RESTRICTED

SOM1-01

TO 12D1-3-11-1
MAJESTIC-12 GROUP SPECIAL OPERATIONS MANUAL

EXTRATERRESTRIAL ENTITIES AND TECHNOLOGY, RECOVERY AND DISPOSAL

TOP SECRET/MAJIC
EYES ONLY

WARNING! This is a TOP SECRET-MAJIC EYES ONLY document containing compartmentalized information essential to the national security of the United States. EYES ONLY ACCESS to the material herein is strictly limited to personnel possessing MAJIC-12 CLEARANCE LEVEL. Examination or use by unauthorized personnel is strictly forbidden and is punishable by federal law.

---

*MAJESTIC-12 GROUP * APRIL 1954*

MJ-12 4838B-Mar 270435°-54-1

TOP SECRET / MAJIC EYES ONLY

**REMOVAL AND / OR REPLACEMENT OF PAGE(S) ATTACHED TO THE
DOCUMENT REQUIRES WRITTEN AUTHORIZATION FROM THE MAJIC-12
OPERATIONS OFFICER AND WILL BE RECORDED BY THE DOCUMENTS/
RECORDS OFFICER FOR EACH INSTANCE.**

PAGE(S)	REMOVED TIME/DATE	REMARKS	INITIALS	REPLACED TIME/DATE	INITIALS
32-40	0920/12OCT54	MJ/04	EWL	1135/12OCT54	EWL
35	1595/10NOV54	MJ/04	EWL	1015/11NOV54	EWL
18.19	1425/08FEB55	MJ/01	EWL	0800/10FEB55	EWL

PAGES 31-40 INCLUSIVE REMOVED PERMANENTLY FROM DOCUMENT
BY ORDER MJ-12 COMMAND 0930/ 12 APRIL 1955 (MJ/031-54)

PAGE(S)	REMOVED TIME/DATE	REMARKS	INITIALS	REPLACED TIME/DATE	INITIALS
8-10	1200/31MAY55	MJ/04	EWL	1415/31MAY55	EWL
5.20	0959/03JUL55	MJ/04	EWL	0830/12JUL55	EWL
5.6	1304/10MAY56	MJ/04	JRT	0900/14MAY56	JRT
17-19	1050/16AUG56	MJ/04	JRT	1635/16AUG56	JRT
6.12. 18	0919/05FEB 57	MJ/01	JRT	1105/05FEB57	JRT

MJ-12 4838B

i

TOP SECRET / MAJIC EYES ONLY
REPRODUCTION IN ANY FORM IS FORBIDDEN BY FEDERAL LAW

TOP SECRET/MAJIC
EYES ONLY

WARNING! This is a TOP SECRET-MAJIC EYES ONLY document containing compartmentalized information essential to the national security of the United States. EYES ONLY ACCESS to the material herein is strictly limited to personnel possessing MAJIC-12 CLEARANCE LEVEL. Examination or use by unauthorized personnel is strictly forbidden and is punishable by federal law.

Removal of any page(s) from this document for examination by authorized person requires written authorization from the MJ-12 OPNAC OPERATIONS OFFICER. Reproduction in any form or the taking of written or transcribed notes is strictly forbidden.

Clinton Laird

Special Operations Manual   MAJESTIC-12 GROUP
No. 1- 01   Washington 25, D.C., *7 April 1954*

EXTRATERRESTRIAL ENTITIES AND TECHNOLOGY, RECOVERY AND DISPOSAL

MJ-12 4838B

1

70

TOP SECRET / MAJIC EYES ONLY

CHAPTER 1

OPERATION MAJESTIC-12

Section I. PROJECT PURPOSE AND GOALS

1. Scope

This manual has been prepared especially for Majestic-12 units. Its purpose is to present all aspects of Majestic-12 so authorized personnel will have a better understanding of the goals of the Group, be able to more expertly deal with Unidentified Flying Objects, Extraterrestrial Technology and Entities, and increase the efficiency of future operations.

2. General

MJ-12 takes the subject of the UFOBs, Extraterrestrial Technology and Extraterrestrial Biological Entities very seriously and considers the entire subject to be a matter of the very highest national security. For that reason everything relating to the subject has been assigned the very highest security classification. Three main points will be covered in this section.

   a. The general aspects of MJ-12 to clear up any misconceptions that anyone may have.
   b. The importance of the operations.
   c. The need for absolute secrecy in all phases of operations.

3. Security Classification

All information relating to MJ-12 has been classified MAJIC EYES ONLY and carries a security level 2 points above that of Top Secret. The reason for this has to do with the consequences that may arise not only from the impact upon the public should the existence of such matters become general knowledge, but also the danger of having such advanced technology as has been recovered by the Air Force fall into the hands of unfriendly foreign powers. No information is released to the public press and the official government position is that no special group such as MJ-12 exists.

4. History of the Group

Operation Majestic-12 was established by special classified presidential order on 24 September 1947 at the recommendation of Secretary of Defense James V. Forrestal and Dr. Vannevar Bush, Chairman of the Joint Research and Development Board. Operations are carried out under a Top Secret Research and Development - Intelligence Group directly responsible only to the President of the Unites States. The goals of the MJ-12 Group are as follows:

   a. The recovery for scientific study of all materials and devices of a foreign or extraterrestrial manufacture that may become available. Such material and devices will be recovered by any and all means deemed necessary by the Group.
   b. The recovery for scientific study of all entities and remains of entities not of terrestrial origin which may become available through independent action by those entities or by misfortune or military action.
   c. The establishment and administration of Special Teams to accomplish the above

2
TOP SECRET / MAJIC EYES ONLY
REPRODUCTION IN ANY FORM IS FORBIDDEN BY FEDERAL LAW

TOP SECRET / MAJIC EYES ONLY

operations.

d. The establishment and administration of special secure facilities located at secret locations within the continental borders of the Unites States for the receiving, processing, analysis, and scientific study of any and all materials and entities classified as being of extraterrestrial origin by the Group of the Special Teams.

e. Establishment and administration of covert operations to be carried out in concert with Central Intelligence to effect the recovery for the United States of extraterrestrial technology and entities which may come down inside the territory of or fall into the possession of foreign powers.

f. The establishment and maintenance of absolute top secrecy concerning all the above operations.

5.   Current Situation

It is considered as far as the current situation is concerned, that there are few indications that these objects and their builders pose a direct threat to the security of the United States, despite the uncertainty as to their ultimate motives in coming here. Certainly the technology possessed by these beings far surpasses anything known to modern science, yet their presence here seems to be benign, and they seem to be avoiding contact with our species, at least for the present. Several dead entities have been recovered along with a substantial amount of wreckage and devices from downed craft, all of which are now under study at various locations. No attempt has been made by extraterrestrial entities either to contact authorities or to recover their dead counterparts or the downed craft, even though one of the crashes was the result of direct military action. The greatest threat at this time arises from the acquisition and study of such advanced technology by foreign powers unfriendly to the United States. It is for this reason that the recovery and study of this type of material by the United States has been given such a high priority.

TOP SECRET / MAJIC EYES ONLY

CHAPTER 2
INTRODUCTION

Section I. GENERAL

6. Scope

a. This operation manual is published for the information and guidance of all concerned. It contains information on determination, documentation, collection, and disposition of debris, devices, craft, and occupants of such craft as defined as Extraterrestrial Technology or Extraterrestrial Biological Entities, EBEs in Section II of this chapter.

b. Appendix I-Ia contains a list of current references, including technical manuals and other available publications applicable to these operations.

c. Appendix II contains a list of personnel who comprise the Majestic-12 Group.

7. Forms and Records

Forms used for reporting operation are listed in Appendix I.

Section II. DEFINITION AND DATA

8. General

Extraterrestrial Technology is defined as follows:

a. Aircraft identified as not manufactured in the United States or any terrestrial foreign powers, including experimental military or civilian aircraft. Aircraft in this category are generally known as Unidentified Flying Objects, or UFOBs. Such aircraft may appear as one of several shapes and configurations and exhibit extraordinary flight characteristics.

b. Objects and devices of unknown origin or function, manufactured by processes or of materials not consistent with current technology or scientific knowledge.

c. Wreckage of any aircraft thought to be of extraterrestrial manufacture or origin. Such wreckage may be the results of accidents or military action.

d. Materials that exhibit unusual or extraordinary characteristics not consistent with current technology or scientific knowledge.

Extraterrestrial Biological Entities (EBEs) are described as:

a. Creatures, humanoids or otherwise, whose evolutionary processes responsible for their development are demonstrably different from those postulated or observed in homo sapiens.

9. Description of Craft

Documented extraterrestrial craft (UFOBs) are classified in one of four categories based on general shape, as follows:

a. Elliptical, or disc shape. This type of craft is of a metallic construction and dull aluminum in color. They have the appearance of two pie-pans or shallow dishes pressed together and may have a raised dome on the top or bottom. No seams or joints are visible on the surface, giving the impression of one-piece construction. Discs are estimated from 50-300 feet in diameter and the thickness is approximately 15 per cent of the diameter, not including the

TOP SECRET / MAJIC EYES ONLY
REPRODUCTION IN ANY FORM IS FORBIDDEN BY FEDERAL LAW

dome, which is 30 per cent of the disc diameter and extends another 4-6 feet above the main body of the disc. The dome may or may not include windows or ports, and ports are present around the lower rim of the disc in some instances. Most disc-shaped craft are equipped with lights on the top and bottom, and also around the rim. These lights are not visible when the craft is at rest or not functioning. There are generally no visible antenna or projections. Landing gear consists of three extendible legs ending in circular landing pads. When fully extended this landing gear supports the main body 2-3 feet above the surface at the lowest point. A rectangular hatch is located along the equator or on the lower surface of the disk.

 b. Fuselage or cigar shape. Documented reports of this type of craft are extremely rare. Air Force radar reports indicate they are approximately 2 thousand feet long and 95 feet thick, and apparently they do not operate in the lower atmosphere. Very little information is available on the performance of these craft, but radar reports have indicated speeds in excess of 7,000 miles per hour. They do not appear to engage in the violent and erratic maneuvers associated with the smaller types.

 c. Ovoid or circular shape. This type of craft is described as being shaped like an ice cream cone, being rounded at the large end and tapering to a near-point at the other end. They are approximately 30-40 feet long and the thick end diameter is approximately 20 per cent of the length. There is an extremely bright light at the pointed end, and this craft usually travels point down. They can appear to be any shape from round to cylindrical, depending upon the angle of observation. Often sightings of this type of craft are elliptical craft seen at an inclined angle or edge-on.

 d. Airfoil or triangular shape. This craft is believed to be new technology due to the rarity and recency of the observations. Radar indicates an isosceles triangle profile, the longest side being nearly 300 feet in length. Little is known about the performance of these craft due to the rarity of good sightings, but they are believed capable of high speeds and abrupt maneuvers similar to or exceeding the performance attributed to types "a" and "c".

10. Description of Extraterrestrial Biological Entities (EBEs)

 Examination of remains recovered from wreckage of UFOBs indicates that Extraterrestrial Biological Entities may be classified into two distinct categories as follows:

 a. EBE Type I. These entities are humanoid and might be mistaken for human beings of the Oriental race if seen from a distance. They are bi-pedal, 5-5 feet 4 inches in height and weigh 80-100 pounds. Proportionally they are similar to humans, although the cranium is somewhat larger and more rounded. The skin is a pale, chalky-yellow in color, thick, and slightly pebbled in appearance. The eyes are small, wide-set, almond-shaped, with brownish-black irises with very large pupils. The whites of the eyes are not like that of humans, but have a pale gray cast. The ears are small and set low on the skull. The nose is thin and long, and the mouth is wider than in humans, and nearly lipless. There is no apparent facial hair and very little body hair, that being very fine and confined to the underarm and the groin area. The body is thin and without apparent body fat, but the muscles are well-developed. The hands are small, with four long digits but no opposable thumb. The outside digit is jointed in a manner as to be nearly opposable, and there is no webbing between the fingers as in humans. The legs are slightly but noticeably bowed, and the feet are somewhat splayed and proportionally large.

TOP SECRET / MAJIC EYES ONLY

b. EBE Type II. These entities are humanoid but differ from Type I in many respects. They are bi-pedal, 3 feet 5 inches - 4 feet 2 inches in height and weigh 25-50 pounds. Proportionally, the head is much larger than humans or Type I EBEs, the cranium being much larger and elongated. The eyes are very large, slanted, and nearly wrap around the side of the skull. They are black with no whites showing. There is no noticeable brow ridge, and the skull has a slight peak that runs over the crown. The nose consists of two small slits which sit high above the slit-like mouth. There are no external ears. The skin is a pale bluish-gray color, being somewhat darker on the back of the creature, and is very smooth and fine-celled. There is no hair on either the face or the body, and these creatures do not appear to be mammalian. The arms are long in proportion to the legs, and the hands have three long, tapering fingers and a thumb which is nearly as long as the fingers. The second finger is thicker than the others, but not as long as the index finger. The feet are small and narrow, and four toes are joined together with a membrane.

It is not definitely known where either type of creature originated, but it seems certain that they did not evolve on earth. It is further evident, although not certain, that they may have originated on two different planets.

11.   Description of Extraterrestrial Technology

The following information is from preliminary analysis reports of wreckage collected from crash sites of extraterrestrial craft 1947-1953, excerpts from which are quoted verbatim to provide guidance as to the type of characteristics of material that might be encountered in future recovery operations.

a. Initial analysis of the debris from the crash site seems to indicate that the debris is that of an extraterrestrial craft which exploded from within and came into contact with the ground with great force, completely destroying the craft. The volume of matter indicates that the craft was approximately the size of a medium aircraft, although the weight of the debris indicates that the craft was extremely light for its size.

b. Metallurgical analysis of the bulk of the debris recovered indicates that the samples are not composed of any materials currently known to Terrestrial science.

c. The material tested possesses great strength and resistance to heat in proportion to its weight and size, being stronger by far than any materials used in military or civilian aircraft at present.

d. Much of the material, having the appearance of aluminum foil or aluminum-magnesium sheeting, displays none of the characteristics of either metal, resembling instead some kind of unknown plastic-like material.

e. Solid structures and substantial beams having a distinct similarity in appearance to very dense grain-free wood, was very light in weight and possesses tensile and compression strength not obtainable by any means known to modern industry.

f. None of the material tested displayed measurable magnetic characteristics or residual radiation.

g. Several samples were engraved or embossed with marks and patterns. These patterns were not readily identifiable and attempts to decipher their meaning has been largely unsuccessful.

h. Examination of several apparent mechanical devices, gears, etc. revealed little or nothing of their functions or methods of manufacture.

TOP SECRET / MAJIC EYES ONLY
REPRODUCTION IN ANY FORM IS FORBIDDEN BY FEDERAL LAW

CHAPTER 3
RECOVERY OPERATIONS

Section I. SECURITY

12.   Press Blackout

Great care must be taken to preserve the security of any location where Extraterrestrial Technology might be retrievable for scientific study. Extreme measures must be taken to protect and preserve any material or craft from discovery, examination, or removal by civilian agencies or individuals of the general public. It is therefore recommended that a total press blackout be initiated whenever possible. If this course of action should not prove feasible, the following cover stories are suggested for release to the press. The officer in charge will act quickly to select the cover story that best fits the situation. It should be remembered when selecting a cover story that official policy regarding UFOBs is that they do not exist.

a. Official Denial. The most desirable response would be that nothing unusual has occurred. By stating that the government has no knowledge of the event, further investigation by the public press may be forestalled.

b. Discredit Witnesses. If at all possible, witnesses will be held incommunicado until the extent of their knowledge and involvement can be determined. Witnesses will be discouraged from talking about what they have seen, and intimidation may be necessary to ensure their cooperation. If witnesses have already contacted the press, it will be necessary to discredit their stories. This can best be done by the assertion that they have either misinterpreted natural events, are the victims of hysteria or hallucinations, or are the perpetrators of hoaxes.

c. Deceptive Statements. It may become necessary to issue false statements to preserve the security of the site. Meteors, downed satellites, weather balloons, and military aircraft are all acceptable alternatives, although in the case of the downed military aircraft statement care should be exercised not to suggest that the aircraft might be experimental or secret, as this might arouse more curiosity of both the American and the foreign press. Statements issued concerning contamination of the area due to toxic spills from trucks or railroad tankers can also serve to keep unauthorized or undesirable personnel away from the area.

13.   Secure the Area

The area must be secured as rapidly as possible to keep unauthorized personnel from infiltrating the site. The officer in charge will set up a perimeter and establish a command post inside the perimeter. Personnel allowed on the site will be kept to the absolute minimum necessary to prepare the craft or debris for transport, and will consist of Military Security Forces.

Local authorities may be pressed into service on traffic and crowd control. *Under no circumstances* will local official or law enforcement personnel be allowed inside the perimeter and all necessary precautions should be taken to ensure that they do not interfere with the operation.

a. Perimeter. It is desirable that sufficient military personnel be utilized to set up a perimeter around the site large enough to keep both unauthorized personnel and the perimeter

TOP SECRET / MAJIC EYES ONLY

personnel from seeing the site. Once the site is contained, regular patrols will be set up along the perimeter to ensure complete security, and electronic surveillance will be utilized to augment the patrols. Perimeter personnel will be equipped with hand communication and automatic weapons with live ammunition. Personnel working at the site will carry sidearms. No unauthorized personnel will be allowed into the secure area.

b. Command Post. Ideally, the command post should be as close to the site as is practical to efficiently coordinate operations. As soon as the command post is operational, contact with the Majestic-12 Group will be established via secure communications.

c. Area Sweep. The site and the surrounding area will be cleared of all unauthorized personnel. Witnesses will be debriefed and detained for further evaluation by MJ-12. *Under no circumstances* will witnesses be released from custody until their stories have been evaluated by MJ-12 and they have been thoroughly debriefed.

d. Situation Evaluation. A preliminary evaluation of the situation will be completed and a preliminary report prepared. The MJ-12 Group will then be briefed on the situation at the earliest possible opportunity. The MJ-12 Group will then make a determination as to whether or not a MJ-12 RED TEAM or OPNAC Team will be dispatched to the area.

Section II. TECHNOLOGY RECOVERY

14.   Removal and Transport

As soon as communication is established, removal and transport of all material will commence under order from MJ-12.

a. Documentation. If the situation permits, care should be taken to document the area with photographs before anything is moved. The area will be checked for radiation and other toxic agents. If the area cannot be kept secure for an extended period of time, all material must be packed and transported as quickly as possible to the nearest secure military facility. This will be accomplished by covered transport using little-traveled roads wherever possible.

b. Complete or Functional Craft. Craft are to be approached with extreme caution if they appear functional, as serious injury may result from exposure to radiation and electrical discharges. If the craft is functioning, but appears to be abandoned, it may be approached only by specially trained MJ-12 RED TEAM personnel wearing protective clothing. Any device that seems to be functioning should also be left to MJ-12 RED TEAM disposal. Complete craft and parts of crafts too large to be transported by covered transport will be disassembled, if this can be accomplished easily and quickly. If they must be transported whole, or on open flatbed trailers, they will be covered in such a manner as to camouflage their shape.

c. Extraterrestrial Biological Entities. EBEs must be removed to a top security facility as quickly as possible. Great care should be taken to prevent possible contamination by alien biological agents. Dead EBEs should be packed in ice at the earliest opportunity to preserve tissues. Should live EBEs be encountered, they should be taken into custody and removed to a top security facility by ambulance. Every effort should be taken to ensure the EBE's survival. Personnel involvement with EBEs alive or dead must be kept to an absolute minimum. (See Chapter 5 for more detailed information dealing with EBEs.)

TOP SECRET / MAJIC EYES ONLY
REPRODUCTION IN ANY FORM IS FORBIDDEN BY FEDERAL LAW

TOP SECRET / MAJIC EYES ONLY

15.   Cleansing the Area

Once all material has been removed from the central area, the immediate area will be thoroughly inspected to make sure that all traces of Extraterrestrial Technology have been removed. In the case of a crash, the surrounding area will be thoroughly gone over several times to ensure that nothing has been overlooked. The search area involved may vary according to local conditions, at the discretion of the officer in charge. When the officer in charge is satisfied that no further evidence of the event remains at the site, it may be evacuated.

16.   Special or Unusual Conditions

The possibility exists that extraterrestrial craft may land or crash in heavily populated areas, where security cannot be maintained or where large segments of the population and the public press may witness these events. Contingency Plan MJ-1949-04P / 78 (TOP SECRET-EYES ONLY) should be held in readiness should the need to make a public disclosure become necessary.

TOP SECRET / MAJIC EYES ONLY
REPRODUCTION IN ANY FORM IS FORBIDDEN BY FEDERAL LAW

TOP SECRET / MAJIC EYES ONLY

17. Extraterrestrial Technology Classification Table

No.	Item	Description or condition	MJ—12 Code	Receiving Facility
1	Aircraft.	Intact, operational, or semi-intact aircraft of Extraterrestrial design and manufacture.	UA-002-6	Area 51 S-4
2	Intact device.	Any mechanical or electronic device or machine which appears to be undamaged and functional.	ID-301-F	Area 51 S-4
3	Damaged device.	Any mechanical or electronic device or machine which appears to be damaged but mostly complete.	DD-303N	Area 51 S-4
4	Powerplant.	Devices and machines or fragments which are possible propulsion units, fuel and associated control devices and panels.	PD-40-8G	Area 51 S-4
5	Identified fragments	Fragments composed of elements or materials easily recognized as known to current science and technology, i.e.. aluminum, magnesium, plastic, etc.	IF-101-K	Area 51 S-4
6	Unidentified fragments.	Fragments composed of elements or materials not known to current science and technology and which exhibit unusual or extraordinary characteristics.	UF-103-M	Area 51 S-4
7	Supplies and provisions.	Non-mechanical or non-electronic materials of a support nature such as clothing, personal belongings, organic ingestibles, etc.	SP-331	Blue Lab WP-61
8	Living entity.*	Living non-human organisms in apparent good or reasonable health.	EBE-010	OPNAC BBS-01
9	Non-living entity.	Deceased non-human organisms or portions of organisms, organic remains and other suspect organic matter.	EBE-XO	Blue Lab WP-61
10	Media.	Printed matter, electronic recordings, maps, charts, photographs and film.	MM-54A	Building 21 KB-88
11	Weapons.	Any device or portion of a device thought to be offensive or defensive weaponry.	WW-010	Area 51 S-4

*Living entity must be contained in total isolation pending arrival of OPNAC personnel

TOP SECRET / MAJIC EYES ONLY
REPRODUCTION IN ANY FORM IS FORBIDDEN BY FEDERAL LAW

MJ-12 4838B

TOP SECRET / MAJIC EYES ONLY

18. Use of Inventory System

 a. The identification is performed as a duty of the officer making an inventory of the Extraterrestrial Technology or entities with the assistance of MJ Forms 1-006 and 1-007. (Fig. 1 and 2.) Instructions for the use of each form appear on the reverse side of the forms.

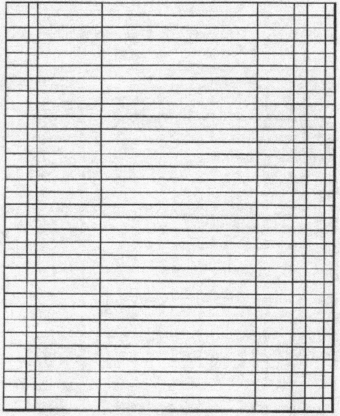

SOM 01 - 1

Figure 1. MJ Form 1-006

MJ-12 4838B   **11**

TOP SECRET / MAJIC EYES ONLY
REPRODUCTION IN ANY FORM IS FORBIDDEN BY FEDERAL LAW

TOP SECRET / MAJIC EYES ONLY

SOM 01 - 2

Figure 2. MJ Form 1-007

19. Packaging and Packing Data

    a. Domestic Shipment. Individual items are tagged and wrapped in a moisture-vaporproof barrier and heat sealed. They are then placed in a corrugated fiberboard box. The voids within the box are packed thoroughly with a neutral cellulose wadding to prevent

MJ-12 4838B   12

TOP SECRET / MAJIC EYES ONLY
REPRODUCTION IN ANY FORM IS FORBIDDEN BY FEDERAL LAW

TOP SECRET / MAJIC EYES ONLY

movement of the items. The box closure is sealed with gummed Kraft tape. MJ Form 1-007 is placed in a sealed manila envelope marked "MAJIC-12 ACCESS ONLY" and is firmly taped to the top of the box. The box is then cushioned at each corner and at the top and bottom with fiberboard inserts and is placed within a large corrugated fiberboard box. The entire outer box closure is sealed with gummed Kraft tape. A label is affixed to the outer box bearing the following information: destination, shipping code number, and the warning, "MAJIC-12 ACCESS ONLY."

   b. Overseas Shipment. Items are packaged as described above except that a dessicant and humidity indicator are included within the inner corrugated fiberboard box. Next, the box is wrapped in a moisture-vaporproof barrier and heat sealed. Then, packaged items are placed within a second waterproof carton sealed with waterproof tape. This second carton is marked "MAJIC-12 ACCESS ONLY" on all sides and is placed within a water-grease proof lined wooden shipping container. The lining is sealed with waterproof tape and the wooden shipping container is screwed shut. The shipping container is reinforced further by nailing two [3/4]-inch metal caps about 8 inches from each end. Shipping information is then stenciled on the surface of the wooden shipping container.

   Note. The packaging and packing procedure detailed above applies to non-organic items only. Data for handling, packaging, packing, and shipping of organic matter and non-living entities is provided in Chapter 5, Section II of this manual.

TOP SECRET / MAJIC EYES ONLY
REPRODUCTION IN ANY FORM IS FORBIDDEN BY FEDERAL LAW

TOP SECRET / MAJIC EYES ONLY

CHAPTER 4
RECEIVING AND HANDLING

Section I. HANDLING UPON RECEIPT OF MATERIAL

20.   Uncrating, Unpacking, and Checking

(Fig. 3)

Note. The uncrating, unpacking, and checking procedure for containers marked "MAJIC-12 ACCESS ONLY" will be carried out by personnel with MJ-12 clearance. Containers marked in this manner will be placed in storage in a top security area until such time as authorized personnel are available for these procedures.

a. Be very careful when uncrating and unpacking the material. Avoid thrusting tools into the interior of the shipping container. Do not damage the packaging material any more than is absolutely necessary to remove the specimens; these materials may be required for future packaging. Stow the interior packaging material within the shipping container. When uncrating and unpacking the specimens, follow the procedure given in (1) through (11) below:

(1)   Unpack the specimens in a top security area to prevent access of unauthorized personnel.

(2)   Cut the metal wires with a suitable cutting tool, or twist them with pliers until the straps crystallize and break.

(3)   Remove screws from the top of the shipping container with a screw driver.

(4)   Cut the tape and seals of the case liner so that the waterproof paper will be damaged as little as possible.

(5)   Lift out the packaged specimens from the wooden case.

(6)   Cut the tape which seals the top flaps of the outer cartons; be careful not to damage the cartons.

(7)   Cut the barrier along the top heat-sealed seam and carefully remove the inner carton.

(8)   Remove the sealed manila envelope from the top of the inner carton.

(9)   Open the inner carton and remove the fiberboard inserts, dessicant and humidity indicator.

(10)   Lift out the heat-sealed packaging containing the specimens; arrange them in an orderly manner for inspection.

(11)   Place all packaging material in the shipping container for use in future repacking.

TOP SECRET / MAJIC EYES ONLY
REPRODUCTION IN ANY FORM IS FORBIDDEN BY FEDERAL LAW

TOP SECRET / MAJIC EYES ONLY

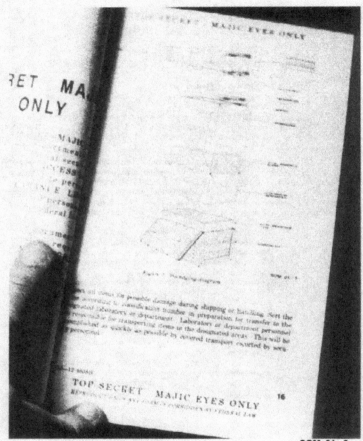

Figure 3. Packaging diagram

SOM 01 - 3

b. Thoroughly check all items against the shipping documents. Carefully inspect all items for possible damage during shipping or handling. Sort the items according to classification number in preparation for transfer to the designated laboratory or department. Laboratory or department personnel are responsible for transporting items to the designated areas. This will be accomplished as quickly as possible by covered transport escorted by security personnel.

MJ-12 4838B   15

TOP SECRET / MAJIC EYES ONLY

CHAPTER 5
EXTRATERRESTRIAL BIOLOGICAL ENTITIES

Section I. LIVING ORGANISMS

21.   Scope

a. This section deals with encounters with living Extraterrestrial Biological Entities (EBEs). Such encounters fall under the jurisdiction of MJ-12 OPNAC BBS-01 and will be dealt with by this special unit only. This section details the responsibilities of persons or units making the initial contact.

22.   General

Any encounter with entities known to be of extraterrestrial origin is to be considered to be a matter of national security and therefore classified TOP SECRET. Under no circumstances is the general public or the public press to learn of the existence of these entities. The official government policy is that such creatures do not exist, and that no agency of the federal government is now engaged in any study of extraterrestrials or their artifacts. Any deviation from this stated policy is absolutely forbidden.

23.   Encounters

Encounters with EBEs may be classified according to one of the following categories:
a. Encounters initiated by EBEs. Possible contact may take place as a result of overtures by the entities themselves. In these instances it is anticipated that encounters will take place at military installations or other obscure locations selected by mutual agreement. Such meetings would have the advantage of being limited to personnel with appropriate clearance, away from public scrutiny. Although it is not considered very probable, there also exists the possibility that EBEs may land in public places without prior notice. In this case the OPNAC Team will formulate cover stories for the press and prepare briefings for the President and the Chiefs of Staff.
b. Encounters as the result of downed craft. Contact with survivors of accidents or craft downed by natural events or military action may occur with little or no warning. In these cases, it is important that the initial contact be limited to military personnel to preserve security. Civilian witnesses to the area will be detained and debriefed by MJ-12. Contact with EBEs by military personnel not having MJ-12 or OPNAC clearance is to be strictly limited to action necessary to ensure the availability of the EBEs for study by the OPNAC Team.

24.   Isolation and Custody

a. EBEs will be detained by whatever means are necessary and removed to a secure location as soon as possible. Precautions will be taken by personnel coming in contact with EBEs to minimize the risk of disease as a result of contamination by unknown organisms. If the entities are wearing space suits or breathing apparatus of some kind, care should be exercised to prevent damage to these devices. While all efforts should be taken to assure the well-being of the EBEs, they must be isolated from any contact with unauthorized personnel. While it is not clear what provisions or amenities might be required by non-human entities, they should be

TOP SECRET / MAJIC EYES ONLY

provided if possible. The officer in charge of the operation will make these determinations, as no guidelines now exist to cover this area.

b. Injured or wounded entities will be treated by medical personnel assigned to the OPNAC Team. If the team medical personnel are not immediately available, First Aid will be administered by Medical Corps personnel at the initial site. Since little is known about EBE biological functions, aid will be confined to the stopping of bleeding, bandaging of wounds and splinting of broken limbs. No medications of any kind are to be administered as the effect of terrestrial medications on non-human biological systems are impossible to predict. As soon as the injuries are considered stabilized, the EBEs will be moved by closed ambulance or other suitable conveyance to a secure location.

c. In dealing with any living Extraterrestrial Biological Entity, security is of paramount importance. All other considerations are secondary. Although it is preferable to maintain the physical well-being of any entity, the loss of EBE life is considered acceptable if conditions or delays to preserve that life in any way compromises the security of the operations.

d. Once the OPNAC Team has taken custody of the EBEs, their care and transportation to designated facilities become the responsibility of OPNAC personnel. Every cooperation will be extended to the team in carrying out duties. OPNAC Team personnel will be given TOP PRIORITY at all times regardless of their apparent rank or status. No person has the authority to interfere with the OPNAC Team in the performance of its duties by special direction of the President of the United States.

Section II. NON-LIVING ORGANISMS

25. Scope

Ideally, retrieval for scientific study of cadavers and other biological remains will be carried out by medical personnel familiar with this type of procedure. Because of security considerations, such collection may need to be done by non-medical personnel. This section will provide guidance for retrieval, preservation, and removal of cadavers and remains in the field.

26. Retrieval and Preservation

a. The degree of decomposition of organic remains will vary depending on the length of time the remains have been lying in the open unprotected and may be accelerated by both local weather conditions and action by predators. Therefore, biological specimens will be removed from the crash site as quickly as possible to preserve the remains in as good a condition as possible. A photographic record will be made of all remains before they are removed from the site.

b. Personnel involved in this type of operation will take all reasonable precautions to minimize physical contact with the cadavers or remains being retrieved. Surgical gloves should be worn or, if they are not available, wool or leather gloves may be worn provided they are collected for decontamination immediately after use. Shovels and entrenching tools may be employed to handle remains provided caution is exercised to be certain no damage is done to the remains. Remains will be touched with bare hands only if no other means of moving them can be found. All personnel and equipment involved in recovery operations will undergo decontamination procedures immediately after those operations have been completed.

TOP SECRET / MAJIC EYES ONLY
REPRODUCTION IN ANY FORM IS FORBIDDEN BY FEDERAL LAW

TOP SECRET / MAJIC EYES ONLY

c. Remains will be preserved against further decomposition as equipment and conditions permit. Cadavers and remains will be bagged or securely wrapped in waterproof coverings. Tarpaulins or foul weather gear may be used for this purpose if necessary. Remains will be refrigerated or packed with ice if available. All remains will be tagged or labeled and the time and date recorded. Wrapped remains will be placed on stretchers or in sealed containers for immediate removal to a secure facility.

d. Small detached pieces and material scraped from solid surfaces will be put in jars or other small capped containers if available. Containers will be clearly marked as to their contents and the time and date recorded. Containers will be refrigerated or packed with ice as soon as possible and removed to a secure facility.

TOP SECRET / MAJIC EYES ONLY

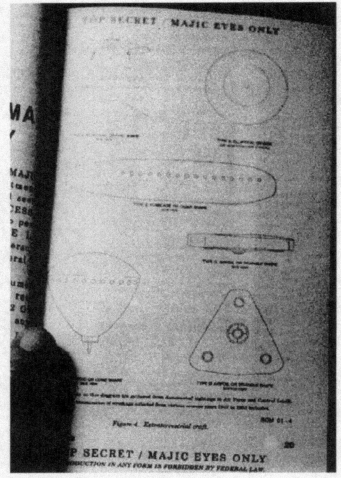

Note: Illustrations in this diagram are gathered from documented sightings in Air Force and Central Intelligence and from Examination of wreckage collected from various sources years 1947-1953 inclusive.

SOM 01 - 4

Figure 4. Extraterrestrial Craft

MJ-12 4838B   19

TOP SECRET / MAJIC EYES ONLY
REPRODUCTION IN ANY FORM IS FORBIDDEN BY FEDERAL LAW

CHAPTER 6
GUIDE TO UFO IDENTIFICATION

Section I. UFOB GUIDE

27. Follow-up Investigations

A UFOB report is worthy of follow-up investigation when it contains information to suggest that positive identification with a well-known phenomenon may be made or when it characterizes an unusual phenomenon. The report should suggest almost immediately, largely by the coherency and clarity of the data, that there is something of identification and / or scientific value. In general, reports which should be given consideration are those which involve several reliable observers, together or separately, and which concern sightings of greater duration than one quarter minute. Exception should be made to this when circumstances attending the report are considered to be extraordinary. Special attention should be given to reports which give promise to a "fix" on the position and those reports involving unusual trajectories.

28. Rules of Thumb

Each UFOB case should be judged individually but there are a number of "rules of thumb", under each of the following headings, which should prove helpful in determining the necessity for follow-up investigation.

a. Duration of Sighting. When the duration of a sighting is less than 15 seconds, the probabilities are great that it is not worthy of follow-up. As a word of caution, however, should a large number of individual observers concur on an unusual sighting of a few seconds duration, it should not be dismissed.

b. Number of Persons Reporting the Sighting. Short duration sightings by single individuals are seldom worthy of follow-up. Two or three competent independent observations carry the weight of 10 or more simultaneous individual observations. As an example, 25 people at one spot may observe a strange light in the sky. This, however, has less weight than two reliable people observing the same light from different locations. In the latter case a position-fix is indicated.

c. Distance from Location of Sightings to Nearest Field Unit. Reports which meet the preliminary criterion stated above should all be investigated if their occurrence is in the immediate operating vicinity of the squadron concerned. For reports involving greater distances, follow-up necessity might be judged as being inversely proportional to the square of the distances concerned. For example, an occurrence 150 miles away might be considered to have four times the importance (other things being equal) than one that is 300 miles away.

d. Reliability of Person or Persons Reporting. In establishing the necessity of follow-up investigation only "short term" reliability of individuals can be employed. Short term reliability is judged from the logic and coherency of the original report and by the age and occupation of the person. Particular attention should be given to whether the occupation involves observation reporting or technical knowledge.

e. Number of Individual Sightings Reported. Two completely individual sightings, especially when separated by a mile or more constitutes sufficient cause for follow-up, assuming previous criterion have not been violated.

TOP SECRET/MAJIC EYES ONLY

f. The Value of Obtaining Additional Information Immediately. If the information cannot be obtained within seven days, the value of such information is greatly decreased. It is of great value to obtain additional information immediately if previously stated criteria have been met. Often, if gathered quickly, two or three items (weather conditions, angular speed, changes in trajectory, duration, etc.) are sufficient for immediate evaluation. If investigation is undertaken after weeks or months, the original observers cease to be of value as far as additional new information is concerned. Generally, late interrogation yields only bare repetition of facts originally reported plus an inability on the part of the observer to be objective.

g. Existence of Physical Evidence (Photographs, Material, Hardware). In cases where any physical evidence exists, a follow-up should be made even if some of the above criteria have not been met.

29. Conclusion - UFOB Guide.

It is understood that all above criteria must be evaluated in terms of "common sense." The original report, from its working and clarity will almost always suggest to the reader whether there is any "paydirt" in the report.

Section II. IDENTIFICATION CRITERIA

30. General

When a UFO report meets, in large measure, the criteria projected in Section I and a follow-up investigation is instituted, then the interrogator should ask what physical object or objects might have served as the original stimulus for the report. The word "object" here includes optical phenomena such as reflections from clouds, sundogs, etc. Frequently one or perhaps two solutions will be immediately suggested by the nature of the report. The word "solution" cannot be used here in the scientific sense. A solution in UFOB work means that a hypothesis has been arrived at which appears to have the greatest probability of having given rise to the given report. Following is a group of hypotheses or examples which should prove helpful in arriving at solutions. A check should be made to see how many of the items are satisfied by the report and how many are missing. An effort should be made to obtain any missing items as soon as possible. Each typical hypothesis is listed in a separate paragraph.

31. Aircraft

a. Shape. From conventional to circular or elliptical.

b. Size. Pinpoint to actual

c. Color. Silver to bright yellow (night - black or color of lights).

d. Speed. Generally only angular speeds can be observed. This depends on distance but small objects crossing major portion of sky in less than a minute can be ruled out. Aircraft will not cross major portion of sky in less than a minute whereas a meteor certainly will.

e. Formation. Two to twenty. Numbers greater than 20 more likely birds than aircraft.

f. Trails. May or may not have (vapor and exhaust).

g. Sound. Zero to loud shrill or low depending on altitude.

h. Course. Steady, straight or gently curving (not erratic - may appear still if approaching head-on). Right angle turns and sudden reversals, changes in altitude ruled out. Note: Although report may indicate erratic course, if other items check, follow-up should proceed on basis of aircraft because of psychological tendencies of excited people to exaggerate course changes.

 i. Time In Sight. More than 15 seconds, generally of the order of a minute or two.

 j. Lighting Conditions. Night or Day.

 k. Radar. Should show normal aircraft returns.

32.   Balloons

 a. Shape. Round to cigar or pinpoint.

 b. Size. Balloons up to a hundred feet will generally appear from pinpoint to size of a pea held at arm length.

 c. Color. Silver, white or many tints. It may possibly appear dark as when projected against the clouds.

 d. Speed. Large scale erratic speed ruled out. In general, hovering to slow apparent speed.

 e. Formation. Single to cluster.

 f. Trail. None.

 g. Sound. None.

 h. Course. Straight with a general gradual ascent, unless falling.

 i. Time In Sight. Generally long. Note: Balloons may suddenly burst and disappear.

 j. Lighting Conditions. Night or day but especially at sunset.

 k. Radar. No return except when carrying sonde equipment.

33.   Meteor

 a. Shape. Round to elongated.

 b. Size. Pinpoint to size of moon.

 c. Color. Flaming yellow with red, green or blue possible.

 d. Speed. Crosses large portion of sky in few seconds except if coming head-on.

 e. Formation. Generally single - can break into shower at end of trajectory. Occasionally (but rare) small groups.

 f. Trail. At night almost always a luminous train which can persist as long as a half hour (rarely). Daytime meteors are much less frequently observed. In daytime, leaves a whitish to dark smoke trail.

 g. Sound. None, although occasionally reported (believed psychological).

 h. Course. Generally streaking downward, but not necessarily sharply downward. Can on rare occasion give impression of slight rise.

 i. Time In Sight. Longest report about 30 seconds, generally less than 10.

 j. Lighting Conditions. Day or Night. Mostly night.

 k. Radar. Return from meteor itself is highly improbable, however, the train left by a meteor, is a good radar reflector.

 l. Other. An exceptionally bright meteor is called a fireball. These are rare but extremely spectacular and on occasion have been known to light surroundings to the brightness of daylight.

34.   Stars or Planets

The planets, Venus, Mars, Jupiter, and Saturn are generally brighter than any star, but they twinkle very much less (unless very close to horizon). Stars twinkle a great deal and when near the horizon can give impression of flashing light in many colors.

a. Shape. Pinpoint - starlike.

b. Size. Never appreciable.

c. Color. Yellow with rainbow variations.

d. Speed. Stars apparent speeds carry them from east to west in the course of the night but they are often reported as erratic. The effect is psychological, most people being unable to consider a point as being stationary. Occasionally turbulence in the upper atmosphere can cause a star to appear to jump (rare) but somehow twinkling gives the impression of movement to many people.

Note: Just because the report says the light moves does not rule out the possibility of it being a star unless motion is from one part of sky to another relatively short time.

e. Formation. There are no clusters of very bright stars but faint stars are grouped in their familiar constellations. Note: a report of 4 or 5 bright clustering lights would rule out stars.

f. Trail. None.

g. Sound. None.

h. Course. Always describe 24 hour circle around pole of sky from east to west.

i. Time In Sight. When clear, stars are always visible. Most stars rise or set during the course of the night. Stars low in western sky set within an hour or two. Stars in east, always go higher in sky.

j. Lighting Conditions. Night - twilight.

k. Radar. None.

35.   Optical Phenomena

This can cover a multitude of things. Original scanning of the report should be made to attempt to determine whether it more likely describes a material object or an optical phenomenon. Optical phenomena which have been reported as UFOBs run from reflections on clouds and layers of ice crystals (sundogs) to the many types of mirages. No one set of optical phenomena can be set down as representation for the whole class. There is no limit to the speed of optical phenomena. Reflections can travel from incredible speed, as in the case of a search-beacon on high clouds, to stationary. These cases if well reported will almost always warrant follow-up. Their variety and connection with upper atmospheric conditions make these observations especially valuable scientifically.

a. Shape. Generally round but can be elliptical or linear.

b. Size. Starlike to large luminous glow.

c. Color. Generally yellow.

d. Speed. Stationary to fantastic.

e. Formation. Any.

f. Trail. None.

g. Sound. None.

h. Course. Any.

i. Time In Sight. Any.

j. Lighting Conditions. Day and night.

k. Radar. No return. In special cases, radar response will occasionally have to do with

TOP SECRET/MAJIC EYES ONLY

unusual clouds, and meteorological phenomena such as described in Minnaert's book "Light and Color in the Open Air."

    l. Other. One of the standard types is the "sundog." In this a large luminous halo is seen around the sun with one to four images of the sun placed along the halo circle at intervals of 90 degrees. Another report often has to do with a bright planet or even the moon shining through a light overcast. Mirages reflections are said to occur frequently when temperature inversions exists in the atmosphere. If an optical phenomena is suspected, routine check of the meteorological records should be made to establish whether such inversions existed.

TOP SECRET/MAJIC EYES ONLY

TOP SECRET/MAJIC EYES ONLY

APPENDIX I
REFERENCES

For the availability of items listed, check SR 310-20-3, SR 310-20-4, SR 310-20-5 and SR 310-20-7.

---

1. [Applicable] Regulations

AR 380-4	Military security (Safeguarding Security Information).
AR 750-4	Maintenance of Supplies and Equipment, Maintenance Responsibilities and Shop Operation.

2. Supply

SR 725-405-5	Preparation and Submission of Requisitions for Supplies.

3. Other Publications

XX 219-20-3	Index of Training Manuals.
XX 310-20-4	Index of Technical Manuals, Technical Regulations, Technical Bulletins, Supply Bulletin Lubrications Orders, and Modification Work Orders.
XX 310-20-5	Index of Administrative Publications.
XX 310-20-7	Index of Tables of Organization and Equipment, Reduction Tables, Tables of Organization, Tables of Equipment, Type Tables of Distribution and Tables of Allowance.

4. Test Equipment References

TM 11-664	Theory and Use of Electronic Test Equipment.

5. Photographic References

TM 11-404A	Photographic Print Processing Unit AN/TFQ-9.
TM 11-405	Processing Equipment PH-406.
TM 11-401	Elements of Signal Photography.
TM 11-2363	Darkroom PH-392.

TOP SECRET/MAJIC EYES ONLY
REPRODUCTION IN ANY FORM IS FORBIDDEN BY FEDERAL LAW

TOP SECRET/MAJIC EYES ONLY

Author Caveats

This manual is a replica of one that was photographed by an unknown person.

The Tri-X negatives were mailed to Mr. Don Berliner, postmarked March 7, 1994. Don provided copies to the GAO. He took early initiative to determine their authenticity. Presently in November 1998, although he has not been able to review the arguments summary, he is not inclined to regard SOM 1-01 as genuine.

The 1st generation print copies became a basis for this replica. It is very accurate, and includes faithful replication of the few errors missed by the original proofreaders. Through page 21 was on the film, but pages 22-25 about the UFOB Guide were found in an unclassified FOIA released document provided to Mr. Brian Parks from Maxwell Air Force Base, referring to the transmittal of such a guide in an unclassified letter dated 14 Jan 1955.

This manual SOM 1-01 is now in the public domain, having been largely reprinted in a book, "TOP SECRET/MAJIC" by Mr. Stanton T. Friedman. That version, however, is incomplete, contains typesetting errors, and does not replicate the six by nine-inch format that was used.

A number of arguments have been proposed to question the authenticity. It is the authors' opinions that they have all been dealt with, and that there is no question at all that this is a genuine manual used for the purposes stated therein.

These points of discussion will be treated in detail in an upcoming book by the authors noted below.

© Robert M. Wood & Ryan S. Wood October 1998
P.O. Box 2272, Redwood City, CA 94064-2272

Email: drbobwood@aol.com & rswood@igc.apc.org

James Vincent Forrestal and the Majestic Twelve

James Forrestal, a former highly respected Secretary of the Navy, had shown no signs of mental instability the day of his crucial meeting with Truman in the Oval Office on 24 September 1947. In the wake of the Roswell recoveries, a panel of 16 military and civilian appointees recommended the creation of a "Fully funded and operational Top Secret Research and Development intelligence gathering agency" called Majestic Twelve (MJ-12). This recommendation was approved at the meeting with Forrestal in the Oval Office. Truman issued a memorandum on the same date (which leaked in 1983) instructing Forrestal to begin funding and organizing the MJ-12 initiative.

In early 1948, in the same month as the Aztec, New Mexico, UFO crash retrieval incident, aides began to notice that Mr. Forrestal was developing a range of nervous mannerisms. His mind drifted elsewhere during meetings and he lost the narrative. He began to believe he was being followed and his home phone wire-tapped. Not only Forrestal, but also his right hand man, Vannevar Bush, began to have mental problems as well. The problems seemed to begin around the time of the Aztec crash where a disabled craft was found on an isolated plateau 12 miles from the small New Mexico town in March 1948. Bush supervised the alien craft retrieval on site with a large group of scientists that he had hand-picked for the highly secret operation. Bush developed headaches and trembling. He thought he had Parkinson's disease. He suffered from sleepless nights and underwent numerous medical tests. In the end, unlike Forrestal, he appears to have made a complete recovery and, by all accounts, was involved in the MJ-12 reverse-engineering program well into the 1950s.

Today we know from the Rendlesham Forest, Suffolk, England Incident of December 26-28, 1980 the injuries to Forrestal and Vannevar Bush were caused from "Unidentified Aerial Phenomena Radiation" (UAP). UAP is caused from being within close proximity to a UFO craft. Both James Penniston and John Burroughs, Air Force police officers at the Royal Air Force Bentwaters Base investigating the UFO incident suffered from the same type of radiation. In 2006, the United Kingdom declassified an intelligence study on UFOs (PROJECT CONDIGN - classified as Secret UK Eyes Only) which stated that the Bentwaters UFOs to be real, and have UAP radiation effects.

When UFOs are operating, they emit a certain electromagnetic field that is known to cause UAP radiation. Other than biological effects, the neurological effects may be the clue to solve some human behavior after exposure to alien spacecraft. Unlike other parts of the brain, the temporal cortex can be tendered electrically unstable. It is clear that the recipients of these effects are not aware that their behavior/perception of what they are observing is being modified. Little is understood about UAP radiation, but since 1986, much research is being conducted by the military, sadly, in order to produce microwave weapons. It is important to note that the effect of UAP radiation on humans takes very little time to manifest.

At around 2 a.m. on the morning of May 22, 1949, America's first Secretary of Defense, James Vincent Forrestal, fell to his death from a small window of the 16th floor of the Bethesda Naval Hospital.

There is no question that Forrestal suffered from a mental breakdown during 1948 and 1949. Throughout the autumn and winter of 1948, Forrestal's mental health, physical condition, and effectiveness as Secretary of Defense deteriorated. Friends commented on his growing paranoia. He was convinced that "foreign-looking men" were following him. Forrestal's condition eventually came to the attention of Truman and Secret Service Chief U. E. Baughman, who decided that Forrestal was suffering from "a total psychotic breakdown." On January 11th, 1949, Truman informed Forrestal that Louis Johnson would soon replace him as Secretary of Defense. Forrestal finally left office in a formal ceremony on March 28th, his last public appearance.

What followed after the ceremony adds to the mystery. Air Force Secretary Stuart Symington told Forrestal, "There is something I would like to talk to you about," and accompanied him privately during the ride back to the Pentagon. What Symington said is not known, but Forrestal emerged from the ride deeply upset, even traumatized. Friends of Forrestal implied that Symington said something that "shattered Forrestal's last remaining defenses." When someone entered Forrestal's office several hours later, the former Secretary of Defense did not notice. Instead, he sat rigidly at his desk, staring at the bare wall, incoherent, repeating the sentence, "you are a loyal fellow," for several hours.

Forrestal was taken home, but within a day, the Air Force flew him to Hobe Sound, Florida, home of Robert Lovett (a future Secretary of Defense).

Forrestal's first words were "Bob, they're after me." He met with Dr. William Menninger, of the Menninger Foundation, and a consultant to the Surgeon General of the Army. Captain George N. Raines, chief psychologist at the U.S. Naval Hospital at Bethesda, soon arrived. He stated that upon his arrival, Forrestal told him that the day before, "He had placed a belt around his neck with the intention of hanging himself, but the belt broke." Menninger found no marks on Forrestal's neck or body, nor did anyone find broken belts of any kind. Menninger considered Forrestal's claim to be a nightmare. That's about all we can know for sure.

On April 2, 1949, Forrestal's coterie flew him to Bethesda, "for security reasons," During the trip from the Air Field to the hospital, Forrestal made several attempts to leave the moving vehicle, and was forcibly restrained. He talked of suicide, of being a bad Catholic, and several times about those "who are trying to get me." He was admitted to Bethesda Naval Hospital under the care of Raines, who had diagnosed Forrestal's illness as "complicated." Melancholia, which is a depressive condition sometimes seen in people reaching middle age, often who saw their life as a failure, was also identified. Upon arrival at Bethesda, Forrestal declared that he did not expect to leave the place alive. In a highly unusual decision for a suicidal patient, Forrestal's doctor was instructed by "the people downtown" (National Security?) to place him in the VIP 16th floor suite.

Throughout Forrestal's hospitalization, access to him was severely restricted. One-time visitors were his wife, his two sons, Sidney Souers (a former DCI, NSC Executive Secretary and MJ-12 member), Louis Johnson, Truman, and Congressman Lyndon Johnson. Menninger visited twice. Although Forrestal was presumably glad to see his sons, he was not close to any of these visitors, and had a political antipathy to his government colleagues who came by. However, Forrestal was not permitted to see the several people he continually asked to see: his brother Henry, a friend, and two priests. Henry Forrestal, for example, repeatedly tried to see his brother but was refused until he threatened to tell the newspapers and sue the hospital. Ultimately, he was able to visit his brother four times. Henry told Raines and the hospital's commandant, Captain B. W. Hogan, that his brother wanted to talk with a close friend, Monsignor Maurice Sheehy. Hogan replied that he was aware of this, but still would not allow the visitation. Indeed, Sheehy had tried seven times to see Forrestal. Each time, he was told that his timing was "not opportune." (What kind of hospital policy denies a patient the right to see a priest, minister, or rabbi?)

Sheehan, a former Navy chaplain, argued several times with Raines, and had the impression that Raines was acting under orders. Another priest, Father Paul McNally of Georgetown University, was also barred from seeing Forrestal, as was at least one other (unnamed) friend of the former Secretary.

By May, Forrestal's condition seemed to be improving. When Henry finally got to see him, he thought his brother was "acting and talking as sanely and intelligently as any man I've ever known." On May 14, 1949, Raines decided that he would leave Washington in four days to attend a meeting of the American Psychiatric Association. After their last meeting on the morning of the 18th, Raines wrote that Forrestal was "somewhat better than on the corresponding day of the preceding week." Forrestal continued in good spirits throughout all of the 20th and 21st. He showed no signs of depression, was well dressed, shaved, and in good appetite.

But the more Henry Forrestal thought about his brother being shut up at Bethesda and denied the right to see Father Sheehy, the more it bothered him. He decided he was going to take his brother to the countryside to complete his recovery, and made train reservations to return to Washington on May 22. He also reserved a room at the Mayflower Hotel for that day, then phoned the hospital to announce that he would arrive on May 22 to take his brother. He was too late.

The official account of Forrestal's death runs as follows: During the night of May 21/22, Forrestal was awake at 1:45 a.m., copying a chorus from Sophocles' Ajax from a book of world literature. (The New York Times added that Forrestal had been asleep at 1:30, then awake at 1:45.) A Navy corpsman named Robert Wayne Harrison, Jr., responsible for guarding Forrestal's room, checked in, as was his job every fifteen minutes. Forrestal told Harrison that he did not want a sedative, as he intended to stay up late and read. Harrison reported Forrestal's refusal to the psychiatrist – Raines' assistant, Dr. Robert Deen – sleeping next door. They returned five minutes later to an empty room. Deen later claimed that Forrestal had sent Harrison out on a "brief errand." During this time, Forrestal walked to the diet kitchen across the hall, tied one end of his bathrobe cord to the radiator, the other end around his neck, removed a flimsy screen, and jumped from the 16th floor. The cord came untied, and he fell to his death after hitting part of the building on the way down.

Some believed Forrestal's death to be "very much desired by individuals and groups who, in 1949, held great power in the United States." Others went further, and maintained that Forrestal was murdered. Henry Forrestal, for one, believed strongly that "they" murdered his brother.

Father Sheehy had reason to suspect murder. When he arrived at Bethesda Naval Hospital after learning of Forrestal's death, an experienced-looking hospital corpsman approached him through the crowd. In a low, tense voice he said, "Father, you know Mr. Forrestal didn't kill himself, don't you?" Before Sheehy could respond or ask his name, others in the crowd pressed close, and the corpsman quickly departed.

There are several odd elements concerning Forrestal's final moments. First, the young corpsman guarding Forrestal, Harrison, was a new man, someone Forrestal had never seen before. The regular guard during the midnight shift was absent without leave and, the story goes, had gotten drunk the night before. Harrison was the only person to have had direct contact with Forrestal in the moments before his death, and ultimately it was on his word only that the official account rested.

Also, Forrestal never finished writing the chorus from Sophocles, and in fact stopped in the middle of a word. Quite possibly, Forrestal had not even written the fragment that evening, especially if he had been asleep at 1:30 a.m. How reasonable is it to suppose that, sometime between 1:30 a.m. and 1:45 a.m., he woke up, got out some writing material, located a bleak poem within a huge anthology, copied 17 lines, put on his robe, crossed the hall to the kitchen, then tightly wrapped and knotted his bathrobe cord around his neck and presumably tied the loose end to the radiator under the window; then climbed up on the window sill and jumped.

There is an odd juxtaposition of a tightly knotted bathrobe cord around Forrestal's neck and the assumption that he tied the other end so loosely to a radiator that it immediately came untied and allowed him to fall to his death. This radiator was a rather improbable gallows: it was about two feet long, the top was six inches below the sill, and it was attached to the wall with its base a good fifteen inches above the floor. There was no evidence that the bathrobe cord had ever been tied to the small radiator in the first place. If the cord had snapped under Forrestal's weight, one end would have been found still fastened to the radiator. The cord did not break, however, and there was not a mark on the radiator to indicate it had ever been tied there. Does this sound odd? Forrestal was in a secure facility, the VIP suite of the prestigious Bethesda Naval Hospital, under 24-hour suicide watch, being checked each 15 minutes, and the regular guard being replaced by a new guard on his first night on the job. Not to mention the bizarre method of committing "suicide.". All of this circumstantial evidence sure sounds a lot like the modern day American financier and convicted sex offender, Jeffrey Epstein's "suicide" on August 10, 2019 at the Metropolitan Correctional Center in New York. Has this become the standard method of staged suicide by our Government?

Forrestal's room shared a bath with his supervising doctor; he fell through a small, unsecured, window in the Diet Kitchen. Moreover, if Forrestal wanted to hang himself, why choose a tiny window by anchoring himself to a radiator, when he much more easily could have done the job from a door or sturdy fixture, such as the shower curtain rod in his own bathroom? On the other hand, if Forrestal wanted to go out the window, why bother with a cord? Why not simply jump, a far easier proposition? Jumpers jump and people, who want to hang themselves, hang themselves. They don't try to hang themselves out of a window of a 16 floor building. Lastly, we do not know that the cord had ever been tied to the radiator, but we do know is it was tied tightly to Forrestal's neck.

Later inspection found heavy scuff marks outside the window sill and cement work. Proponents of the suicide theory claim these were made by Forrestal's feet while he was hanging by the neck from the radiator, and perhaps that he belatedly changed his mind and tried to climb back in. But the scuff marks confirm no such thing. They could just as easily have been made by his struggle with someone pushing him out the window.

There are many other suspicious elements to this story, such as the decision to place Forrestal on the 16th floor. This was exactly opposite what ordinary medical opinion dictated. The bottom floor of a nearby annex had been the first choice of his caretakers, but was dismissed by unnamed individuals in Washington. Also, the official investigation of the hospital labeled his death a suicide before any investigation took place; the county coroner rushed to confirm the hospital statements. In cases where there is even a slight possibility of murder, it is normal for a coroner to delay signing a death certificate until an investigation, an autopsy, and an inquest had been completed. This did not happen with the Forrestal case. Since the death occurred on a U.S. Naval reservation, local police did not investigate.

Instead, the head of the Naval Board of Inquiry immediately announced he was "absolutely certain" that Forrestal's death "could be nothing else than suicide." The committee's full report, regarding Forrestal's death, was held secret for 55 years and was not released until 2004. The official report, in fact, did not conclude that Forrestal committed suicide. It concluded only that the fall caused his death, and that no one in the U.S. Navy was responsible for it.

UFOs constitute the great hole of contemporary history. We know, at the very least, that this was a topic of great concern to those at the top of American national security policy, despite the near-complete absence of public references to it. It is the proverbial "elephant in the room" that no one wishes to discuss. There are several reasons to consider a UFO connection to Forrestal's death.

In the first place, Forrestal's position within the defense community made him a de facto key player in the formulation of UFO policy. Because of the strategic importance, even urgency, associated with this topic in policy formulation during the late 1940s, we must assume that Forrestal knowledgeable in this area. The sensitivity of the UFO problem meant that Forrestal's mental deterioration was a real security risk. One might even wonder whether Forrestal learned a truth about UFOs that contributed to his breakdown.

Secondly, Forrestal's concern about being followed by "foreign-looking men is a common description of the legendary-to-the-point-of-cliché Men in Black. He never stated clearly just who he believed to be following him, at least not consistently. Others assumed that he was talking about Communists, Jews, and Washington insiders, but they could only assume.

An explanation centering on the UFO phenomenon accounts surprisingly well for the complete unhinging of a successful and brilliant individual, and more importantly, the need to silence someone who could no longer be trusted. Perhaps Forrestal's psychological state was such that he did commit suicide. Although the facts of his death do not point toward this conclusion, we do not have definitive knowledge, either.

Ronald Reagan UFO Briefing

According to an unverified internet transcript, in March of 1981, President Reagan met with CIA Director William Casey and a select team of advisors at Camp David were briefed on the subject of unidentified flying objects and extraterrestrial visitation of planet Earth. It is not the intent of this article to determine the truthfulness of this transcript but to simply, leave it up to the reader to evaluate its validity for themselves.. The following is a condensed version of the original transcript do to the original transcripts length.

Along with William Casey, Reagan was briefed by an agency operative introduced simply as "The Caretaker". This man claimed to be custodian of the UFO secrets for thirty-one years, and that he had briefed Presidents Nixon and Ford as well. President Carter, he said, was NOT in the 'loop'.

The CARETAKER: The United States of America has been visited by Extraterrestrial Visitors since 1947. We have proof of that. However, we also have some proof that Earth has been visited for many THOUSANDS OF YEARS by various races of Extraterrestrial Visitors. Mr President, I'll just refer to those visits as ETs. In July, 1947, a remarkable event occurred in New Mexico. During a storm, two ET spacecraft crashed. One crashed southwest of Corona, New Mexico and one crashed near Datil, New Mexico. The U.S. Army eventually found both sites and recovered all of the debris and one live Alien. I'll refer to this live Alien as "EBE 1." [Note: This is different from our understanding of the Roswell crash. Perhaps one UFOs had an explosion scattering debris over the Corona site then crashed into the ground on the Plains of San Agustin then the second UFO crashed near Datil, New Mexico.]

PRESIDENT: What does that mean? Do we have codes or a special terminology for this?

The CARETAKER: Mr President, EBE means "Extraterrestrial Biological Entity It was a code designated to this creature by the U.S. Army back in those days. This creature was not human and we had to decide on a term for it. So, scientists designated the creature as EBE 1. We also referred to it as "Noah." There was different terminology used by various aspects of the U.S. military and intelligence community back then.

PRESIDENT: Do we or did we have others? The number "1" would seem to indicate we had others.

The CARETAKER: Yes, we had others. Back then, the term was EBE and no number designation. We'll explain how the others came into our knowledge.

PRESIDENT: OK, sorry, I was just wondering and I guess, well, I'm sure the briefing will cover this. Please continue.

The CARETAKER: All the debris and EBEs recovered from the first crash site were taken to Roswell Army Air Field, Roswell, New Mexico. EBE was treated for some minor injuries and then taken to Los Alamos National Laboratories, which was the safest and most secure location in the world. Special accommodations were made for EBE. The debris was eventually transferred to Dayton, Ohio, home of the Air Force Foreign Technology Division. The second crash site wasn't discovered until 1949 by some ranchers. There were no live Aliens at this site. All this debris went to Sandia Army Base in Albuquerque, New Mexico.

PRESIDENT: OK, a question, regarding the first site, how many aliens were in the spaceship?

The CARETAKER: Five (5) dead aliens and one (1) alive. The bodies of the dead aliens were transported to Wright Field in Ohio and kept in a form of deep freeze. They were later transported to Los Alamos where special containers were made to keep the bodies from decaying. There were four (4) dead aliens in the second crash site. Those bodies were in an advanced state of decaying. They had been in the desert for the past two (2) years. Animals and time got to those bodies. The remains were transported to Sandia Base and eventually onto Los Alamos. We determined both crashed spaceships were of similar design and the bodies of the aliens were all identical. They looked exactly the same. They had the same height, weight and physical features. Here are the photographs of the aliens.

PRESIDENT: Can we classify them? I mean can we... well, connect them with anything Earthly?

The CARETAKER: No, Mr President. They don't have any similar characteristics of a human, with exception of their eyes, ears and a mouth.

Their internal body organs are different. Their skin is different, their eyes, ears and even breathing is different. Their blood wasn't red and their brain was entirely different from human. We could not classify any part of the Aliens with humans. They had blood and skin, although considerably different than human skin. Their eyes had two different eyelids probably because their home planet was very bright.

The CARETAKER: Thank you, Mr President. EBE stayed alive until 1952 when it died. We learned a great deal from EBE. Although EBE did not have voice organs like humans, it was able to communicate with an operation performed by military doctors. EBE was extremely intelligent. It learned English quickly, mainly by listening to the military personnel who were responsible for EBE's safety and care.

PRESIDENT: Excuse me, but you are referring to this creature as an IT. Did it have a gender?

The CARETAKER: I'm sorry Mr President, but yes, it was male. Within EBE's race they had males and females.

The CARETAKER:. EBE did explain where he lives in the universe. We call this star system Zeta Reticuli, which is about 40 light-years [38.42] from Earth. EBE's planet was within this star system.

The CARETAKER: It took the EBE spaceship nine (9) of our months to travel the 40 [38.42] light-years. Now, as you can see, that would mean the EBE spaceship traveled faster than the speed of light. But, this is where it gets really technical. Their spaceships can travel through a form of "space tunnels" that gets them from point "A" to point "B" faster without having to travel at the speed of light. I cannot fully understand how they travel, but we have many top scientists who can understand their concept.

The CARETAKER: We recovered two alien spacecraft from New Mexico. Both were heavily damaged, but we were able to examine them. The two craft were considered technological marvels by our scientists. However, the operating instrumentation was so advanced that our scientists could not decipher it. The two craft were stored in a special security location in the West. We gained a large volume of technological data from these craft.

The CARETAKER: It was felt that public awareness of these projects would have jeopardized the future space program of the United States. Releasing our secrets about UFOs and alien visitation would also cause a PANIC AMONG RELIGIOUS LEADERS around the world. Therefore, MJ-12 decided that an independent scientific study of the UFO phenomena would be needed to satisfy the public curiosity.

The CARETAKER: Thank you, Mr President. I will continue. In the 1976 MJ-12 report, it was estimated that the aliens' technology was many thousands of years ahead of ours. Our scientists speculated that until our technology develops to a level equal to the aliens, we cannot understand the large volume of scientific information we have gained from the aliens' craft. This advancement of our technology may take many hundreds of years.

PRESIDENT: Well, I have a lot of questions, so let me ask a few and then we can move on. I guess the first question I have is their life span. How old is EBE 1?

The CARETAKER: Mr President, the alien civilization that EBE came from [is what] we call the Eben Society. It wasn't a name they gave us; it was a name we chose. Their life span is between 350-400 years, but that is Earth years.

PRESIDENT: Is time the same on their planet as on ours?

The CARETAKER: No, Mr President, time is very different on the Eben Planet, which, by the way, we call SERPO. Their day is approximately 40 hours. That is measured by the movement of their two (2) suns. The solar system containing SERPO is a binary star system, or two suns, rather than one, like our solar system.

PRESIDENT: Oh, well, your answer creates more questions. OK, as I understand it, their planet has two suns. Wouldn't that mean the planet was hot? I guess that explains their eyes, having two eyelids.

The CARETAKER: Yes, Mr President. Their suns do not set, like ours. There is daylight during their entire day, with the exception of a short time period where both suns hit the horizon.

PRESIDENT: What is life like on Serpico?

The CARETAKER: Well, Mr President, the distance from Earth to SERPO is about 40 light-years. They can travel that in about nine (9) of our months. I am no scientist, but as I mentioned earlier, they can travel that great distance by means of space tunnels. They seem to be able to bend the distance from one point in space to another. Just how they do this, must be explained scientifically.

PRESIDENT: OK, well, very interesting. Are the laws of physics on their planet the same as our planet?

The CARETAKER: Not exactly. There seem to be a little different laws, especially when it comes to the movement of their planet in relationship to their two suns. Our scientists don't understand it because it defies some of our laws of physics.

PRESIDENT: Do they use nuclear power, or what type of power do they have in those ships?

The CARETAKER: Mr President, we understand very little about their propulsion system. There seem to be two different propulsion systems. One they use within our atmosphere and one they use once they exit our atmosphere. They do not have nuclear power. Their propulsion system does have some type of low level radiation emissions, but nothing that would endanger us. It isn't like our radiation, but we call it radiation because we have nothing else to compare it with.

PRESIDENT: OK, well, then Bill, that presents a very disturbing feeling for me. Are you telling me there are different races or species, as you said, visiting Earth at the same time?

The CARETAKER: At least five (5).

PRESIDENT: Are they all friendly?

ADVISER #1: Mr President that is a very difficult question to answer. There are many parameters that we follow to evaluate the threat. However, we have little intelligence on four (4) of the five (5). We have plenty of intel on the Ebens... gee... they've given us everything we asked for! They have also helped us to understand the other four (4) species. I'm afraid to say, Mr President and please don't misunderstand my words, but we think ONE

OF THE SPECIES IS VERY HOSTILE. WM CASEY: Mr President, do you wish for us to continue on this track or would you like something more private, as to the discussion of this topic?

PRESIDENT: For Christ sakes, I'm the President of the United States. I should know if we are endangered by some THREAT FROM OUTER SPACE. If you have something to say about a threat posed by this one species of aliens, then I WANT TO HEAR IT.

WM CASEY: Mr President, we have intelligence that would indicate this one (1) species of aliens have ABDUCTED PEOPLE FROM EARTH. They have performed scientific and medical tests on these humans. To the best of our knowledge, NO humans have been killed. But, as ADVISER #1 stated, the intelligence is from witnesses and we haven't thoroughly evaluated this intelligence.

ADVISER #4: Now, as for the other four (4) species. We know they have visited us in the past and will visit us in the future. We are like a petri dish within the universe. We are a diverse planet. We must be very interesting to other extraterrestrials. I'm SURE other intelligent life forms in the universe must have some sort of communications among the [sentient] life forms. Maybe they broadcasted that Earth has intelligent life. Maybe that is why we are [being] visited.

PRESIDENT: Do you have a... huh... name for them, I mean the bad ones?

The CARETAKER: Thank you, Mr President. We call the hostile aliens simply that, HAV, meaning Hostile Alien Visitors. MJ-12 placed that code on them back in the '50s.

The CARETAKER: OK, thank you. Mr President, the five (5) species are called, Ebens, Archquloids, Quadloids, Heplaloids and Trantaloids. These names were given to the alien's species by the intelligence community, specifically MJ-5. The Ebens are friendly; the Trantaloids are the dangerous ones. [

PRESIDENT: My God, just knowing we have names for these things are amazing. Which one did we capture?

WM CASEY: Mr President, we have a Trantaloid, but it is dead. We captured it in 1961 in Canada and we had it in captivity until 1962, when it died.

The CARETAKER: OK, Mr President, I'll keep this in general terms. I just want to assure you that all of the information is safely tucked away at secure locations, including the devices and flying craft that we have.

PRESIDENT: May I assume one of these places is located in California?

The CARETAKER: Some of the items are tested at Livermore and flown around Edwards, but they are kept in Nevada.

The CARETAKER: In order to protect all this information and the fact that the United States Government has evidence of our planet being visited by Extraterrestrials, we developed over the years a very effective program to safeguard the information. We call it "Project DOVE." It is a complex series of [disinformation] operations by our military intelligence agencies to disinform the public. As you know, Mr President, we have some highly classified aircraft.

The CARETAKER Mr President, in 1964, we were able to have our very first controlled encounter with the Ebens. Let me first give you the background. EBE was a mechanic, not a scientist. He was still able to teach us some of the Eben language. Their language was very difficult for our linguists to learn because it consisted of tones, not words.

However, we were able to translate some basic words. EBE showed us their communications device. It was a strange looking device that had three (3) parts. Once assembled, the device sent out signals, something like our Morse code system, although there was a problem. During the crash in 1947, one part of this communication system was broken. EBE was unable to repair it until our scientists found some items that could be used in place of the broken parts. Once the communication device was repaired, EBE sent our messages. We had to trust EBE as to the contents of those messages.

PRESIDENT: Excuse me, did EBE receive any return messages?

The CARETAKER: Getting back to the messages, Mr President, EBE sent out six (6) messages. One letting his home planet know that he was alive and his comrades were dead, another explaining the two crashes, the third was a request to be rescued, the fourth was a message suggesting a meeting between his leaders and our leaders. The last message suggested some form of an EXCHANGE program.

PRESIDENT: (not understood)... what... the exchange program?

The CARETAKER: Mr President, we don't think he did, but we could not be entirely certain. But, our scientists fine-tuned our efforts over the next 18 months and finally sent two (2) messages in 1955 that were received. We received a reply. We were able to translate about 30 percent of the message. We turned to several linguist specialists from several different universities and even several from foreign universities. Finally, we were able to translate most of the messages. We decided to reply in English and see if the Ebens could translate our language easier than we could theirs.

The CARETAKER: Mr President, the first message we received acknowledged our message and asked questions about the crew of the two missing craft. It also gave a series of numbers that we think were some type of coordinates.

PRESIDENT: OK, so they wanted to know the coordinates of the crash sites on Earth? I'm sure they wanted to know about their crew. Did we tell them all but one was dead? No, wait; I'm sure when EBE sent his messages that is probably the first thing he sent. Was EBE a military person or what?

The CARETAKER: Mr President, we believe EBE was a member of their air force or maybe something like NASA.

PRESIDENT: OK, please continue.

The CARETAKER: Thank you, Mr President. Finally we were able to translate most of the messages. As I said, we decided to respond in English. Approximately four months later, we received a reply in broken English. Sentences contained nouns and adjectives, but no verbs. It took us several months to translate the message. We then sent Eben our typed English lessons in a series of one sheet formats.

Without going into the technical description of the Eben communications device, it was like a television screen and a key pad, but the pad contained several different Eben characters depending on the number of times you held down one key. We were able to transpose our English-typed words into the second part of the device, which was similar to our facsimile transmission system. It took our scientists some time to perfect this, but it worked. Six months later, we received another English message. This time it was clearer, but not clear enough. Ebens were confusing several different English words and still failed to complete a proper sentence.

The CARETAKER: Yes, Mr President, I cannot imagine living on a planet with just one language. But we were able to provide the basic skill level for them to communicate in English. It took time, but they realized our efforts. In one message, they provided us with a form of the Eben alphabet with the equivalent English letter. Our linguists had a very difficult time figuring this out. The written Eben language was simple characters and symbols, but our linguists had a difficult time comparing the two written languages.

Over the next five (5) years, we were able to perfect our understanding of the Eben language somewhat and the Ebens were able to better understand English. However, we had a major problem. Trying to coordinate a date, time and location for an Eben landing on Earth. Even though we could basically understand some Eben and the Ebens could understand some English, we could not understand their time and date system and they could not understand ours. We sent them our Earth's rotation schedule, revolution, date system, etc.

The CARETAKER: Thank you. When EBE was alive, he showed us two devices. One was a communication system and one was an energy device. The communication system did not work without the energy device. Eventually, a scientist from Los Alamos figured out the two systems and connected them. After EBE died, we were able to send transmissions, as I said earlier. EBE built up a strong friendship with a U.S. Army Major, who was his guardian.

Over a period of a few years, we could send and receive information. We finally received a startling message from the Ebens. They wanted to visit Earth, retrieve their spacemen bodies and meet with Earthlings. They provided a time, date and location. We figure that the Ebens were continually visiting Earth and had probably mapped it. However, the date was about eight (8) years in the future. Our military figured something was wrong and that maybe the Ebens were confusing Earth time with Eben time. After a long series of messages, it was determined the Ebens would land on Earth on Friday, April 24, 1964.

The CARETAKER: Our government, specifically, MJ-12 met in secret to plan the event. Decisions were made, then changed many times. We had just about 25 months from the time we finally received their message of the date to prepare for their arrival. Several months into the planning, President Kennedy decided to approve a plan to exchange a special military team. The USAF was tasked as the lead agency.

The USAF officials picked special civilian scientists to assist in the planning and crew selection. The team members' selection process was the hardest to accomplish. Several plans were suggested and then changed. It took months for the planners to decide on the selection criteria for each team member. They decided that each member must be military, single, no children and a career member. They had to be trained in different skills.

The CARETAKER: Mr President, a team of 12 men were selected. However, during this time period, President Kennedy died. The nation was shocked, as you know....

The CARETAKER: President Johnson continued the program. When it came time for the meeting, we were ready. The landing occurred in New Mexico. We had everything prepared. We had a hoax landing location just in case it was leaked. The landing occurred and we greeted the Ebens. However, a mix up happened. They were not prepared to accept our exchange personnel. Everything was placed on hold. Finally in 1965, the Ebens landed in Nevada and we exchanged 12 of our men for one of theirs.

The CARETAKER: Mr President. Our team of 12 went to the Eben planet for 13 years. The original mission called for a 10-year stay, however, because of the strange time periods on their planet, the team stayed three (3) additional years. Eight [seven] returned in 1978. Two died on the planet and two decided to stay.

[NOTE: Team Member #308 (Team Pilot #2) died of a pulmonary embolism enroute to SERPO on the 9-month journey; 11 arrived safely. See Release 14]

PRESIDENT: OK, this is just AMAZING! I can see, about that movie. The movie was based on a real event. I saw that movie. 12 men left, along with Richard Dreyfuss.

["Close Encounters of The Third Kind," 1977]

WM CASEY: Mr President, yes, the movie was similar to the real event, at least the last part of the movie.

PRESIDENT: What's with New Mexico? The aliens seem to like that state. Do we know why?

The CARETAKER: New Mexico is similar to the home planet of the Ebens. Since we do not know which planet the Trantaloids come from....

The homeworld of the HAV, the TRANTALOIDS, is the THIRD PLANET out from the star Epsilon Eridani in the constellation Eridanus at 10.5 light-years away. Although somewhat cooler and fainter than our sun, it is very similar

Nearby Star EPSILON ERIDANI has an Earth-like Planet! Is this the homeworld of the hostile ET species, the TRANTALOIDS?!

PRESIDENT: So that means they can travel like the Ebens travel? I mean using those black holes or whatever you call them?

ADVISER #4: Yes, Mr President, they can travel in the same fashion as the Ebens. However, according to the Ebens, the Trantaloids use a different form of propulsion. Something like matter versus antimatter.

ADVISER #4: I was just going to say that we know that when matter is placed next to antimatter, there is a great deal of energy released. If one could harness that into a propulsion system that would be great. But we don't have the capability to do that.

PRESIDENT: Do we have one of their spaceships?

The CARETAKER: Yes, well, partially. A crashed one.

PRESIDENT: OK, can we or do we have the technical knowledge to understand it?

WM CASEY: No, Mr President, we don't.

ADVISER #4: Mr President, their technology is probably 1,000 years more advanced than ours... maybe even more. They have different materials to work with. Some of their materials are not found on this planet.

PRESIDENT: What do you mean, like iron or elements?

ADVISER #4: Yes, Mr President. We found many metals and other things that are not found on this planet. Maybe they have more than 104 elements or maybe they are different than ours.

PRESIDENT: The hostile ones or the Ebens?

ADVISER #4: Mr President that goes for each species although the Ebens do have similar elements as [those found on] Earth. But the Trantaloids have strange materials... nothing like [those found on] Earth. These ALIENS CAN IMITATE HUMANS. They CAN LOOK LIKE BLOND HUMANS. However, they are not blond, but UGLY-LOOKING INSECTS.

WM CASEY: They are pretty nasty looking.

ADVISER #4: Well, Mr President, they have the ability to change their bodies. As I said before, they are 1,000 years ahead of us in technology and probably every other science.

PRESIDENT: They can be killed?

ADVISER #4: Yes, they are just flesh and blood, like a human body. They can be killed. But their spaceships have a force field around them. They can be shot down, but it takes some doing on our part.

WM CASEY: Mr President, we have to use a small-style nuclear missile to shoot them down, but we haven't actually done that yet. We have experimented in Nevada on the captured craft we have of theirs.

PRESIDENT: Can we intercept their radio transmissions? Do we know their language?

ADVISER #1: We know or we can recognize their language, which is entirely different than the Ebens. They use a very high-band radio system. But they have different frequencies and it is difficult for NSA to track them.

[Bolling AFB is where all of the "Project SERPO" files are located which include thousands of photographs of the Eben civilization in several large photo album books, animal, plant and soil samples, audio recordings of the Eben music, and photos of other alien species that visited/were cloned on SERPO.]

Area 51, S- 4

Area 51 is a United States military base located in a remote area of Nevada. Leading researcher and whistleblower information strongly suggest that the Area 51 section known as "S-4" (Site Four) is where retrieved extraterrestrial artifacts are kept. On the surface, the more well-known Area 51 (Dreamland, Skunkworks, or Groom Lake draws attention away from the alien secrecy of S-4 by just being an aircraft testing area for advanced aircraft.

Area 51

Employment at S4 is through recommendations of other scientists, many from Los Alamos National Laboratory, California Institute of Technology, or Massachusetts Institute of Technology. To be employed at S4 a scientist is required to sign a secrecy agreement and an agreement to waive their constitutional rights. They also have to sign an agreement which allows the Government to perpetually monitor the scientist's activities and phones.

Travel to Area 51 by scientists and employees are provided by a private airline whose Air Traffic Control call sign is "Janet". Due to the airline's secretive nature, little is known about its organization. It is operated for the USAF by infrastructure and defense contractor AECOM through AECOM's acquisition in 2014 of URS Corporation, which acquired EG&G Technical Services in 2002. Janet boards at a special, secure area of McCarran International Airport (LAS) in Las Vegas Nevada. Employees board the unmarked, windowless planes from a passenger terminal on the northwest side of the airport. This makes them readily recognizable, and the red stripe across the windows on the fuselage is the only one of its kind. Only employees of Area 51 and the Tonopah Test Range are allowed to travel on the airline.

The purpose of Janet is to pick up the employees at their home airport, and take them to their place of work. Then, in the afternoon, they take the employees back to their home airports. The airline primarily serves the Nevada National Security Site Area 51 and the Tonopah Test Range..

The Airline consists of a Fleet of six Boeing 737 aircraft (tail numbers N319BD, N869HH, N859WP, N273RH, N365SR, N288DP), and a fleet of smaller executive aircraft, including two turboprop Beechcraft 1900 Executive Liners (tail numbers N20RA, N623RA) and the smaller Beechcraft twin turboprop (tail numbers N661BA, N662BA, and N654BA). Due to its secrecy, Janet uses the code TTR for Tonopah Test Range and XTA for Area 51. Each week about 20 flights in each direction between Las Vegas and Area 51 or the Tonopah Test Range transport between 1,000 to over 1,500 workers. The first Janet plane leaves Las Vegas at about 4:00 am with the last plane leaving Area 51 at about 8:00 pm. Flight time is approximately 25 minutes one-way to either prime location. While Las Vegas is Janet's home base, at times, it also operates flights between Palmdale, California and other airports.

Travel to Section S-4 from Area 51 is restricted only to those with the proper security badges. At least at one time, the badge was white with two blue hash marks across the upper left side. Below these hash marks, along the very bottom, were the codes allowing the person access to different parts of the facility. The code would say (S4), then the special area of concern, like (ETL) Extraterrestrial Laboratory, later changed to (EBL) for Extraterrestrial Biological Laboratory. Other codes included (DX) for Departmental Transfer; and (WX) for Engineering Transfer. Directly above the (S4) was a star shaped punch. On the right side of the badge was MAJ spelled vertically. The badges also displayed the photo of the scientist, and below, his name, assignment, and badge number. On the reverse side of the badge was a black magnetic strip, similar to those on credit cards.

Large, modern air-conditioned busses with the blacked out windows drive the scientists on a 15-mile bumpy dirt/gravel road to S-4. The S-4 site is a combination of buildings, and underground hangars built completely into the side of a mountain. The underground structures consisted of 5 levels, each floor conducting different types of scientific research.

Approaching S-4, the bus passes nine concealed sand textured aircraft hangars, with the doors built into a mountainside, then a sharp left turn to the drop-off site. The scientists exit the bus, and are escorted to the facility's entrance. This has been described as simply a steel door in the side of the mountain. The coordinates of the hangar doors are N 37° 01' 40", W 115° 46' 35". Employees would pass guards holding snarling dogs. These dogs were different from "normal" dogs, in that they had their vocal chords cut out to avoid being detected.

Once inside, there was a single guard sitting at a desk in an empty room, with a door behind him. The entrants were checked-in, then led to another small room with a palm-reader and yet another door. A long hallway which ran the length of the hangar doors led to briefing rooms, restroom, and nurse's station. The scientist's work areas were colored differently, and the scientists under guard were only allowed into the area of color that their research was performed. Even when using the restroom, the scientists were escorted by two guards. The programs at S-4 were compartmentalized, with each group separated from the others. People in the program worked on a limited "buddy system". The scientists worked in teams and were obviously not allowed to chat in the lunch room about what everybody was doing.

The first day at S-4, scientists are taken to the nurse's office and asked to submit to a dermal allergen test. A grid was drawn on the arm, and diluted solutions of various substances were placed in each section. On the next visit to S-4, the arm was checked for any skin eruptions or other adverse reactions to the allergens.

Scientists were also given a substance to drink, and were told that it would bolster their immune system response to the alien materials with which they might come into contact. The liquid had been described as, "smelling like pine." Later, many scientists complained about suffering severe abdominal cramps, which were undoubtedly related to the substance they drank.

The hangars were equipped with typical tools and extensive electronic equipment. The hangars that contained a disc were at the end of a long row of 9 identical hangars. This is where the UFOs were stored. Each had a sliding door between them and the trademark "sloped" door, commensurate with the slope of the mountain. Each hangar had a machine with an X-ray warning emblem on it. An overhead gantry-type crane rated at 20,000 pounds could lift the disc up and out of the hangar. Equipment in a particular hangar was marked with a black number 41 with a white circle around it.

On the first two underground floor levels of the structure, scientists worked on PROJECT GALILEO. The project dealt with UFO Propulsion Systems. Scientist studied the role of gravity as the propulsion medium, harnessing, amplifying, and lensing the basic Gravity 'A-wave, and which has many other possibilities for application.

On the third underground floor level, scientists worked on PROJECT SIDEKICK. The project dealt with the beam weapon potential of the craft, and the attempt to prototype one of the units using gravity and lensing, it in order to collimate and align the beam. Once the beam is focused in a triangulated manner on a specific point, the options for destructiveness are endless.

On the forth underground floor level, scientists worked on PROJECT LOOKING GLASS. The project dealt with the physics of understanding the effects of an artificially-produced gravity wave on the dimension of time. This embraced the control of gravity, and therefore, the control of Space/Time as the key element.

On the fifth underground floor level, scientists worked on PROJECT AQUARIUS, a covert and aggressive action to collect data on the extraterrestrial UFO phenomenon. Its main objective was to capture one of the extraterrestrials and assimilate their technology. In 1953, PROJECT

GLEEM was initiated by order of President Eisenhower, under control of the National Security Council and Majestic 12, as it was alleged the UFOs presented a threat to the national security of the United States. GLEEM was renamed PROJECT AQUARIUS in 1966.

When someone is indoctrinated to S-4, they are exposed to at least part of that knowledge base. A scientist would randomly be taken into a small room which contained a table, chair, and be left there to read 120-or so blue briefing folders. These folders contained a wide spectrum of information, mostly relating to aliens and alien technology. The reports appeared to be an overview of alien information which could be used to provide an overview of all of the projects, not just focused their specific specialty. The papers stated the aliens came from a planet in Zeta Reticuli binary star system and included autopsy pictures of a dead alien.

These reports included information about human history, philosophy, theology, and the role that aliens play in bringing disc technology to humankind. Much of this information was alarming, even shocking. The most frightening were reports of the aliens' involvement with the human race over the last 10,000 years!

In the early years of S-4, the Russian scientists worked with the U.S. scientists at the site, but in 1989, the U.S. scientists had made a discovery which was a major step forward in understanding disc technology and gravity propulsion. Rather than share this advanced knowledge with the Russians, they dismissed them from further S-4 activities. It is unknown if the Russians were allowed to actually work with the alien hardware, but they had been involved in mathematical and physical calculations. Needless to say, the Russians were not pleased about being left out.

According to Dr. Michael Wolf and Bob Lazar's co-worker, Barry Castillo, on May 1, 1975 during one such technology exchange in Nevada, a demonstration of a small ET antimatter reactor was performed. The lead Grey ET asked the Colonel in charge of the Delta Forces guarding them to remove all their rifles and bullets from the room, so that they would not accidentally discharge during the energy emissions. The guards refused, and in the ensuing commotion a guard opened fire on the Greys. One alien, two scientists and 41 military personnel were killed. One guard was left alive to attest that the ETs apparently used "directed mental energy" in self-defense to kill the other attacking Delta Forces. Dr. Wolf states that "This incident ended certain exchanges with the Greys."

Badging got a little more complicated as you advanced to the lower level labs. No one was supposed to know who you were as you got down into AQUARIUS. When a scientist was in that sub-level, he was required to place his badge into a plastic bag-like container which went into a decontamination device. When the badge came out, it was returned to the scientist, but it had been laminated. The badge was then carried over to a badge wall, and put on a hook where the front was facing the wall so that nobody could read it. Anonymity was key to the process in AQUARIUS. The scientist would then take a blue numbered badge that corresponded to the badge hook. This blue badge had only a number on it, like "Scientist #5" for example. Bottle washers and general support personnel, most of whom were non-scientists, were similarly numbered. This served to isolate the different levels of workers from one another which maintained compartmentalization. Nobody used proper names at that level.

The information above was obtained from the following whistleblowers: Robert Scott Lazar (Bob Lazar) an American scientist hired in the late 1980s to reverse-engineer extraterrestrial technology.

Dr. Barry Castillo was Bob Lazar's co-worker at S-4. He is recognized for his outstanding performance in analyzing foreign weapons systems, and reporting them to senior policymakers and leadership of major offices in three CIA directorates regarding arms control issues.

Connor O'Ryan was a pseudonym used by Derek Hennessy, a US Marine who, for eleven years was in Special Forces assigned to CIA in the 1980s. In 1990-1991 he worked for 9 months as a guard at S-4. Hennessy worked on the second level of the S-4 facility. S-4 employed approximately 75 personnel on levels 1 and 2. He said he was aware of further levels of the facility, but was never allowed to enter them. He said that approximately 12-15 personnel worked at Levels 3 & 4. His primary duty was to guard the elevators which required three keys, a thumbprint and a retinal scan to open. He was told to do his duty without wandering eyes.

David Adair is a rocket scientist. In the past, he had worked for NASA. Nowadays, David Adair is the president of Intersect, Inc., which is a space technology consulting agency. He had examined a large engine that came out of a flying disk. at Area 51.

Dr. Michael Wolf served as an Air Force Colonel, pilot, flight surgeon and counter-intelligence officer for the CIA and NSA. He was in charge of a Majestic 12 team known as Alphacom, whose function was to assess the number and types of ET visitors, the extent of visitation, the reasons behind Earth visitations. The assessments included the extent of human interactions with extraterrestrials in the past, and information regarding the cultures of the various off-world visitors, and how we can negotiate with them. Dr. Wolf has an M.D. in Neurology, a Ph.D. in Theoretical Physics and a D.Sc. in Computer Science. Now dying of untreatable cancer, Dr. Wolf has decided to reveal what he has learned about the aliens.

Dr. Wolf claims that in the 1950s, the U.S. entered into treaty terms with the so-called Grey ETs from the fourth planet of the star system Zeta Reticuli, but these treaties were never ratified as constitutionally required. He said the Greys shared certain of their technological advances with military/intelligence scientists, apparently often while they were prisoner "guests" within secure underground military installations in Nevada and New Mexico. The extraterrestrials have given the U.S. government some of their antigravity craft and a huge amount of fuel (element 115). According to Dr. Wolf, several confederations of extraterrestrial civilizations are visiting us in loosely-coordinated fashion. Dr. Wolf had concerns about the how religion on Earth was created, and how the knowledge of aliens would be received by the Vatican. Would such an announcement threaten organized religions?

Dr. Dan Burisch is a microbiologist. He was born as Danny Benjamin Crain, but in 1995 Dan legally changed his last name from Crain to Burisch to match his stepchild's legal last name. In 1989, as Dan Crain graduated from Stony Brook University with a Ph.D. in Microbiology and Molecular Genetics, he was at the same time employed by the U. S. Navy's DOD Naval Research Laboratory. His rank was Captain and his title Microbiologist IV. In 1994, he was assigned to work in an underground laboratory at S-4, on the fifth floor under the Papoose Mountain installation. The fifth floor is accessible only by one secure elevator.

To work on floor sub-level 5, a scientist was suited like an astronaut, with breathing and urination hoses. His assignment was to enter a round "clean sphere" filled with a cold hydrogen atmosphere of 4%, and an unknown gas(s). In this atmosphere, Dr. Burisch worked with an extraterrestrial named "J-Rod", who was one of two ETs captured from a recovered

UFO that crashed near Kingman, Arizona in On May 21, 1953. There were three extraterrestrial in the craft, one of which was dead. They came from the fourth planet of the star system Zeta Reticuli. The other live extraterrestrial was taken to Los Alamos National Laboratory (LANL) and worked with Bill Uhouse on flight simulator equipment.

Dr. Burisch was told there was a serious medical problem with J-Rod and his species, and that MJ-12 wanted Dan to extract tissue from the being's arm for microscopic study. A serious peripheral neuropathy was diagnosed and Dr. Burisch said that in 1994, he collected more than 100 tissue samples in an effort to study J-Rod's nerve damage, and he hoped to develop a treatment.

Colonel Steve Wilson, U.S. Air Force (ret.), former head of PROJECT POUNCE, commanded an elite Air Force/National Reconnaissance Organization Special Forces unit who retrieve downed UFOs. Colonel Wilson reports that "The first successful U.S. antigravity flight took place July 18, 1971 at S-4, wherein light-bending capabilities were also demonstrated in order to obtain total invisibilities." Present at this flight were notables such as Admiral Bobbie Ray Inman, former National Security Agency director, who is now head of Science Applications International Incorporated (SAIC), a large U.S. military contractor who work on the antigravity drives. Colonel Wilson says that the military began flying their enormous Black Triangle antigravity craft, the TR-3B, in January 1994, which was back-engineered from extraterrestrial UFOs.

Colonel Wilson states that a super-secret mobile unit within Delta Force at the National Reconnaissance Office has been deployed with the "Equalizer". This is an exotic-looking cannon, 6-feet in length, and 1-foot in diameter. This device uses low-frequency pulsed microwave energy, and is mounted on a pedestal on the back of a military truck that is used to shoot down UFOs. The Equalizer is built by LTV (Ling-Temco-Vought) at Anaheim, CA. It is interesting to note that retired Air Force Lt. Col. Richard French said that an electronic pulse-type weapon fired from experimental U.S. airplane over White Sands, N.M. brought down the UFO that crashed at Roswell, New Mexico on July 2, 1947.

Thomas Mack Is a retired Air Force Major. He served from 1972 to 1994 as an Air Force Intelligence officer. He served with the Air Force Scientific Advisory Group at (S-4) Groom Lake, Nevada, from June 1975 to April 1983, and from March 1988 to October 1994, he worked on numerous special projects. All involved the reverse engineering of captured UFOs and the collection of UFO related intelligence. He worked with Dr. Dan Burisch on AQUARIUS. "R-4800" was the specific program that he worked on, along with JAROD (J-Rod), an extraterrestrial biological entity "EBE" who was referred to as the "Puppet Master."

When JAROD arrived at S-4 he had no verbal language interface with humans. A series of symbols were shown to test the alien's reactions. Some of the symbols looked like letters and others were geometric shapes. The first symbol the alien pointed to looked like a "J." The other was an "inertial-bar" that looked like a rod. So, humans called the alien "J-Rod." Later as communication was established he reveal that his name was Chi'el'ah.

Mr. Mack claims that J-Rod is the most perfect non-human being in the Universe. He said J-Rod actually had a good sense of humor, and could imitate anyone's voice. The entire program, COSMIC-MAJIC, was classified above Top Secret, and operated under the control of Majestic-12. He stated that an extraterrestrial known as EBE-1 from the Roswell UFO crash lived from 1947 to 1952.

Richard Doty is a retired Special Agent who worked for the U.S. Air Force of Special Investigations. At one time he was part of a disinformation project with the government. He confirmed the Roswell UFO Crash of 1947 and described exactly what they found inside. The craft was egg-shaped, not saucer-shaped, and the interior did not have any readily discernable controls even though there were creatures present. The beings were about four feet in length and some had sustained massive injuries. He was later told that they were taken to Kirkland Air Force Base, Albuquerque before going to Los Alamos, then to S4.

Bill Uhouse was a test pilot and mechanical engineer at Area 51 who retired in 1987. He was partnered with an extraterrestrial called "Jarod 2" from 1966 to 1979, who was one of two aliens captured from a recovered UFO impact near Kingman, Arizona on May 21, 1953. The other extraterrestrial had been taken to S4. Bill Uhouse and Jarod 2 worked on building a flight simulator in order to train Air Force pilots to fly advanced stealth reconnaissance craft. Bill Uhouse died in 2009 in Pennsylvania.

Chapter 4

UFO Propulsion System

What We Know About UFO's

The following material is from NASA aeronautical engineer Paul R. Hill's book, "Unconventional Flying Objects: A Scientific Analysis" (written in the 1970s, published post- posthumously 1995), and other sources.

Propulsion
Scientists have analyzed every physically possible methods of UFO propulsion and compared them with the observed performance. This includes the behavior in flight and hovering, the glow seen around and below the objects, and the reported physical effects. Through a process of elimination, impulse power, magnetic fields, electrical fields, neutrino and photon propulsion, and all other possible driving forces were ruled out except one in which a form of a gravitational field known as "anti-gravity". This field can be focused to provide a repelling force in order to counter the earth's gravity. It does so by moving molecules of air out of the way well before they could physically encounter a UFO.

The engine produces a static field that repels all mass. This field follows the inverse-square law of gravity or photon fields, and is focused to provide propulsive force. Using this field, the amount of energy to move a UFO to any particular position above the earth's gravitational is only equal to energy required to lift it to that altitude, which is a very small value. This field has an electromagnetic component, or expression, in the range between x-rays and gamma rays. This explains the radiation effects described in many cases on those who get too close to hovering

UFO's, while at the same time, it is consistent with the lack of residual radioactivity at UFO landing sites.

Gravity-like force fields are used externally for propulsion and airflow-control (shockwave suppression and drag reduction) and internally, for acceleration neutralization during maneuvers. As in this case, the UFO occupants can withstand the tremendous accelerations which would certainly kill a human pilot. The force fields consist of at least two types: the propulsive force field may be thought of as being long-range, narrow and focused; and the UFO airflow-control force field may be thought of in terms of short-range and continuous, and having components which are uniformly distributed with respect to direction.

It is the precise energy wavelength that creates the glow surrounding UFO's when in operation. This is a result of excitation of air molecules, and shifts from dull red through orange, yellow, and then to intense welding-arc white as the electromagnetic component shifts from soft x-rays up to the lower portion of the gamma-ray spectrum. The plasma generated by this wavelength of radiation is cold which is consistent with the lack of intense heat reported in UFO encounters.

Ionization and Quantum Light Processes

At low altitudes, atmospheric gas molecules such as nitrogen and oxygen consist of two atoms each, like dumbbells held together by the sharing of their outer electrons. The electrons of such molecules, unless disturbed by a collision with an energetic particle or photon, remain in their lowest energy state, called the GROUND STATE. Above the various electron ground-state energy levels are numerous energy-level vacancies.

When a sufficiently energetic wave (photon) or particle generated by the UFO collides with a molecular electron in the surrounding atmosphere, the electron is impelled past all energy-level vacancies and outside the molecule. The electron becomes a free entity, rattling around between molecules. The molecule that lost the electron is said to be IONIZED; it is a positive ion. If the freed electron attaches to a neutral molecule, a negative ion is formed. If a free electron enters a positive ion, it usually enters one of the normally vacant energy levels and gives off a light quanta (photon) having an energy equal to that given up by the electron. Thus a relatively fast electron would give off a relatively energetic photon, say in the ultraviolet, or blue range.

This electron, occupying what is normally an energy-level vacancy, is in an unstable state. It can't remain because it is attracted toward lower states by the central positive charges. The molecule containing the unstable electron is said to be EXCITED. The electron may cascade down through successively lower energy levels until it arrives at the unfilled ground state, successively giving off light quanta with energies just equal to each change of energy level by the electron. These emissions from the excited molecule depend strongly on the atomic structure and energy-level vacancies of the particular element involved, but are modified by molecular spin.

In excited atoms, the energy transitions are distinct, as are the atomic spectral lines. In excited molecules, on the contrary, the temperature-dependent energy of the rotating "dumbbell" is enough to make the spectra appear to be a continuum, having peaks at high energy concentrations and valleys in the frequency regions in between, where few photons are emitted.

Radiation

Electromagnetic radiation is coincident with the UFO's "gravity-like" force fields. Gravity-like waves used for propulsion and airflow control, and ionizing electromagnetic radiation waves go together. In other words UFOs emit invisible electromagnetic wave energy with the ionizing process. The generations of force field waves are simply a side effect of the propulsive waves which have an electromagnetic component. The existence of the ionized air around UFOs confirms this high-intensity electromagnetic radiation from the UFO. The radiation is in a range between the bottom of X-ray band and the lower end of Gamma-ray band X-rays from a UFO hovering near ground level would also penetrate a few inches of soil giving up their energy to plant-root depths.

Soil being a thermal insulator, the heat would escape slowly and the temperature would build up with time below a low-hovering UFO. Saucer-type UFOs are known to focus their force fields and accompanying ionizing radiation downward with considerable accuracy creating an "ion cones" which has given us much data on ground heating. Mild Gamma-rays are suspected for symptoms similar to radiation sickness in witnesses who have closely approached UFOs. However, lasting radioactivity, which indicates the presence of particle radiation, has not been found at landing sites. There is not much infra-red radiation since there is an absence of heat near a UFO with only a mild sensation of warmth.

Air Plasma (Aura Glow)

A plasma sheath can causes a glow of the air around UFOs, much like what happens inside a neon-lamp. It is a sheath of ionized and excited air molecules often called AIR PLASMA. The phenomenon of ionized and excited atmospheric molecules around a UFO accounts for the general nighttime appearance of the UFO producing many observed colors and the fiery neon-like self-illuminating look. It produces a fuzzy or even indiscernible outline, yet has an appearance of solidity behind the light. It accounts for the general lack of heat radiation despite the fact that they sometimes look like a flaming ball of fire. Ultraviolet burns sometimes can be received by those close to the UFOs with blue plasma.

In the daytime, the same plasma is present, but usually invisible. Morning and evening, it is partly visible. The ion sheath accounts for some daytime UFO shimmering haze or smoke-like effects sometimes observed when high contaminant concentrations and chemical actions may be presumed to be present. The cause of the plasma sheath is a power-plant-connected, ionizing, wave-type radiation from the UFO.

Color

The observed atmospheric colors are a by-product of the power plant radiation which is quite dependent on the properties of the atmosphere. The energy the electron imparts to each photon determines its wavelength and color. Air molecules can radiate in a kaleidoscope of colors, any color of the spectrum.

The following equation, in slightly different form, was first used by Einstein in 1905 to explain the photoelectric effect. It is basic to all light phenomena.

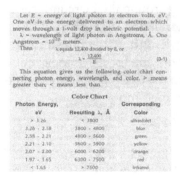

All UFO colors stem from energetic, ionizing radiation (s) generated by the UFO, which ionizes the air. Of all the visible colors, red and orange correspond to the least energy. They are also the two most common colors associated with UFO low-power operation, such as hovering or low-power maneuvers. The electrons have been given the ionization energy, but not much more, and cascade down in small energy drops corresponding to red or orange. This is statistically probable, as there are more small drops available than big ones. According to the color chart, blue requires relatively high activation energy. Blue, white and blue-white are the common colors at high-power operation. The blue of the high-power maneuver or high-speed operation corresponds to the strong radiation peaks of nitrogen. A blend of all the colors tends to be white; but with the blues predominating, the blend gives a blue-white, as with an electric arc.

Brightness

When a hovering UFO starts to maneuver, it necessarily increases thrust (lift) and power. In such a circumstance, the UFO is generally observed to brighten rather than change color. This brightness would be the result of an increase in the activation power that the UFO puts out while the energy levels of individual events stay fixed. This concept is simply standard quantum mechanics, which explains the changes in brightness, as well as the color of the air molecules surrounding a UFO at night. The brightness change together with the UFO power change clearly shows that the UFO radiation causing the brightness is an integral part of the power system.

Illumination

Sometimes a UFO's illumination is described as "running lights", "portholes", "windows" or "vents" etc, which may output steadily, or blink multi-colored in a sequence. Discoid UFOs may have such lights arranged in a band/ring around their circumference; sphere-shaped UFOs may be lit in an equatorial ring; cigar-shaped UFOs may have "brightly lit windows" along their length. Others have suggested that the rotating components of UFOs may be for gyroscopic stabilization. However they also could be related to the UFO's propulsion. Some UFOs have strobe-like flashing "beacons" on their top or bottom.

Maneuverability

All UFO maneuvers obey the known laws of physics. UFOs often fly in a manner as if their drive is perpendicular to the plane of the disc. They tilt in the direction of the force to be applied to accelerate or decelerate. They sit level to hover, tilt forward to move forward, tilt backward to stop, bank to turn. In cruise mode, the slight saucer tilt is opposite that of a wing producing lift. This slight tilt is necessary to overcome both air drag and the negative lift a saucer creates. UFO's descend with a wobble like a coin falling in water. It swings from side to side while descending. This maneuver is observed at the end of a rapid descent as the UFO initiates hovering. This wobble continues when hovering or moving slowly in a sinusoidal path typically about 30°, ±15° from centerline in an undulating "rocking" motion, like a gyroscope or a toy top. They ascend or descend in a spiral or corkscrew path. When they want to fly away fast, they tilt typically at 45° with the plane of the disc directed forward, and accelerate at a high speed.

At low speed, UFO motion seems jittery. This could be an optical effect rather than a real jitter, an optical distortion effect seen in daylight due to the surrounding plasma.

UFO movements are not smooth, like those of an airplane, but are in steps appearing to move in a jerky fashion. They shoot forward, then stop or change direction similar to skipping a flat rock on water. UFOs often travel in a zig-zag, or execute an acute-angle turn with rapid stop at the vertex, then sudden reversal of direction. The movements may be abrupt and rapid, with sudden changes of direction and speed, such as reversals (180° turns) and right-angle turns without perceptible slowing down. On these turns the craft travels through the air tilted, then reverses the tilt to level off and again tilts in the new direction. All this is accomplished in less than a few seconds giving the appearance of an instantaneous 180° or right-angle turn. These violent and erratic high speed maneuvers caused many eye-witnesses to notice them as something beyond their normal experience. This movement is caused by creating a gravity field around a UFO repelling the earth's gravitational influence. Inside the craft, this gravity field protects the occupants from extreme G-forces since the occupants do not have to overcome the inertia of their own weight. They only feel a residual fraction of the G-forces to give them a 'feel' for their craft's maneuvers. This gravity field lets the UFO hover in similar manner as a helicopter by maintaining a constant distance from the ground surface for long periods of time. Hovering is common, and can be done at any altitude. The gravity field also lets them hug the terrain while moving forward.

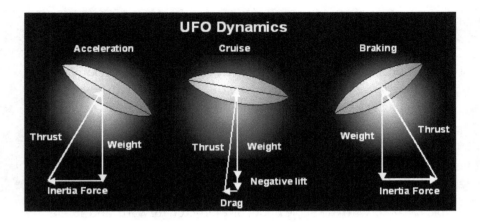

Shapes

Most UFOs are symmetrical objects, typically with smooth and featureless, seamless surfaces. Sometimes UFOs have windows or portholes which emanate light. The surfaces of the UFO are not very hot; nothing is even close to "red hot." The texture of the skin seems to "ripple" or be "wobbly" like jelly". Appearance in daylight is usually described as white or "metallic", ranging from dull gray "brushed aluminum" to bright "polished silver". It can appear as a "mirror reflecting sunlight", probably due to plasma surrounding the UFO emitting light directly or via reflection off of its skin. Some UFOs appear non-reflective matte black or dark, especially all triangle and boomerang shaped objects, while others are described as "glossy black, like black plastic."

There are a great variety of shapes:

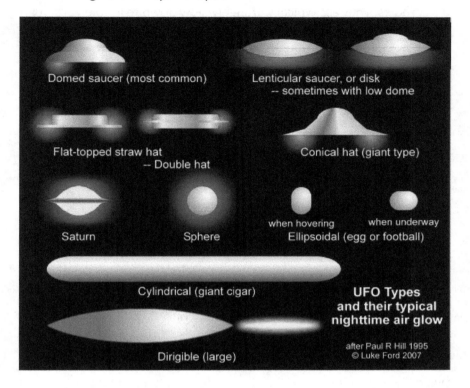

Discoid saucer in many variations

Common descriptions include the flat-bottomed saucer, convex on one side. Sometimes the convex side is shallow, similar to an "upside-down saucer". At other times, it has more depth, looking hemi-spherical as a "silver dome" or bell-shaped.

Lenticular saucers are convex on either sides or "lens-shaped", occasionally with a dome.

Flat-top discs, described as, "like a silver dollar" or a coin with a rim similar to a "straw hat.

Other configurations seem to be "like a mushroom" or a "bowl with dome". Even "a cup upside-down on a saucer".

Spheroid saucers are the common "orange balls of light" in night-time UFO reports. They are typically orange/yellow or white in color, although sometimes red, green or blue. Appearance may be due to a spherical shell of luminous ionized air around the UFO itself.

Perfectly spherical "shiny silver spheres" have white or amber light-balls, from baseball to beach ball in size, and are reported all over the world. During WWII many night-time sightings of "foo-fighters" were described as luminous spheres 3ft in size, which would pace allied aircraft in several war zones, particularly China.

A sphere with a protruding "band" or "ring" around the equator has been recorded.

Oblate spheroid or flattened spheres are quite commonly reported. These often have an equatorial ring, similar to the planet Saturn.

Other UFO descriptions include:

Walnut-shaped, "like two soup bowls rim to rim"

Crown shaped.

Ovoid ("orange ovals of light" similar as the night-time reports of spherical UFOs)

Elliptical or ellipsoidal; football-shaped; smaller egg-like objects; and acorn-shaped.

Oval UFOs, with a stripe around its base with "hieroglyphic" symbols, estimated. 10-12ft long, 8ft diameter.

Conical

Giant disc objects, similar to a shallow cone.

Medium-size

Small-size like a toy "top".

Cylindrical or Cigar flying objects are typically "bright silvery metallic", or white, like a fluorescent tube lamp. They fly in the direction of its long axis. Large cigar-shaped UFOs are often reported to be surrounded by a luminous "foggy haze" and may also have one or more rings of different color around them. Some sightings report seeing portholes or windows along their length, often emitting light.

Triangular or boomerang UFOs are reported nearly always as dark black or charcoal grey in appearance. Typically shaped as equilateral or isosceles triangles, they sometimes have rounded corners. Most are reported to have three lights on their underside and one at each corner which shine downward. Sometimes they are reported to also have other lights, like a pulsating light at their center. Sightings of triangular UFOs started in the 1950's, but increased in the late 1960s, and became very common in the 1980s. One was witnessed by famous Lockheed aeronautical engineer Clarence "Kelly" Johnson who designed the U-2 and SR-71 spy planes. Johnson described it as "boomerang shaped."

Today some people believe that these are ultra-top secret U.S. Military vehicles known as the TR3B "Astra", an anti-gravity craft which is nuclear-powered. Astra is built by the Skunk Works at the Lockheed-Martin's plant in Palmdale, California, and at Boeing Phantom Works in Seattle, Washington. It is housed in Utah. The pulsating light at their center are said to be a electromagnetic-pulse laser cannon.

Size
There are great variations in the size of UFOs, as described:

The "typical" flying saucer is 10 feet – 40 feet in diameter. They land, leaving burnt or depressed areas in an irregular configuration. Larger discs typically have a retractable landing gear, three legs positioned in the configuration of an equilateral triangle.

Smaller hemispherical (dome, helmet, mushroom) / spherical / conical objects, from 4 feet-12 feet in diameter, sometimes with "vents" or "extensions". They rarely touch the ground, but remain stationary 1-5 feet above the ground surface. They generally leave behind circular areas which are depressed, burnt or dehydrated.

Small egg-shaped objects 6-8 feet long which hovers with the long axis vertical.

A spherical object about 15 feet in diameter.

Elongated cylinders without external appendages, about 230 feet long, comparable in size to the body of a modern jet fighter aircraft, and flying in the direction of its long axis.

Oval or Egg-Shaped objects 16-20 feet in length, with visible landing legs, generally four, on occasion six.

These make ground contact, leaving burnt areas, imprints, and some tree damage. Small humanoid beings are often reported as associated with these vehicles.

Triangles 10 to 1,000 feet per side.

Boomerangs ("V") up to 2,625 feet (0.5 mile)

Conical "coolie hat" discs about 650 feet

Dirigibles about 325 feet to 2 miles.

Physiological Effects

Witnesses who come close to a UFO may experience a prickling sensation. In some incidences a heating or burning sensation is felt, and in other cases a temporary paralysis manifested. After-effects of close encounters may include sunburned-like skin and eye irritation, extreme dryness of the nasal area and of the throat, nausea, vomiting, headaches, and general weakness. There have been a few cases of people and animals that stood directly under a UFO who experienced symptoms similar to radiation sickness. People who have stared at glowing UFOs at close range have suffered temporary loss of vision and even lasting eye damage. Occasionally, odors have been reported, described as "ozone-like", "foul stench", "pungent", and "Sulphur-like stink" etc.

Effects of EM Interference have been observed which include interruption of electrical circuitry and radio communications, magnetic and gyro compasses that gyrate and wobble, and prematurely burned-out batteries. Car gasoline engines have been known to stop, but oddly, diesel engines are apparently unaffected. Aircraft pilot UFO sightings indicate strong magnetic field s and EM-effects.

Flight Characteristics
UFO's use an antigravity field that is focused to provide a repelling force to counter the earth's gravity, and move molecules of air or water out of the way well before they encounter a moving UFO. For this reason UFOs can travel through air and underwater known as USOs (Unidentified Submerged Objects), as well as in the vacuum of space.

Weight
UFOs are quite massive. Soil compression testing from imprints of 18-30 foot saucers indicated a range between 8-10 tons. Its density is estimated to be about 60.24 lb/ feet^3 (note: 62.4 lb/feet^3 is the density of fresh water), which is like that of modern nuclear submarines, but much more than that of jet aircraft.

Wakes/Trails
Generally, UFOs don't create visible trails in daylight. Large UFOs like dirigibles and cylinders may have plume-like wakes when accelerating rapidly or moving at high speeds. They can move slowly at 100 mph without generating a wake. These wakes are gray to straw-colored in daylight, red or green flame-colored at night.

What is described as "flames" or "exhaust" or "sparks" at night-time is probably a cold zone of ionized air (plasma), whose plume shape is controlled by the ionization and ion-relaxation processes. Daylight trails are possibly vapor condensation due to the airflow-control force fields.

Speed
At relatively low altitude, hypersonic speeds of about Mach 5 (3,806 miles per hour) are reported, but there are several multi-radar cases of speeds of Mach 6.5 (5,000mph). At higher altitudes, speeds of Mach 12 (9,000mph) to Mach 15.7 (12,000 mph) have been recorded by military radar. For comparison, the fastest United States jet, the SR-71, has an estimated maximum speed 2,200mph.

Acceleration
UFOs can accelerate and decelerate at over 100 G's, or 3,217 feet per second squared.

Sound

UFO's are almost completely silent. Seconds before and during take-off, sounds may rise in both pitch and intensity, or it can be silent. During motion, a light swish-of-air sound may be heard, or it can run completely silent. Some witnesses report a "cone of silence" where all other background sounds from the environment such as birds, insects etc. cease, and everything seems to be totally silent. Witnesses have reported an intense, penetrating humming sound.

Groups of UFO sounds that might be heard are:

1) Low pitch like a **hum** or buzz similar to swarm of bees. It can be felt as well as heard.
2) High pitch like a whine, hissing, shrill, or hum.
3) Highest pitch like a shrieking or piercing whistle.
4) Rush or release of air like a swishing or fluttering but rarely heard.
5) Violent like a thundering roar, bang or loud explosion.
6) Electrical or crackling sound.

A UFO's gravity-like propulsive force field has a cyclic component that induces vibrations in nearby air at a hum frequency. This explains why the UFO hum can be heard as well as felt. Rarely, shock waves appear to be generated just before take-off or at rapid acceleration which produces a violent explosive noise. It might be created as the air is pushed away from the UFO in order to create a near-vacuum. Or, it can be the result of the rare occasion when the cyclic "hum" frequency coincides with the natural frequency of the air column under the UFO.

UFOs traveling several times the speed of sound produce no shock waves or 'sonic boom'. One theory for this is that the control of airflow by the UFO's acceleration-type force field, results in a constant-pressure, compression-free zone without shockwave, in which case the vehicle is surrounded by a subsonic flow-pattern of streamlines and subsonic velocity ratios.

Disappearance / Invisibility

This is probably the most disputed aspect of reported UFO behavior. Many eyewitness report UFOs as "vanishing" or "instantly emerging" in plain sight and in broad daylight. This might be caused by the craft accelerating out of the picture so quickly that witnesses simply fail to notice them. Perhaps a better explanation causing the "invisibility" might be due to some sort of "gravitational lensing" phenomenon that uses gravity-like force field technology to bend light This would explain why many night-time cases report UFOs change their angular diameter, as if they seemed to implode. There are also reports of a UFO bending car headlight beams.

Weapons

It is speculated that UFOs can use their gravity-like force field technology as a highly destructive weapon by focusing such a beam on the target, and increasing the cyclic component to a very high frequency. This causes the target's material to vibrate so quickly that it effectively disintegrates. UFOs have spotlight beams which are used to light terrain and objects at night. However, some luminous beams may be weapons that also project heat, causing he disruption of electric and electronic equipment. The luminous beams have been reported to alter packets of light (photons), and produce hallucinations in witnesses or even the temporary paralysis of individuals that are in close proximity to it.

Levitation

It has been observed that UFOs can use their gravity-like force field to lift, repel, or move objects. This is not the same as used in the movie "Star Trek", where a person or object hit by the gravity-like force field dematerializes then rematerializes inside the spacecraft. Used here, the UFO's gravity-like force overcomes the Earth's natural gravity and produces a lifting or levitation force. It has been reported to lift people as well as water into the vehicle.

Water Connection

It is estimated that over 50% of the UFO sightings occurred over, coming from, or plunging into bodies of water. These include lakes, reservoirs, rivers and the oceans. They frequently cruise at low altitude or hover near the water surface. There are many cases of UFOs seemingly "sucking" water from lakes, rivers or reservoirs.

Covert Reconnaissance

UFOs are seen more frequently near military installations, particularly nuclear weapons-related areas, but also nuclear energy generation facilities, as well as hydroelectric dams.

Habits

UFOs are most often observed at dusk or early in the evening. They are frequently seen travelling or maneuvering over water, just off shore. They often return to a given area within minutes or hours of their departure, as though they had not concluded their Earthly observations. Seemingly, UFOs prefer to surveille lone individuals, small groups, and isolated cars. They are sometimes attracted by blinking light signals, such as the classic scene at a railroad crossing in the Spielberg movie. UFOs appear mostly at night, but they are present in daylight hours, but are difficult to see because of their light-bending characteristics.

Formation

When multiple UFOs are observed, they are often reported to maintain a formation, much like our military aircraft. When there are three, they often maintain an equilateral triangle formation. This sometimes might be interpreted as a "huge triangular craft" or "boomerang" shaped UFO.

Carrier Deploy/Recover

Spheres and saucers leave and enter large cylinders, dirigibles and cones. Very small spheres and discs are thought to be remotely controlled sensing devices, and round, discoid, or egg-shaped craft of a few yards in size are seen as "scout ships". They are typically seen on or near the ground, sometimes with occupants, and are dispatched from larger craft thought to be "mother ships" which typically stay at high altitudes.

Merging/Splitting

UFOs have been reported as "splitting" into smaller objects, in a soundless, but bright "explosion.". An explanation for this might be that when UFOs fly in close formation, their antigravity or propulsion fields combine, producing one air plasma sheath (Aura Glow) which looks like one object.

Rotation/Spin

Be it UFOs having a round cross-section, or spheres, discs, ovals, cones, and cylinders are often reported to exhibit a rotary motion. Many discoid UFOs have luminous "portholes" or "windows arranged in a circular band around their circumference. These often give the illusion of rotation by blinking multi colors in sequence, or in a single color, but each light will individually pulse brighter periodically. Rotation of "lights" at the rim of saucers is practically always reported to be counter-clockwise or left to right as seen from the side. A few UFOs have been reported to have two rotating sections, which counter-rotate. Some discoid UFOs saucers have been reported to have a rotating outer rim, which is described as spinning independently from the central part, which remains stationary. UFOs are almost never reported to completely rotate, despite popular myth.

Time Anomalies/Distortion

There are reports from people who have come close to a UFO who experience "missing time" or "gravitational time dilation", the effect of time passing at different rates. This is most likely due to the craft's gravity-like force field. We know from Einstein's Theory of Relativity that time is a function of gravitational waves. For instance, a person who is wearing a wristwatch inside of a UFO gravity wave will experience a different time than that shown on a watch outside..

Alien Visitors

Described as humanoids about 3 1/2 feet tall, the otherworldly aliens are of thin build, with grayish or yellowish skin, and a bit Asian-looking. They have large, black eyes, only a slit for a mouth, small, flat noses, and small ears. The beings have extra-long arms with less than five digits on the hands, which are like non-human animal claws. The feet have three stubby, webbed toes. Some have been reported to be 5 to 6 feet tall, and a few are said to be 8 or 9 feet tall. Very small portions are reported as hard, tough, hair-covered, non-human animal-like creatures, with claws and large, glaring yellow eyes. There have been reports from California, New Mexico, Arizona, Washington and Mexico, of flying humanoid beings coming from UFOs,

Estimated Number of UFO Sightings

The estimated number of UFO sightings in the U.S. in 2009 is over 6000 reports. After intense investigations, nearly 2000 of those cases were listed as "unknowns", or 32% of all cases for that year.

Statistics on the Top 20 States Reporting UFOs

	State	Count	Pop	Perc
1	CA	2192	36,961,664	0.0059%
2	TX	1531	24,782,302	0.0062%
3	FL	1100	19,541,453	0.0056%
4	PA	920	12,604,767	0.0073%
5	NY	759	19,541,453	0.0039%
6	MI	756	9,969,727	0.0076%
7	AZ	748	6,595,778	0.0113%
8	CO	715	5,024,748	0.0142%
9	IN	661	6,423,113	0.0103%
10	OH	622	11,542,645	0.0054%
11	IL	579	12,910,409	0.0045%
12	OR	456	3,825,657	0.0119%
13	WA	429	6,664,195	0.0064%
14	NC	391	9,380,884	0.0042%
15	GA	372	9,829,211	0.0038%
16	NJ	360	8,707,739	0.0041%
17	MO	340	5,987,580	0.0057%
18	NV	323	2,643,085	0.0122%
19	MA	306	6,593,587	0.0046%
20	VA	301	7882590	0.0038%

Sorted by number of sightings reported

	State	Count	Pop	Perc
1	CO	715	5,024,748	0.0142%
2	NV	323	2,643,085	0.0122%
3	OR	456	3,825,657	0.0119%
4	AZ	748	6,595,778	0.0113%
5	IN	661	6,423,113	0.0103%
6	MI	756	9,969,727	0.0076%
7	PA	920	12,604,767	0.0073%
8	WA	429	6,664,195	0.0064%
9	TX	1531	24,782,302	0.0062%
10	CA	2192	36,961,664	0.0059%
11	MO	340	5,987,580	0.0057%
12	FL	1100	19,541,453	0.0056%
13	OH	622	11,542,645	0.0054%
14	MA	306	6,593,587	0.0046%
15	IL	579	12,910,409	0.0045%
16	NC	391	9,380,884	0.0042%
17	NJ	360	8,707,739	0.0041%
18	NY	759	19,541,453	0.0039%
19	VA	301	7882590	0.0038%
20	GA	372	9,829,211	0.0038%

Sorted by percentage of sightings per population

Statistics on the Top 20 Towns Reporting UFOs

	Town	Counts	Pop	Perc
1	Phoenix	193	1,500,000	0.013%
2	Philadelphia	118	1,540,000	0.008%
3	Denver	110	610,345	0.018%
4	Las Vegas	104	558,383	0.019%
5	Chicago	93	2,800,000	0.003%
6	Austin	89	757,688	0.012%
7	Houston	86	2,200,000	0.004%
8	Portland	81	582,130	0.014%
9	Wilmington	81	72,826	0.111%
10	Tucson	79	541,811	0.015%
11	Los Angeles	70	3,800,000	0.002%
12	London	67	7,556,900	0.001%
13	Fort Worth	64	703,073	0.009%
14	Stephenville	64	14,921	0.429%
15	Albuquerque	62	521,999	0.012%
16	New York	58	8,300,000	0.001%
17	Pittsburgh	58	316,718	0.018%
18	Tampa	58	340,882	0.017%
19	San Antonio	57	1,351,305	0.004%
20	San Diego	56	1279329	0.004%

Sorted by number of sightings reported

	Town	Counts	Pop	Perc
1	Stephenville	64	14,921	0.429%
2	Wilmington	81	72,826	0.111%
3	Las Vegas	104	558,383	0.019%
4	Pittsburgh	58	316,718	0.018%
5	Denver	110	610,345	0.018%
6	Tampa	58	340,882	0.017%
7	Tucson	79	541,811	0.015%
8	Portland	81	582,130	0.014%
9	Phoenix	193	1,500,000	0.013%
10	Albuquerque	62	521,999	0.012%
11	Austin	89	757,688	0.012%
12	Fort Worth	64	703,073	0.009%
13	Philadelphia	118	1,540,000	0.008%
14	San Diego	56	1279329	0.004%
15	San Antonio	57	1,351,305	0.004%
16	Houston	86	2,200,000	0.004%
17	Chicago	93	2,800,000	0.003%
18	Los Angeles	70	3,800,000	0.002%
19	London	67	7,556,900	0.001%
20	New York	58	8,300,000	0.001%

Sorted by percentage of sightings per population

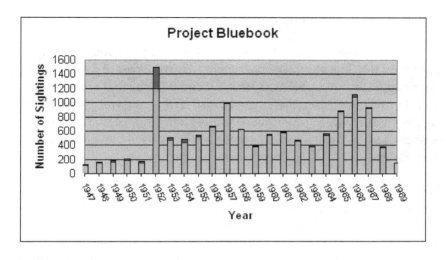

Note: The reddish-brown portion of each is the number of unidentified sightings

Studies have established that between 5% to 20% of UFO sightings can be classified as "unidentified." The majority of UFOs are observations of real, but conventional objects. Most commonly seen Unidentified Flying Objects are: aircraft, balloons, or astronomical objects such as meteors, or even bright planets like Venus in the low sky that have been misidentified by the observer. The idiom, "When a person wants to believe, they stop thinking" often comes to mind with UFO sightings. A small 5% are reported as (sometimes elaborate) UFO hoaxes.

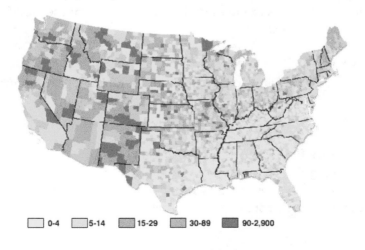

Map of UFO Hotspots

Antigravity Propulsion Systems

Gravity-controlled propulsion research has been the subject of widely published UFO literature. The documented testimonies of whistleblowers have suggested that scientists have successfully reverse engineered the vehicle retrieved from the second crash site at Roswell, New Mexico, to the point at which three Alien Vehicles had been reproduced by 1981. Branches of the military and defense agencies have denied and refuted such claims.

The propulsion research had started in the 1950s at which time Air Force researchers fully realized the astounding possibilities for aerospace companies and technical laboratories, many of them under secret government contracts. Every year, the number of these projects has increased. In 1965, forty-six unclassified "G-Projects" were confirmed by the Scientific Information Exchange of the Smithsonian Institution. Thirty-three of the total forty-six projects involved gravity-control technology.

There have been advances beyond antigravity field propulsion. Quantum physics is now used to update a variety of aerospace craft and their weapons systems. While relativity theory is great at describing the universe on visible scales, quantum physics tells us about the way things work on the atomic level, involving subatomic particle regimes. According to quantum theory, if one examines the fabric of space-time close enough, it is made of infinitesimal grains of information.

Scientific research has found the following methods for the modification of gravitational fields:

Electrogravitics
By using millions of volts in order to disrupt the ambient gravitational field produces an antigravity field resulting in an 89% reduction in gravitational influence.

Magnetogravitics (Dynamic Counterbary)
Generating high-energy doughnut-shaped fields, spinning at incredible revolutions per minute disrupts the ambient gravitational field to an extent that counters Earth's gravitational pull.

Magnetic Field Disrupter

Both Sandia and Livermore National Laboratories have developed Magnetic Field Disrupter technology. A circular, plasma-filled accelerator ring, called the Magnetic Field Disrupter, surrounds the rotatable crew compartment. The plasma, mercury based, is pressurized at 250,000 atmospheres at a temperature of 150 degrees Kelvin, and accelerated to 50,000 rpm to create super-conductive plasma with the resulting gravity disruption reducing almost all of the pull of gravity and effects of inertia. The Magnetic Field Disrupter generates a magnetic vortex field, which disrupts or neutralizes the effects of gravity on a body of mass within its proximity by 89 percent. The mass of the circular accelerator and all mass within the accelerator, such as the crew capsule, avionics, Magnetic Field Disrupter systems, fuels, crew environmental systems, and the nuclear reactor, are reduced by 89% making a vehicle extremely light with the ability to outperform and outmaneuver other aircraft.

Nuclear Strong Force

Two elements, Bismuth (Element 83) and Moscovium (Element 115), have unique gravitational characteristics because of their particular distinctive atomic nucleic configuration (the 'Magic Number' of 184 neutrons). In them the Strong Force Field naturally extends slightly beyond their nuclei. It does so much more powerfully in the case of Moscovium than with Bismuth. These two elements have stable isotopes which generate their own gravitational fields, secondarily and independently of Earth's gravitational field. By amplifying the secondary gravitational field, a craft's gravitational force field becomes a very powerful engine. This field provides the craft's body mass with an integrated secondary force field. A pilot aboard the craft using power from an antimatter reactor can direct the secondary force to lift the craft from the ground, then switch to powering the craft through manipulation of the secondary field polarity, creating an inherent attraction to, or repellency from, Earth's gravitational field.

A description of how a Nuclear Strong Force works and its potential comes from Bob Lazar, a scientist that was hired in the late 1980s to reverse-engineer extraterrestrial technology. In his gravity generators, he used the fuel "Moscovium" with atomic chart as "Mc" and atomic number of 115 which was discovered in August 2003. It is a "super heavy" element having an atomic number over 110. Moscovium functioned as a gravity wave generator for UFOs, being "stepped up" (excited) through the use of Livermorium proton bombardment. Livermorium's decay products include gravitons, a "pure" gravity wave.

The term "Gravity Generator" is used to describe the capability of producing a gravitational field, But a more accurate term might be to "amplify" a gravitational field. In a gravity generator, Moscovium is machined into about 223 gram triangles which is just under a half pound. This trivial amount is sufficient to operate the craft for 30 to 45 years! It is inserted into the top of the reactor, with the base of the reactor being a highly sophisticated particle accelerator similar to a cyclotron.

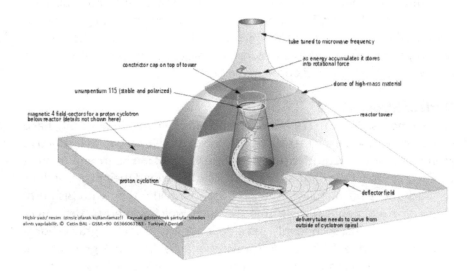

Protons are accelerated to high speed and deflected up a small tube that is aimed at the Moscovium. The protons are transmuted and become an atom of element 116, which immediately decays and produces a radiation. Each atom of element 116 decays, release two antiprotons (anti-hydrogen), producing a form of antimatter. The flux of antimatter particles produced in the reactor are guided down an evacuated, tuned tube (which keeps it from contact with the matter that surrounds it), and reacts with a gaseous matter target. When matter and antimatter react, they convert to 100 percent energy. The two more common nuclear reactions, Fission and Fusion, are dwarfed by the power and efficiency of the annihilation reaction. The reaction between the gaseous matter target and the antimatter particles produces a continuous release of tremendous amounts of heat. This heat is converted directly into electricity by the use of a Thermionic Generator. This electricity is used to power electrical items in the craft without the need for wires. It functions as a compact, lightweight, and efficient, onboard power source.

The Thermionic Generator is only secondary to the primary function of the reactor. The antiparticle flux emitted from the transmuting element 115 is not the only energy radiated during the operation. This is the point at which the small (micro) gravity waves known as the "strong nuclear force" is first produced. The gravity wave emitted by the 115 reaction appears on the hemisphere of the reactor, propagating up the tuned waveguide in a fashion very similar to the way microwaves behave. This then goes to a series of amplifying cavities, then through the projectors at the bottom of the craft. There is no thermic radiation endangering the crew in that the thermo-electrical generator is 100% efficient. This process violates our first law of thermodynamics, but in fact, it works. The gravity generator produces a wave which is similar to what the Earth produces, however the phase shifts away from the craft, where it will work against the natural gravity wave of the Earth and produce lift.

For purposes of demonstration, we will use the smaller disc shaped UFO craft which is most likely used as a scout vehicle. There are three gravity generators located on the bottom of the vehicle. The craft can lift off from the ground or fly using one of the gravity generators. The way it is propelled is by two different configurations, one known as 'Omicron', the other, a 'Delta' configuration. In the omicron configuration it uses one gravity generator, and in the delta configuration it uses all three gravity generators. Delta configurations are used for space travel. The craft tilts up on its side and focuses the three gravity generators to a single point.

Travel near the surface of Earth requires only one amplifier in the Omicron configuration. The gravity wave, which propagates outward from the disc, is phase shifted into the gravity wave, which propagates outward form the earth, thus creating lift. The craft then floats on the gravity field surrounding the Earth, like a ship on water. Note that this is not anti-gravity. It is simply using the natural gravity that exists within every atom, accessing it, amplifying it, and returning it as another form of gravity. It is important to understand that this process is not generating gravity or anti-gravity. Everyone is searching for the concept of obtaining energy from nothing, or 0-point energy, in an effort to "generate" gravity.

The gravity amplifiers of the disc can be focused independently, and they are pulsed in a rotational pattern that is not in continuous operation. The amplifiers pulse individually at 7.46 Hz, as this cycle revolves around the disc. Changing the phase of the one wave against the phase of the other, (much like "tuning-in" a microwave signal) is what constitutes lift, or attraction. This means that the craft uses only one gravity amplifier to hover over the ground, and the other two to levitate objects, or to create "wave fronts" for lateral movements.

0 to 90° Phase Shifts = Lift or Repulsion; 90 to 180° Phase Shifts = Amount of Attraction.

In the Omicron configuration, one amplifier is pointed toward the earth allowing the craft to float on the neutral area established by aiming these two gravities at each other and changing the phase. In this case, the other two amplifiers are free to bias the craft in a lateral direction, as well as being used to levitate objects, or to function as a beam weapon. When the gravitational field around the disc is so intense that the space-time around the disc achieves maximum distortion, the disc can't be seen from any vantage point and, for all practical purposes becomes invisible. All that can be seen is the environment around it.

Moving around the Earth's gravity creates a problem, as it is interference to the craft. So instead of fighting it, UFOs work with that interference by using only one gravity generator to lift it off the ground. This creates a high voltage discharge on the bottom of the craft which dissipates after it is about 30 feet in the air, but other than that, produces no exhaust. The sound from the high voltage discharge was recorded by the Saint Helens, Oregon Police Department on March 17, 1981, as well as by others.

Unlike a conventional aircraft that uses thrust or some type of force out the back of it in order to propel a plane forward, the UFOs work completely opposite from that. Once they are hovering in the air, they swing the two remaining gravity generators up in front of them and create a downhill distortion, allowing the craft to "roll downhill." It is always chasing a little distortion which makes them look goofy at low speeds, since the gravity field around the Earth is not completely constant or stable, depending on Earth's density and mineral composition passing beneath the moving craft. In low speed mode, the UFO is somewhat unstable for the most part.

The craft generates its own gravitational field. Being inside that field you are influenced only by its gravitational field - inertia has no effect. Gravity distorts both time and space, so there is a lack of physical effect once you are in this field. This process enables 90 degree turns at high speeds without its occupants being thrown against the crafts walls.

When all three amplifiers are being used for travel, they are in the Delta configuration, which is used for Interstellar Travel. Assuming that a vehicle can generate a strong gravitational field forming a wave sufficient to shoot a vector in any direction and therefore distort space-time in its path. But to define a point in space-time and compressing the space-time between the vehicle and that point, the vehicle would need at least 2 or 3 separately-generated gravity wave vectors. This is due to the need for triangulation of the three synchronized beams of gravity to focus on a distant point where they intersect. One example of a triangulation program that uses separate, but synchronized vectors exists in the 3D motion picture industry which provides film special effects. Another example is seen in sound based programs that can detect the exact point of origin of a sniper's position simply by listening to the gunshot from three to six differently-spaced microphones. Similarly, we can generate intense gravitational fields which distort the space/time, and in turn, the distance between the point where we are and the 'point' where we want to be. We can then position ourselves at the point where we want to be, a very small move at this stage, and then stop generating the gravitational field allowing space/time to return to its natural form. We would now be at that new point, potentially millions of miles from where we started an instant ago.

With the effects of gravity from so many sources in space, it is safe to assume that light wouldn't travel in a straight line in a natural, linear fashion. So to shoot too far in the distance could be disastrously off the target by millions of miles. These crafts travel in zig-zag patterns or "small chunks" to maintain a sense of its position in space. Only the most sophisticated navigation system could keep track of these jump points. Remember, the star charts that we have become accustomed to here on Earth are only valuable from our terrestrial point of view. One powerful jump into space, and all those star charts would be fairly useless. Distance from earth to the star as a cross reference would not be nearly accurate enough because that assumes that light is traveling in a straight line, unaffected by gravitational forces.

We reason that the shortest distance between two 2-dimensional points is a straight line, but in our multi-dimensional universe, standard ways or performing terrestrial measurements are out the door. When distorting space-time through the generation of intense gravitational fields, the method of travel between points A and B is to bend the space-time, thereby reducing the distance of travel. Using this concept as described by Bob Lazar, a space craft could travel from one point in our universe to any other point in a very short time if enough force was applied at a small distance ahead of the craft in the direction of travel. Instead of "pushing" forward, it is more like being sucked forward in a vacuum. The more intense the gravitational field, the greater the distortion of space/time and the shorter the distance between points A and B. The speed of light equation is not being violated, in that the light in this warped or reduced distance is less than maximum speed, and it is traveling with the craft. From an observer viewing this from a fixed point in the universe, the light would appear to be traveling faster than the maximum.

As the intensity of the gravitational field around the disc increases, the distortion of space-time around the disc also increases. If you could see the space-time distortion, which we can't, the space-time around the disc not only bends upward, but at maximum distortion, actually folds into almost a heart shape around the top of the disc. This space-time distortion is taking place entirely around the disc, creating a volume of distortion. Looking at the disc from the top, the space/time distortion would be in the shape of a donut as it enclosed the disc. When the gravitational field around the disc is so intense that the space/time around the object achieves maximum distortion, the disc can't be seen from any vantage point, and for all practical purposes, is invisible. All that would be seen is the sky around it. At various angles prior to the disc achieving maximum distortion, the disc may be visible from one vantage point, but not another. All that is seen is the environment around it. This is similar to being able to see stars that are behind the sun, due to the intense gravity of the sun bending the light path between the star and earth. Essentially, this bending process creates a sort of space-time bubble around the craft. "Maximum distortion" is not necessary for standard flight over the surface of a planet, except in the case of rapid "streaks" across the sky. The typical meteorite streaking across the night sky is not the object itself, but rather the air around the object that is ionizing the air molecules and trailing it.

The speed of light is 186,000 miles a second, which translates into roughly 669 million miles an hour. A "Light Year" is the apparent distance traveled in one Earth year at the speed of light, a distance of almost 6 trillion miles. Proxima Centauri, the star nearest us outside of our solar system, is over four light years away, but could be much "closer" if using space/time bending applications of travel.

Our UFO Fleet

When it comes to ultra-high technological aircraft, there is only one (known) facility that tests all types of craft, and that is Area 51, located within the Nevada Test and Training Range. The test operations are administered by a remote detachment from Edwards Air Force Base. Leading in this development, is the "Skunk Works", an official pseudonym for Lockheed Martin's Advanced Development Programs, which is a secret aeronautical research facility located in Burbank, California. It is responsible for a number of aircraft designs, beginning with the P-38 Lightning in 1939, and the P-80 Shooting Star in 1943. Skunk Works engineers subsequently developed the U-2, SR-71 Blackbird, F-117 Nighthawk, F-22 Raptor, and the F-35 Lightning II.

Dr. Benjamin R. Rich was a brilliant scientist, aeronautical engineer and the second Director of Lockheed's Skunk Works from 1975 to 1991. Regarded as the "Father of stealth", Rich was responsible for leading the development of the F-117, the first production stealth aircraft. He also helped develop the F-104, U-2, A-12, SR-71, and F-22, among others. When Benjamin Rich says something about aircraft dynamics and characteristics, he knows what he is talking about.

Before Rich died of cancer, Dr. Rich confirmed to his friend, John Andrews:

1. 1. There are 2 types of UFOs — the ones we build, and ones 'they' build. We learned from crash retrievals and actual "hand-me-downs." The Government knew of UFOs and aliens, and until 1969 took an active part in the administration of that information. After a 1969 Nixon "purge", that type of administration was turned over to an international board of directors in the private sector.
2. 2. Nearly all "biomorphic" aerospace designs were inspired by the Roswell spacecraft — from Kelly's SR-71 Blackbird onward to today's drones, UCAVs, and aerospace craft.

3. 3. It was Ben Rich's opinion that the public should not be told about UFOs and extraterrestrials]. He believed that people could not handle the truth — ever. Only in the last months of his decline did he begin to feel that the "international corporate board of directors" dealing with the "Subject" could present a bigger problem to citizens' personal freedoms, than the knowledge of the existence of off-world visitors themselves.

The statement, "We learned from both crash retrievals and actual "hand-me-downs" clearly means that we have obtained knowledge from UFO crashes and that extraterrestrials have given us UFO vehicles that we have obtained as "hand-me-downs." This corroborates Bob Lazar's S-4 story, and strongly suggests that Eisenhower's extraterrestrial meeting actually took place.

James Goodall, an aerospace journalist, became friends with Ben Rich. Goodall states that he spoke with Rich about 10 days before Rich died. The telephone conversation took place while Rich was in the USC Medical Center in Los Angeles. Goodall claims that Rich said, "Jim, we have things out in the desert that are fifty years beyond what you can comprehend. If you have seen it on Star Wars or Star Trek, we've been there, done that, or decided it wasn't worth the effort."

Ben. Rich attended an Aerospace Designers and Engineers conference in 1993 before his illness overwhelmed him. He stated — in the presence of Jan Harzan, the Orange County Section Director of MUFON, and many others, as related In the MUFON UFO Journal, May 2010 written by Tom Keller:

1) "Inside the Skunk Works - Lockheed's secret research and development entity, we were a small, intensely cohesive group consisting of about fifty veteran engineers and designers and a hundred or so expert machinists and shop workers. Our forte was building technologically advanced airplanes [in] small numbers for highly secret missions."

2) "We already have the means to travel among the stars, but these technologies are locked up in black projects, and it would take an act of God to ever get them out to benefit humanity. Anything you can imagine, we already know how to do."

3) "We now have the technology to take ET home. No, it won't take someone's lifetime to do it. There is an error in the equations... We now have the capability to travel to the stars. First, you have to understand that we will not get to the stars [by] using chemical propulsion. Second, we have to devise a new propulsion technology. What we have to do is find out where Einstein went wrong."

4) When Rich was asked how UFO propulsion worked, he said, "Let me ask you. How does ESP work?" The questioner replied with, "All points in time and space are connected?" Rich responded, "That's how it works!"

Gary McKinnon a Scottish systems administrator and hacker was accused in 2002 of perpetrating the "biggest military computer hack of all time." McKinnon was accused of hacking into 97 United States military and NASA computers over a 13-month period between February 2001 and March 2002. McKinnon hacked into U.S. Space Command computers and learned of the existence of "non-terrestrial officers", "fleet-to-fleet transfers", and a secret program called "SOLAR WARDEN". The Solar Warden Space Fleet operates under the U.S. Naval Network and Space Operations Command (NNSOC), formerly referred to as, Naval Space Command. There are approximately 300 personnel involved at NNSOC, with the figure rising. Solar Warden is said to be comprised of U.S. aerospace Black Projects contractors, but with some contributions of parts and systems from Canada, United Kingdom, Italy, Austria, Russia, and Australia.. It is said that there are approximately eight cigar-shaped motherships, each longer than two football fields end-to-end, and 43 small "scout ships." It may be noted that McKinnon does not say that these vehicles are U.S. vehicles. There are reports that the United States and the aliens signed a treaty, including for them to share some of their technology. We might be in a joint Space Force with the aliens. It has been over 71 years since the Roswell incident, which leads to speculation that Solar Warden may actually exist. Also note that many very large "cigar-shaped" UFOs have been reported in the in the United States and Canada since 1980 to the present.

It is my view that SOLAR WARDEN is very real. Rumors abound that McKinnon let slip the names of two U.S. military spaceships: the USSS LeMay, and the USSS Hillenkoetter. Apparently, USSS stands for "United States Space Ship".

The secretive "Black budget" has been known to hide multiple types of projects from elected U.S. Government officials. With secret code names and hidden figures, the details of the black budget are revealed only to select individuals of Congress, if at all. This budgetary process had been approved by the U.S. National Security Act of 1947, which created the Central Intelligence Agency (CIA), the National Security Council (NSC), and has been used to reorganize some military bases with assistance from the U.S. Department Of Defense (DOD). The U.S. Government claims that the money given to this budget is used to investigate advanced sciences and technologies for military and defense purposes, including the creation of new aircraft, weapons, and satellites. In 2018 the Trump administration asked for an astonishing $81.1 billion for the 2019 black budget.

The Black Triangle

A person could consider the Roswell Incident, "The Conspiracy Theory", Reverse Engineering, Gravity and Light Focusing Beams, Anti-Gravity Propulsion Systems, and the TR-3B "Astra" as being caused by an over-active imagination. However, one must contemplate that for over 40,000 years, UFOs have been characterized as being saucer-shaped, spherical elliptical, or cylindrical-shaped silver objects. Then suddenly in the mid-1950s, a few years after the "Roswell Incident", there appears the "Black Triangle" UFOs. These are nothing like anything seen previously, and they do not match any other reported alien UFOs throughout recorded history. Whether or not it is a secret United States aircraft with characteristics of either the TR-3B "Astra" an alien UFO, or that of an over-active imagination, we need to evaluate the following reports of the "Black Triangle" UFOs and decide for ourselves.

Triangular-shaped UFOs first made their appearance in the mid-1950s, mainly in the United States and United Kingdom. Accounts of enormous black flying triangles, wedges, or boomerangs have increased dramatically since the 1990s. Most Black Triangle reports indicate that the craft are at least 200 feet in length, and similar to the dimensions of a typical football field in width. They appear silently and seemingly "out of nowhere", drifting a few hundred feet or less above the ground. Black Triangles are usually described by witnesses as moving very slowly or hovering in one place for varying periods of time, sometimes even landing. They have been reported to slowly cruise at low altitudes over cities and highways, usually at night and making no attempt to evade detection. These crafts are often described as having "running lights", either bright white lights or pulsing colored lights that appear at each corner of the triangle. The craft are also sometimes reported by witnesses to be capable of sudden, rapid acceleration, often mentioned in descriptions of other types of UFOs. Many have been reported flying over Nuclear Power Stations, before turning back out to sea a few hours later. There is an average of 1, 525 reports of Flying Triangle UFOs seen each year, with 900 of them observed over Nuclear Power Stations.

UK Ministry of Defense researchers conclude that "Black Triangle" UFOs are formations of electrical plasma, the interaction of which creates mysterious energy fields that both refract light and produce optical illusions and even hallucinations to witnesses that are in close proximity. A geographic distribution of sightings within the United States led an American-based investigative organization called, The National Institute for Discovery Science. A July 2002 report suggested that the craft may belong to the U.S. Air Force. Some of the Black Triangles are likely sightings of one or more black projects under development by the U.S. military. However, the fact that triangles are usually reported in and around populated areas, and that they make no effort to evade detection, casts doubt on whether such sightings are secretive military craft.

On the evening of November 18, 1980 in Missouri and Kansas, hundreds of witnesses including police officers watched as a slow moving UFO hovered over the countryside for a period of four hours. Most of the sightings occurred in a broad area between Ridgeway and Edina, Missouri, a distance of about one hundred miles. The enormous craft, described as a "Flying Triangle as big as a football field" appeared to be dropping what a local truck driver described as satellites, appearing to be round and emitting a bluish glow. The entire event was tracked on local radar systems during the four hour period.

On December 26, 1980 at 3:00 a.m. near an American air base at Rendlesham Forest in Suffolk, Britain, a two-man USAF security patrol near the East Gate of RAF Woodbridge observed strange colored lights above the forest in the direction of Orford Ness. The lights were inside the pine forest. Security officers drove on a logging track that led into the forest, and preceded the rest of the way on foot, owing to the icy terrain. All three men closed in on a pyramid-shaped craft that resembled an "aircraft on fire". The team went close enough to see an actual object (being?) looming from within the glow.

Two nights later on the morning 28 Dec 1980, the bizarre lights were spotted again. A small group of five men, headed by the deputy base commander, left the base to investigate, but this time armed with additional equipment. They encountered a red pulsating object that apparently navigated between the trees, which after disturbing nearby animals, silently "exploded" in a flash of bright light, then separated into smaller brightly lit objects. The objects which had broken off the original object moved rapidly in sharp angular movements and one projected pencil-thin "laser-like" beams down onto the ground. One beam landed directly in front of the five man team, causing them great concern. Was it a warning? Was it trying to communicate? Other beams landed near the base Weapons Storage Area.

A huge boomerang-shaped craft was seen over Arizona in January of 1981. One witness proclaimed the object, "was bigger than several football fields!" Oddly, a "football field" seems to be the term that people in the U.S. commonly use in order to gauge the size and dimensions of UFO craft. The V-shaped object was later reported in New York State and Connecticut in March, 1983. Once again the craft was described as being "as big as two football fields" and this time, the craft flashed its lights on and off as though trying to attract attention.

On March 30, 1990 the Belgian Air Force reported that the citizens of Brussels spotted what appeared to be a large black triangular craft hovering silently over the city for several minutes. Local police officials arrived on the scene and observed the object hovering over apartment buildings. One officer reported that the object released a red glowing disk of light from its center which flew down to the ground and darted around several buildings before disappearing. The Belgian Air Force dispatched two F-16 fighters that intercepted a number of the flying triangles, although the jets were completely unable to match the speed and maneuverability of the UFOs, as subsequent cockpit radar film footage displayed.

A huge Flying Triangle craft was seen over Bakewell in Derbyshire, England on the 26th of September 1993. A huge black craft, slowly and silently flew over their town. With a bright white light on each corner of its triangular shape, and numerous smaller lights running along the edges of the craft, the Black Triangle flew low, and at an estimated speed of only 30 mph. The craft performed several slow maneuvers over the town before returning to its original course and flying slowly out of sight. From December 1994 to May 1995 there were 52 Black Triangle incidents recorded in and around the city of Derby. A triangular craft was observed hovering over one of the main traffic ways, Spider Bridge, located on the A-5111 circular road. The craft was seen at night hovering and shining down a white beam of light onto the countryside. The white beam of light sometimes seemed "ending in midair, like a fluorescent tube." Black Triangle craft have been reported entering and leaving the sea off the British eastern coast near Lowestoft. There have been over 25 reports of lights seen moving under the surface of the sea in the same area.

In the U.S., the "Phoenix Lights" are one of the more famous appearances of these craft. On Thursday, March 13, 1997 multiple unidentified objects, many of them Black Triangles, were spotted by the residents of Phoenix, Arizona and videotaped by both the local media and residents. Some of the airborne lights drifted as low as 1000 feet and moved far too slowly for conventional aircraft, and too silently for helicopters. Some of the lights appeared to group into a giant "V" formation that lingered above the city for several minutes. Many residents reported one triangle to be over a mile wide that drifted slowly over their houses blocking out the stars of the night sky. Other reports indicated the craft were spotted flying away from Phoenix as far away as Las Vegas, Nevada and Los Angeles, California.

Beginning shortly after 4:00 a.m. on January 5, 2000, five on-duty Illinois police officers in separate locations sighted and reported a massive, unidentified triangular aircraft. Two of the five officers reported flight characteristics which do not conform to currently known civilian technologies, as the object appeared to move at incredible speeds without making any sound. Sightings in Highland, Illinois, by a civilian who first reported to the local police department and subsequent sightings took place in Lebanon, Summerfield, Shiloh, Millstadt, Dupo, and O'Fallon. Scott Air Force Base public relations office denied any knowledge of the event. To substantiate that the police officers did in fact witness the same unexplained aircraft, and that their reports correlated, all five officers were given a lie detector test and asked various questions about the incident, which all five officers passed. The above are just a few of the most well-known Black Triangle incidents.

Antigravity Vehicles

Lieutenant Colonel Philip James Corso claims that he administered extraterrestrial artifacts which were recovered from the Roswell crash in 1947. Corso confirmed the existence of the covert government group Majestic 12. At the same time, Corso said the U.S. government simultaneously discounted the existence of flying saucers. According to Corso, the reverse engineering of these artifacts indirectly led to the development of accelerated particle beam devices, fiber optics, lasers, integrated circuit chips and Kevlar material. Was Corso a crackpot? Given his background, you decide:

In 1942, Corso served in Army Intelligence in Europe, becoming Chief of the U.S. Counter Intelligence Corps in Rome. In 1945, he was the personal emissary to Giovanni Battista Montini at the Vatican, later to become Pope Paul VI. During the Korean War (1950–1953), Corso performed intelligence duties under General Douglas MacArthur as Chief of the Special Projects branch of the Intelligence Division, Far East Command. Corso was on the staff of President Eisenhower's National Security Council for four years (1953–1957). In 1961, he became Chief of the Pentagon's Foreign Technology desk, Army Research and Development, working under Lt. Gen. Arthur Trudeau.

Reverse engineering of UFOs led to the development of Anti-Gravity Technologies. One of these was a gravity and light focusing beam that alters light and has the potential to produce hallucinations in witnesses that are in close proximity. The spotlight beams can be used to light terrain and objects at night. However, some luminous beams may be used as weapons. It can be used for the purpose of projection of heat, the disruption of electric and electronic equipment, and even the temporary paralysis of individuals. It can also be used to lift, repel, or move objects. Used as a weapon, it had highly destructive powers. Another of these Anti-Gravity Technologies led to its use in propulsive systems.

It took the U.S. 45 years to figure out (with extraterrestrial consultants' assistance) how a UFO "flies." All of these technologies are primitive in comparison with the otherworldly visitors' own craft, which utilize not only Strong Force field propulsion, but also transit through hyperspace harnessing the power of the ambient Zero Point Energy Field, which is everywhere.

By the year 2019, twelve antigravity or reduced-gravity U.S. aircraft and spacecraft according to Dr. Richard Boylan website were known to exist. Dr. Richard Boylan claims that these names of antigravity aircraft were given to him from his Military contacts the reader should use their own judgement to determine accuracy. These human-built crafts that use antigravity technology are:

The B-2 Stealth Bomber, manufactured by Northrop-Grumman. The Air Force describes it as a low-observable, strategic, long-range heavy bomber capable of penetrating sophisticated and dense air-defense shields. The Stealth Bomber has navigation and guidance systems directed by a classified Artificial Intelligence (AI) program. This AI is exotic, involving the connection of PCR-cloned copies of extraterrestrial brain tissue, with advanced integrated circuitry in order to fashion hybrid sentient 'neuro chips'. The B-2 gets extra lift in-flight by employing its electro-gravity fields, running along its wings and fuselage, in order to considerably neutralize the pull of gravity. Now we can begin to see why the U.S. Northrop B-2 stealths cost about a billion dollars each.

The F-22 Raptor advanced Stealth Fighter is built by a joint effort of the Lockheed-Martin Skunk Works and Boeing's Phantom Works. In crude imitation of extraterrestrial star craft, the guidance system of this F-22 aircraft incorporates special Artificial Intelligence (AI) semi-autonomously-functioning guidance system. Additionally, the F-22 uses antigravity weight-reduction capability, which is employed selectively by the pilot, in a mental connection with the AI guidance system, activating the antigravity field generation as needed. In coordination with the F-22's conventional jet engine thrust, the antigravity effect dramatically increases the plane's overall maneuverability.

The F-35 Lightning II advanced Stealth Fighter is built jointly by Lockheed-Martin, Northrop-Grumman and BAE Systems. Similarly, the F-35 incorporates quasi-sentient Artificial Intelligence and antigravity weight-reduction technology, which has been back-engineered from alien technologies, in addition to its conventional jet thrust.

The Aurora is a moderate-size spacefaring vehicle. The late National Security Council scientist, Dr. Michael Wolf of MJ-12, using the cover of "NSC Special Studies Group", has stated that the Aurora can operate on both conventional fuel, and reduced-gravity field-propulsion modes. Dr.

Wolf further stated that the Aurora can travel without booster rockets to the Moon. The Aurora operates out of Area 51 in Nevada.

Lockheed-Martin openly acknowledges its rocket-engine, X-33 'prototype', a single-stage-to-orbit reusable aerospace vehicle referred to as the "National Space Plane." Lockheed's other space plane, the X-33A, (The 'A' suffix stands for antigravity). It incorporates antigravity technology, whose security level is deemed, above-Top Secret. Lockheed-Martin does not say too much about its conventional winged delta-shape X-33 VentureStar. The "VentureStar X-33" has an electrogravitics antigravity system on board

Lockheed's X-22A is a two-man antigravity discoid craft. The late USAF Colonel Steve Wilson stated that military astronauts are trained at a secret aerospace academy adjacent to the regular Air Force Academy at Colorado Springs, CO. These military astronauts go on to operate out of Beale and Vandenberg Air Force Bases in California. From those bases, they regularly fly outside of Earth's atmosphere, and out into deep space. Colonel Wilson had confirmed that one of the aerospace craft used is the X-22A. The X-22A antigravity disc is capable of achieving optical as well as radar invisibility! The original X-22A had had a standard altimeter hard-wired into it, but such an instrument would give faulty readings because of the craft's antigravity field, which bends space-time. Instead, a gradiometer is used, which functions much better for navigational calculations.

The Nautilus is another space-faring craft, a secret military vehicle which operates by magnetic pulsing. It operates clandestinely out of Vandenberg Air Force Base, California. It makes trips several times a week up to the joint-nations secret military-intelligence space station. This undeclared, cloaked space station has been in deep space for the past forty years, manned by U.S., Russian, British, Canadian, Austrian, Australian, Brazilian, and other military astronauts. The Nautilus is also used for super-fast surveillance operations, utilizing its ability to penetrate target-countries from space. Nautilus is manufactured jointly by Boeing's Phantom Works at Nellis Air Force Range, Nevada, and by Airbus Industries, the Anglo-French consortium.

The TR3A "Pumpkinseed" is a super-fast air vehicle. The 'Pumpkinseed' nickname is a reference to its thin oval airframe. It uses Pulse-Detonation Wave Engine technology for propulsion in a sub-hypersonic regime. The

TR3A also employs antigravity technology for reducing the vehicle's mass, and for field propulsion at higher altitude and speed levels. As air breathers, these Pulse Detonation Wave Engines can propel a hypersonic aircraft towards Mach 10 at an altitude in excess of 180,000 feet. The same Pulse-Detonation Wave Engines are capable of lifting the craft to the edge of space when switched to rocket mode.

The TR3B "Astra" is a large triangular anti-gravity craft within the secret U.S. spacefaring fleet. The Astra was built with technology already available in the mid-1980s, so, not every UFO spotted is necessarily of alien origin.

The TR3B is the most "exotic" vehicle, a triangular nuclear Earth-to-space platform manufactured by Boeing that was created under the Aurora Program, funded and coordinated by the NSA, the NRO, and the CIA, and costing over $3 billion. The first operational reconnaissance flight took place in the early 1990s, replacing the SR-71 "Blackbird. The operational model is approximately 600 feet in diameter. The TR3-B does not depend solely or principally on its hydrogen-oxygen rockets. The reduced-gravity field it generates reduces the vehicle's weight by about 90% so that very little thrust is required to either keep it aloft, or to propel it at speeds of Mach 9 or higher. The vehicle's outer coating is electrochemical-reactive, and changes with radio-frequency radar stimulation, thereby modifying reflectiveness, radar absorptiveness, and color. This is also the first US vehicle to use quasi-crystals in the vehicle's skin. This polymer skin, when used in conjunction with the TR3B's Electronic Counter Measures and Electronic Counter-Countermeasures (ECCM), can make the vehicle look like a small aircraft, or a flying cylinder – or even trick radar receivers into falsely detecting a variety of aircraft, no aircraft, or several aircraft at various locations! It is a high-altitude stealth reconnaissance platform with an indefinite loiter time. Once it gets to operational altitude, it doesn't take much propulsion to maintain altitude. Sources say that the performance is limited only by the stresses that its human pilots can endure. Such stresses are greatly reduced, considering that along with the 89% reduction in mass, the inertial G (gravity) forces are also reduced by 89%. The crew can comfortably take up to 40Gs!

Propulsion of the TR3B is provided by three multimode thrusters which are mounted at each bottom corner of the triangular platform. The craft is a sub-Mach 9 vehicle until it reaches altitudes above 120,000 feet – then, free from atmospheric drag, it can go much faster. The reactor heats the liquid hydrogen and injects liquid oxygen into the supersonic nozzle, so that the hydrogen burns concurrently in the liquid- oxygen afterburner. The multimode propulsion system can operate in the atmosphere with lift from the Magnetic Field Disrupter powered by the nuclear reactor and creates propulsion by burning hydrogen; in orbit it uses the combined hydrogen/oxygen propulsion. The engines are reportedly built by Rockwell.

The Northrop Antigravity Disc (military designation unknown) is manufactured by Northrop Grumman Advanced Concepts and Technologies Division, sixty miles north of Los Angeles in the Tehachapi Mountains west of Edwards Air Force Base. There, Northrop has its secret saucer manufacturing works buried deep within the mountain. When energized, these discs emit their characteristic intense bright orange-gold signature. It is reasonable to assume that this is due to strong ionization, and that electrogravitics is part of the methodology of their field propulsion.

Chapter 5

Nuclear Facility's and UFOs

When it comes to investigating crime they say follow the money but when it comes to UFOs you can say follow the nukes. It has been reported that every nuclear facility including nuclear aircraft carriers and nuclear submarines on our planet have reported UFO activity.

The Hanford Site

A nuclear production complex known as "The Hanford Site" operated by the United States federal government on the Columbia River in Benton County, Washington was established in 1943 as part of the Manhattan Project. The site was home to the first full-scale plutonium production reactor in the world. Plutonium manufactured at the site was used in the first nuclear bomb, tested at the Trinity site in New Mexico's White Sands Missile Range and in Fat Man, the atomic bomb that was detonated over Nagasaki, Japan on August 6, 1945. The plutonium produced at The Hanford Site accounted for most of the more than 60,000 weapons built for the U.S. nuclear arsenal.

In the latter part of December 1944 six months before the atomic bomb was detonated over Nagasaki, Japan radar operators at the Naval Air Station, Pasco, Washington, reported UFOs over The Hanford Site and these reports of UFOs continued for three days.

The Navy selected group of pilots to form a new air group to prepare for carrier operations at the Naval Air Station, Pasco, Washington. The base has another mission for the experienced pilots, as well about 60 miles away stands the Hanford plant, its atomic activities un known to them.

These battle-scarred veterans were to protect that plant in the event of an air attack. Although they don't know what this is all about, they will follow orders.

The standby aircraft are always armed and ready to defend the plant, although few pilots seriously believe it will ever come under enemy attack, given the current state of Japan's diminishing effectiveness. On July 1945 about noon time and no planes were in the air. The bullhorn's jarring sound of General Quarters sends the pilots of six F6F "Hellcats fighters rushing to the ready room for a quick briefing and on to the aircraft for immediate takeoff. Radar had detected a fast-moving object that is now in a holding pattern directly above the Hanford plant. It was extremely high and pilots could not see the object as they flew close to the Hanford plant. As they rapidly increase altitude the pilots all spot it at about the same time and head directly for its position.

None of them can recognize it, but they can see it well from their vantage point. It has a saucer-like appearance, is bright, extremely fast, and very high. The F6F has an operating ceiling of 37,000 feet, Pilots pushed their F6Fs to 42,000 feet, which was well above the aircraft's rated ceiling of 37,000, but they were unsuccessful contact with this large unknown craft above them.

The pilots of the "Hellcats" described the UFO as the size of three aircraft carriers side by side, oval shaped, very streamlined like a stretched-out egg and pinkish in color. There was some kind of vapor being emitted around the outside edges from portholes or vents. The object was observed at noon in a clear sky at an estimated altitude of 65,000 feet.

The UFO remained a fixed position above the Hanford Nuclear Reactor for an about twenty minutes,. It doesn't make any overt moves, gave no signals, just hovers there as if observing, staying well enough out of reach. The pilots could not believe its ability to hover like this. When some of the engines begin to fail and fuel consumption went critical, the planes return to base one by one. The UFO disappeared going straight-up

Although a number of people witness this incident, the local newspaper carries no report of it in the days that follow. It can only be surmised that the government stepped in and clamped a lid on the whole affair, according to war security measures.

This was not the end of UFOs reported over the Hanford Site. The UFO Reports continued. On June 24, 1947, pilot Kenneth Arnold sighted nine objects in the sky near Mount Rainier, Washington in route to Mt. Adams for Covert Reconnaissance at the Hanford Site triggering the start to the general public of the modern UFO era even though the Military had long been aware of UFO activity.. This UFO activity at the Hanford Site continues to present day with a prime versing area at the James Gilliland's ranch at Mt Adams. In 2020 it was estimated that a UFO was reported every 45 hours on average in Washington according to the National UFO Reporting Center.

UFOs over Chernobyl Nuclear Plant

The Chernobyl nuclear disaster of April 26, 1986 was quite a disaster but could have been much worse. If the fourth reactor exploded, it could have wiped out the population of much of Europe, and caused much sickness and birth deformities.

One month before the Chernobyl disaster the air traffic controller of the Kharkov airport reported a rising number of UFO observations in the area of the Chernobyl Nuclear Power Station from pilot reports.

When the troublesome events started hundreds of people saw a UFO hovering above the fourth generating unit of the Chernobyl plant. Eyewitnesses say that an UFO was there for six hours.

Three hours after the explosion, a team of nuclear specialists saw in the sky over the station a fiery ball of the color of brass. Mikhail Varitsky, a senior dosimetrician with the Dosimetry Control Department said "I and other people from my team went to the site of the blast at night. We saw a ball of fire, and it was slowly flying in the sky. I think the ball was six or eight meters in diameter. Just before the observation these specialists measured the level of radiation in the place where they were standing. It was measured at 3000 milliroentgens per hour. 'Suddenly two bright rays of crimson color extended from the ball to the reactor... This lasted for some 3 minutes... The rays abruptly faded and the ball slowly floated away in a north-westerly direction, towards Byelorussia. Then we again looked at our radiation monitor. It displayed only 800 milliroentgens per hour.'" The UFO brought the radiation level down. The level was decreased almost four times. This probably prevented a nuclear blast.

Three years later on September 16, 1989, the fourth power-generating unit emitted radiation into the atmosphere. Several hours later, Doctor Gospina saw a UFO in the sky above the Chernobyl plant. Doctor Gospina described it as "amber-like." She said she could see the top and the bottom of it as well.

In October of 1990, a reporter from the newspaper the Echo of Chernobyl, V. Navran, was photographing the machine shop of the Chernobyl plant. "I photographed the top of a hole above the machine shop. I remember everything very well; I did not see any UFO. However, when I developed the film, I clearly saw an UFO that was hovering above the hole in the roof." The object looked like the one doctor Gospina saw.

UFOs over Fukushima Power Plant

While Fukushima may be synonymous with death and tragedy, most people are not aware that it is also the "UFO Capital of Japan," and also has what is claimed to be Japan's only research institute for unidentified flying objects.

UFOs were reported above the Fukushima nuclear plant a few hours before the March 11, 2011 catastrophe happened.

An Asian news outlet provided a video clip to the German media group NDR which published it on YouTube after the March 2011 earthquake and tsunami to show the extensive destruction in the Fukushima nuclear plant. At the 21-second mark, a giant UFO can be seen hovering above the nuclear plant.

On Thursday, August 20, 2019, five very bright orbs of light were captured on video as they hovered or moved slowly and silently over the nuclear facility that was damaged on, by a monster tsunami triggered by an offshore 7.4-magnitude earthquake. The UFOs in the skies above Japan's Fukushima Prefecture were bright enough to be seen in overcast and twilight conditions and impossible to mistake for stars or conventional aircraft.

On June 24, 2021 Japan opened up a research lab dedicated to unexplained phenomena near the site of the Fukushima nuclear disaster. The new lab is located on the grounds of UFO Interactive Hall in Iino, Fukushima Prefecture, just miles from the Fukushima Daiichi Nuclear Power Plant (Fukushima-1) in Okuma, Fukushima. The UFO Interactive Hall was built in 1992 as a central facility. The museum has numerous exhibits on UFOs. For example, exhibits include their history, notable UFO incidents, photo panels, and a 3-D virtual theater. In addition, they have approximately 5,000 items related to UFOs on display. Many of the items come donated from the collection of Kinichi Arai. Mr. Arai was a pioneer in Japanese UFO research. His reputation remains one of the most prominent UFO researchers Japan has ever seen.

According to Japanese news outlet The Mainichi, the International UFO Laboratory will look into a number of sightings that have occurred near the district, which calls itself the 'hometown of UFOs. Iino became host to a number of UFO sightings – including one "light-emitting cone-shaped object" spotted near the area's Mount Senganmori.

Chapter 6

Military Encounters with UFOs

Malmstrom Air Force Base Incident of 1967

The Minuteman strategic weapons system was conceived in the late 1950s, and deployed in the early 1960s, as a result of International tensions between the U.S. and U.S.S.R., known as the 'Cold War'. Minuteman is a land-based ballistic missile with intercontinental range (ICBM). The missiles are dispersed in hardened silos in order to protect against attack, and connected to an underground Launch Control Center (LCC) through a system of hardened cables. The launch center consists of a crew of two officers who monitor around-the-clock alerts. They have instantaneous, direct contact with the National Command Authorities, consisting only of the President and the Secretary of Defense, or their duly-deputized alternates. The current Minuteman Force consists of 450 Minuteman III's, located at four known sites: Warren AFB, Wyoming; Malmstrom AFB, Montana; Minot AFB, North Dakota; and Grand Forks AFB, North Dakota.

A typical Minuteman LCC facility is located on a 6-acre tract of land surrounded by two fences. The outer fence is a standard three-strand wire farm fence built to mark the property line and to keep animals from wandering onto the site. The inner fence is a chain link security fence topped with razor wire that surrounds the LCC. The facility provides living accommodations for the launch crew, a security checkpoint for the Air Police detachment, and housing for the environmental support systems for the underground command center. The support building is a one-story wooden frame structure measuring 33 feet wide and 128 feet long adjacent to it is a large garage.

Forty feet beneath the support building is the LCC that commands ten missiles. To enter, one has to first pass through the Security Control Center, then climb down a 40-foot ladder encased within a lo-foot vertical reinforced concrete passageway. The passageway leads to a reinforced concrete tunnel which leads to an 8-ton steel blast door, the entry into the LCC. The door can only be opened from the inside.

The underground LCC is in the shape of a cylinder with its axis parallel to the earth, approximately 59 feet long and 29 feet in diameter. It consists of a 4-foot thick outer wall built of reinforced concrete and lined with l/4-inch steel plate. Suspended inside it is a box-like enclosure, approximately 12 feet high by 28 feet long that houses the two-person Air Force crew and specialized equipment to monitor and launch the missiles. From this underground command center, two officers keep constant watch over ten missiles, each located in a remote launch silo.

The Launch Facility serves as a temperature- and humidity-controlled, long-term storage area, service platform, and launch site for the Minuteman ICBM, housed in an unmanned, heavily hardened silo. It contains a launch tube, a prefabricated cylinder made of l/4-inch steel plate, 12 feet in diameter and approximately 62 feet long. The lower 52 feet of the tube are surrounded by 14 inches of heavily reinforced concrete. The missile rests within the tube, suspended by a three-point pulley system affixed to a series of shock absorbers mounted on the silo floor. Encircling the upper third of the launch tube is the cylindrical, two-level equipment room built of heavily reinforced concrete with a steel liner. The equipment room houses generators, surge arresters to protect the electronic equipment against electromagnetic pulses (EMP), an artifact from nuclear weapon detonation. Gas generators open the silo's 80-ton reinforced concrete door, while guidance equipment and communications equipment connect the Launch Facility to the LCC. Adjacent to the launch tube is its support building. The support building is an underground structure measuring 16 feet wide, 25 feet long, and 11 feet deep, and provides heating and cooling equipment for the launch facility, as well as generators to serve as the auxiliary power supply.

Security is the utmost concern in and around the Launch Control facilities. Each has its own Security Police, who closely monitor and control access to its missile silos and launch control center. They check visitors' credentials, monitor radio transmissions and observe microwave detection and seismic sensor systems, and act as armed response teams who are dispatched by LCC personnel to actively investigate any breach of security. Armored security vehicles, usually Dodge pickup trucks with an armored body and a turret mounted M60 machine gun, are known as 'Peacekeepers'. The Peacekeepers are a common sight on roads surrounding each of the Minuteman complexes.

Malmstrom Air Force Base is located in western Montana on the outskirts of Great Falls. It initially had 150 Minuteman I missiles placed in the 1960s, but then upgraded to the Minuteman III missiles in 1975. The base is home to the 341st Missile Wing. Two of its Minuteman Launch Control Centers were: Oscar Flight Launch Control Center, located between the towns of Winfred and Hilger, about fifteen miles north of Lewistown; and Echo Flight Launch Control Center, located about a mile south of the town of Roy.

March 16, 1967 was a typical clear, frigid Montana night, with a few inches of snow and ice on the ground. At Oscar Flight Launch Control Center, Security Police noticed strange lights making zig-zag maneuvers over their facility that were clearly not behaving like known aircraft. The lights moved at incredible speeds, then made right-angle turns. These actions continued for some time. Security Police reported this to Robert Salas, who was on duty as a Deputy Missile Combat Crew Commander in the underground capsule. At first Salas thought that this was a joke, but knowing that Security Police were experienced professionals, decided he should take the report seriously.

Commander Salas later received a call from the Air Force Security Police Officer in charge of security, who was stationed at the entrance checkpoint. In a clearly frightened voice, he shouted, "Sir, there's a glowing red saucer shaped object immediately outside the front gate, hovering silently It's just sitting there! We're all just looking at it. What do you want us to do?"

Salas replied, "Make sure the site is secure and I'll phone the Command Post."

The Air Force Security Police Officer sent a security patrol to check the Launch facility and silos. They reported sighting another UFO, but immediately after, lost their radio contact with the security checkpoint. Salas reported the incident to the Command Post, and then phoned the security guard at the entrance checkpoint. He was told by the guard that a security officer approached the UFO and was injured. The guard stated the injuries were not serious, but he was being evacuated by helicopter to the base hospital.

Salas went to his commander, Lt. Fred Meiwald-, who was on a scheduled sleep period, in order to brief him about the incident. In the middle of this conversation, they heard the first alarm klaxon sound throughout the confined spaces. At once, they looked at the panel of annunciator lights glowing on the Commander's station. A 'No-Go' light and two red security lights were lit, indicating problems at one of the missile silos. Meiwald jumped up to determine the cause of the problem. Before he could do so, another alarm went off at another silo, then another, and another simultaneously. Within the next few seconds, they had lost six to eight missiles to a 'No-Go' (inoperable) condition. When their shift ended, Salas and Meiwald were relieved by their scheduled replacement crew, but the Oscar LCC missiles still had not been brought on line by the maintenance teams.

Meanwhile, at Echo Flight LCC, approximately 20 miles northwest of Oscar Flight LCC, missile maintenance crews were completing a day of routine maintenance, and along with the Security teams, were camped at one of the silos, ready for a good night's rest. There were no city lights to detract from the spectacular array of celestial objects in the night sky. They had become accustomed to looking in wonderment at the myriad of stars in the Ecliptic. Their attention turned to concern, as the same zig-zag lights that had been reported at Oscar Flight LCC, were on their way here, becoming brighter and closer until they appeared directly overhead.

The next morning around 8:30 a.m., Captain Don Crawford, the Deputy Crew Commander, was in the process of relieving Captain Eric Carlson and Crew Commander, First Lieutenant Walt Figel in their below ground Launch Control Center capsule. Figel was briefing Carlson on the night's status when the alarm klaxon sounded. One of the Minuteman missiles that they managed had become inoperable. It was at one of the two silos where maintenance crews had camped out. Upset, thinking that the maintenance personnel had not notified him about work being done on a missile, caused the missiles to display a 'No-Go' status.

Figel immediately called the on-site security guard at the missile silo. The security guard reported that maintenance personnel had not yet performed any maintenance that morning. He also reported that a UFO had been hovering over the site.

Suddenly the other missiles started to go off line in rapid succession. Within seconds, the entire flight of ten ICBMs was down! All of their missiles reported a "No-Go" condition and became inoperable. When the checklist procedure had been completed for each missile site, it was discovered that each of the missiles had gone off alert status because their guidance and control systems had malfunctioned for unexplainable reasons. Power had not been lost to the sites.

Two Security Alert Teams were dispatched to the areas where the maintenance crews were present. Figel had not informed the strike teams of the reported UFO. On arrival at the silos, the Security Alert Teams reported back to Figel that UFOs had been seen hovering over the sites in the presence of the maintenance and security personnel. Both Carlson and Figel were visibly shaken by what had occurred. At least one security policeman was so affected by this encounter that he never again returned to missile security duty. Maintenance crews worked on the missiles the entire day and late into the night during Crawford's shift and finally brought them back into 'Alert' status.

An post incident, full scale investigation was made on-site of both incidences. Declassified Strategic Missile Wing documents and interviews with ex-Boeing engineers who conducted tests following the Silo Incident confirm that no cause for the missile shutdowns was ever found. Robert Kaminski was the Boeing Company engineering team leader for this investigation. Kaminski stated that after all tests were done, "There were no significant failures, engineering data or findings that would explain how ten missiles were knocked off alert," and "there was no technical explanation that could explain the event."

The preceding incidences are well-documented, with information obtained from official Air Force, Federal Bureau-Investigation, and Central Intelligence Agency files that had been declassified via the Freedom of Information Act (FOIA), and from the book, 'Faded Giant' by Robert Salas.

Chilean Air Force 1978 Incident with Huge UFO

On December 16, 1978 on the coast of northern Chile Captain Hernan Gabrielli Rojas and Captain Danilo Catalán both flight instructors were flying with two dual F-5 training fighters returning to base from Mejillones to Antofagasta, at an altitude of 35,000 feet after completing their mission, It was noon. Accompanying them were Fernando Gomez, an avionics tech, and another trainee. Suddenly they detected a radar fault and saw a line that ran side to side on the scope. The F-5 is radar-equipped, and a line appeared from side to side – in other words, a trace throughout the bottom side of the screen. A trace for a surface ship, a cruiser, is approximately one centimeter long, but this line went from one side of the screen to another indicating a size of the object as greater than two miles in length. Captain Rojas assumed the radar scope had failed, and told Danilo Catalán, but his radar also "failed". Captain Rojas advised the ground radar at Antofagasta which also had picked up the line. The pilots flying from north to south in the vicinity of Mejillones looked toward the east and saw a deformed cigar-shaped object. Deformed, like a plantain banana. It was swathed in smoke and equal to ten or more aircraft carriers in size. The pilots were frightened, having no missiles or weapons. As the pilots approached parallel to the massive object hovering at 35,000 feet the UFO sped off at an unimaginable speed westward over the Pacific Ocean. All at once, it vanished from the three radar screens

The very next morning the Chilean Air Force scrambled some F5 fighter jets to intercept another very large UFO. The pilots described this one as very bright, and very large. The Chilean Air Force and Captain Hernan Gabrielli Rojas now a Retired General have officially acknowledged these events, but could not explain what had occurred.

Rendlesham Forest UFO Incident of 1980

Most people have heard about Rendlesham Forest, Suffolk, England Incident of December 26-28, 1980, but few know of the binary code received by Sgt. James Penniston. After the incident, U.S. and British government agents provided Penniston a generic cover story, limiting him about discussing details of the incident. As an example, he was told to say that he observed a metallic craft, but that he did not get closer than 50 yards. Penniston was instructed by the agents that an official investigation was underway, and that he is to tell the cover story that was provided to him to all who ask. In 1993 he retired from the USAF and was told that all reference to the Rendlesham Forest Incident were newly unclassified material, and he was free to talk about the events of 1980.

What makes the Rendlesham Forest incident even more important than other UFO events was its close proximity to the RAF Bentwaters, and RAF Woodbridge in Suffolk, England. The bases were separated by a small forest, and used at the time by the United States Air Force (USAF) who stored most of the nuclear weapons in Europe. The atomic weapons held at RAF Bentwaters were stored in what is known as the "Hot Row", concrete bunkers within the secure Weapons Storage Area in the southwest corner of the base. It is believed that the nuclear arsenal at Bentwaters included tactical payloads, presumably including warheads with a neutron bomb physics package. The weapons were ready for deployment at short-notice by pilots of the 81st Wing from hardened hangars.

John Burroughs, an Air Force police officer, and his boss Staff Sgt. Bud Steffens arrived at the East Gate of the Bentwaters Base and noticed blue, red, orange and white lights glowing in Rendlesham Forest. They thought an aircraft had crashed in the forest and reported the incident to 26 year old Staff Sergeant James Penniston, the base security supervisor. Penniston decided to lead a three man USAF Security Police team consisting of himself, John Burroughs and Airman Ed Cabansag to go off base into the Rendlesham Forest to investigate the incident.

They came upon a landed craft of unknown origin. The craft was sitting silently at the bottom of a berm, on the pine forest floor. Airman Cabansag, The driver stayed by the pickup truck while Burroughs and Penniston cautiously approached the triangular, shiny black craft. Penniston said that it was like nothing he had ever witnessed. He was well versed in all types of aircraft, an authorized aircraft observer and crash investigator. As part of his USAF advanced training, he studied both the NATO and WARSAW PACT inventories of aircraft.

Penniston said, "It had a bank of blue lights on it and it was just sitting there, it was completely stationary. I estimated it to be about three meters tall and about three meters wide at the base. There was an area of about 5 meters surrounding the outside of the craft," which he called 'the bubble.' "Within the bubble, static electric pulsed upon my clothes, skin, and hair, and [gave the] appearance of slowing time. The air seemed dead, not transmitting any sound.

"No landing gear was apparent, but it seemed like it was on fixed legs. I noticed the fabric of the shell was like a smooth, opaque, black glass. The bluish lights went from black to grey to blue. The nearer we got to that thing, the more uneasy I felt ... it was as if I was moving in slow motion." Jim Penniston had his USAF issued notebook and camera with him, so he began to take notes about the object which was sitting directly in front of him.

SSgt. Pennington's notes:

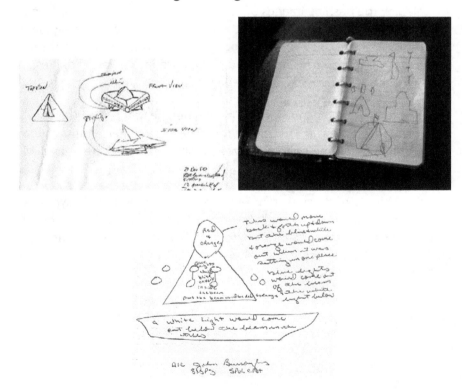

"The top portion is producing mainly white light, which encompasses most of the upper section of the craft. A small amount of white light peers out the bottom. At the left side center is a bluish light, and on the other side, red. The lights seem to be molded as part of the exterior of the structure, smooth, slowly fading into the rest of the outside of the structure, gradually molding into the fabric of the craft'."

Jim Penniston proceeded to touch the landed object, but he quickly realized that it would be brief. "I touched the symbols, and I could feel the shapes, as if they were inscribed or etched or engraved, like a diamond cut on glass." Soon after he touched the symbols, the white light on the object grew brighter. Penniston and Burroughs jumped backwards, then threw themselves to the ground. "The craft moved up off the ground, about three feet, still with absolutely no sound, then maneuvered between the trees, ascended to tree top level and disappeared in the blink of an eye.

Two nights later on December 28, a UFO hovered directly above the nuclear weapons storage bunkers at the NATO base, and fired beams of light at the bunker that burned holes through the hardened storage silos.

Troubled by the flashing images of ones and zeros that he received from touching the glyphs, Penniston felt compelled to write the image in a notebook. As he scribed the numeric symbols into the notebook, each image was erased from his mind. He put the notebook away, and doesn't think too much about again until the year 2010.

During a casual conversation with a researcher, he mentioned the codes that he had written in the notebook. The researchers immediately recognized that the ones and zeros were binary code, and together, seek to decipher the text.

The 8-bit binary number system represents values using two symbols, typically 0 and 1. Computers call these bits. A bit is either off (0) or on (1). When arranged in sets of 8 bits (1 byte) 256 values can be represented (0-255).Using an ASCII chart, these values can be mapped to characters, and alpha text can be deduced.

Pages 1-16 Composite message using my preferred interpretation with appropriate spaces and decimal points:

```
EXPLORATION OF HUMANITY 666 8100
52.0942532N 13.131269W                    (By Brasil)
CONTINUOUS FOR PLANETARY ADVAN???
FOURTH COODINATE CONTINUOT UQS CbPR BEFORE
16.763177N   89.117768W                   (Caracol, Belize)
34.800272N   111.843567W                  (Sedona, Arizona)
29.977836N   31.131649E                   (Great Pyramid in Giza, Egypt)
14.701505S   75.167043W                   (Nazca Lines in Peru)
36.256845N   117.100632E                  (Tai Shan Qu, China)
37.110195N   25.372281E                   (Portara at Temple of Apollo in Naxos, Greece)
EYES OF YOUR EYES
ORIGIN 52.0942532N 13.131269W             (By Brasil)
ORIGIN YEAR 8100
```

Legend:
Blue characters represent those decoded directly from the original binary code.
Red characters represent questionable ones in areas with transmission errors.
Red ? (question marks) represent unintelligible characters due to transmission errors.
Green characters represent those I have interpreted in areas of transmission errors.
Orange . (periods) represent decimal points I have inserted into coordinate values.
Black characters represent my comments.

James Penniston and John Burroughs both suffered injuries from "Unidentified Aerial Phenomena Radiation\" or UAP, caused by their close proximity with the bubble (energy field) on the outside of the craft. Burroughs experienced vision, and throat, but the most serious was damage to his heart which was diagnosed as a shredded anterior mitral valve component, causing atrial fibrillation and potential congestive heart failure.

In 2006 the British Government declassified an intelligence study on UFOs, codenamed PROJECT CONDIGN, which had been classified as 'Secret UK Eyes Only'. The report concluded that UFOs are real, and can impart UAP radiation effects on humans. The spacecraft may emit a certain electromagnetic field that is known to cause injury. When subject to UAP radiation for prolonged periods of time, neurological, rather than biological effects may be manifested. Unlike other parts of the brain, the temporal cortex can be tendered electrically unstable. It is clear that the recipients of these effects are not aware that their behavior/ perception is being modified from that which they are truly observing. Little is understood about UAP radiation, but since 1986 much research is being done by the military in order to produce microwave weaponry. The reported effects of UAP radiation on humans is that it is fast-acting, and cognitively remembered, albeit with a lack of time continuum. In short, the witness often reports an apparent 'gap' or 'lost time' – often not accounting for up to several hours.

In January 2015, the Veterans Administration finally admitted that it was an unidentified aerial phenomenon that caused the injury to John Burroughs. By de facto confirmation of the Condign document, the U.S. military had confirmed the existence of UFOs and UAP radiation and Burroughs was granted full medical benefits.

There is a similarity of this incident to the Japanese folklore Utsuro Bune. On March 24, 1803, at the beach of 'Harato-no-hama' (原舎浜) in the Hitachi province, a strange 'boat' was washed ashore. It reminded the witnesses of a rice cooking pot; around its middle it had a thickened rim. It was also coated with black paint and it had four little windows on four sides. The lower part of the boat was protected by brazen plates which looked to be made of iron of the highest western quality. The height of the boat was about 11 feet and its breadth was about 18 feet. A woman of 20 years came out of the boat. Her body height was about 5 feet tall and her skin was as white as snow. Her long hair dangled smoothly down along her back. Her face was of indescribable beauty. The dress of the woman was of unknown style and material. She spoke a language that no one recognized, and held a small box that no one was allowed to touch.

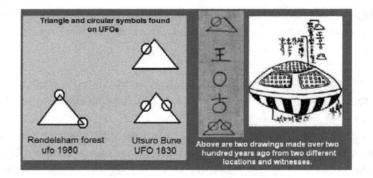

Utsuro Bune and Rendelsham UFO Symbols

The Russian UFO Experiment

Retired Russian Federal Security Service major general Vasily Yeremenko had been in charge of the KGB division that oversaw the air force and aircraft manufacturing. It was his division that was entrusted with the task of collecting all reports of UFO sightings.

In the early 1980s, he realized that UFOs were frequently sighted in areas of "heightened tension" – for instance, during weapons tests, or when there was a lot of military and hardware gathered in one locale.

He devised an experiment to see if UFOs could be summoned by staging military activity at a military range in Astrakhan Region, northwest of the Caspian Sea. He proposed a sharp increase in the number of flights performed by combat aircraft, and a lot of movement of hardware, including nuclear weapons. "The UFOs will appear with a probability of nearly 100 percent!" Yeremenko said. He was correct. Luminous spheres were everywhere over the site, and over time, all the participants in the experiment became so used to these phenomena that they took them for granted. Some even tried to make contact with the objects. "It looked like this: a person on the ground would wave their arms, twice to the right and twice to the left. The ball in the sky would react to it by swinging twice to the right and then twice to the left. We had no idea how to explain that," said Yeremenko. It was obviously a crude form of interaction, but where to go from there?

In the end, the military, together with the scientists who took part in the experiment, came to three main conclusions: First, these may be natural phenomena that modern science is not yet able to explain; second, these may be U.S. or Japanese reconnaissance equipment; and finally, these may be extraterrestrial objects.

Usovo missile Base Incident of 1982

The preceding cases are well-documented, with information obtained from official Russian KGB files. The legal deposition of Russian Major M. Davidovich Kataman, and the January 26, 2010 Open Minds magazine article, "Soviet Nukes and UFOs" by Antonio Huneeus are the main reference sources. The actual names of people involved in the UFO/USO events, and the location of sensitive military areas are used. These are just a few of the many incidents involving UFOs at sensitive nuclear installations in the United States, Russia, and Europe.

Like the United States, the Soviet Union developed an elaborate command and control system which enabled the country's leadership to respond quickly to crisis situations. The nuclear command and control system would usually be activated by the General Staff command post. The Kazbek communications system connects the main military leaders, and was instituted for the purpose of issuing nuclear launch orders. The Kazbek system's terminals are managed by the country's Commander-in-Chief, Minister of Defense, and the military Chief of Staff.

The possibility of launching nuclear strikes without authorization by the Commander-in-Chief can be accomplished, provided that a number of conditions are satisfied. These include a confirmed loss of contact with the Commander-in-Chief; and verified reports of nuclear explosions on Russian territory by outside forces; and the Commander-in-Chief's pre-delegated launch authority. If all three conditions are satisfied, the authorization to use nuclear weapons may be issued at the General Staff's central command posts.

On October 4, 1982 Captain Valery Polykhaev, Lt. Colonel Balanev, Captains Duman Tukmachev, Lt. Colonel Povar, Lt. Colonel Kuzmin and Lt. Colonel Zinkovsky returned to Usovo from the long-range nuclear missile base near Byelokovoriche. At 15:30 they noticed unidentified lights performing acrobatics in the sky.

Captain Valery Polykhaev in his deposition to the Ministry of Defense stated, "After the bus stopped at the cross roads to Usovo, I saw in the clear space above the road, at 5-6 km of altitude, two brightly shining objects resembling very much a New Year's tree garland in its shape. They were shining with bright-golden light and those lights were twinkling.

"There were 6-8 brightly shining spots making a circle in every object. The distance between objects was about 2-3 km. Then a shining small ball separated from the left object and moved to the right one." The lights continued their acrobatics for another 5 to 7 minutes before flying out of sight.

At about the same time, Major Lipezki was driving along the Perebrody-Usovo road with Capt. Ryabinin. In his legal deposition, he states that, "I paid attention to the luminescence of some object straight in front of me somewhere above Usovo. The luminescence came from a group of shining spots forming 5 groups. The lights were disposed on the area approximately equal to the area of the setting sun. It was situated at an altitude of about 30 meters above the edge of a distant forest. The color of the lights was from pale-yellow to red."

Senior Lieutenant Kobulyansky, the Battery vice-commander, driving along the road to Byelokovoriche between 19:30 and 21:00 also saw unidentified lights blink rapidly on and off. At one point, they reported an apparent electromagnetic effect on the car radio, saying, "We were coming under high-voltage lines, but there were no high-voltage lines there."

About 20:00 that evening, Capt. Polykhaev was driving his own car near the railway crossing between Topyilnja station and Zhovtnevo Street with his wife, two children and some friends. Again, he noticed the unusual light show in the skies over Usovo at an altitude of 5-7 km. "A bright light flashed and went out, then it flashed again and after that, 6-8 bright-golden lights flashed around it in the shape of an ellipsis," the deposition read. "A small brightly shining ball separated from them and flew to the earth and on approaching it, went out. In 10 minutes the phenomenon repeated... the shining object began to move quickly in our side, with high speed and rising in size. Then the object suddenly stopped. Our distance to it was about 1-2 km. The children were scared that the object would fall down on us. After it stopped, the light went out slowly as if melting away. Soon, another garland 'flourished' at a large distance and went out again." Captain Kovalenko, who was in the car with Capt. Polykhaev, corroborated the account.

The depositions do not indicate any sign of hostility from the UFOs. On the contrary, what happened at the underground bunker of Military Unit (MU) 52035, which contained nuclear missile launch control panels, is another matter entirely.

At 21:37 Major M. Davidovich Kataman, in charge of the computerized control panels for the long-range nuclear missiles at the Usovo base, was on duty in an underground bunker. Major Kataman was not aware of any UFOs flying above the facility. Suddenly, signal lights on both control panels activated, showing that nuclear missiles were preparing for launch. This normally happens when an order has been transmitted from Moscow. Alarmed, Kataman shouted, "Nyet! Nyet! Nyet!" feeling powerless in the situation. As he stated in his deposition, "I observed spontaneous illumination of all displays ... Someone or something was manipulating the series of precise control codes and control code combinations which regulate the computerized missile control launch panel." For 15 seconds, the base lost control of its nuclear weapons and came just moments away from launching their missiles at the United States, and elsewhere.

In his deposition, he added that, "Testing of apparatus and measurement of parameters according to technical map 1-30 showed no defects. The apparatus was functioning normally."

A nearly identical occurrence happened in the United States at Minot AFB, North Dakota in 1966. According to a former Minuteman missile launch officer, David H. Schuur of the 455th/91st Strategic Missile Wing, most of his 10 missiles were temporarily activated, and were preparing to launch just as the on-site Security police reported a UFO that was hovering rapidly from missile silo to missile silo. With vast numbers of nuclear ICBMs, such incidents pose a potential threat to the future of the human race, over and above that which is already stored in the silos.

The USS Nimitz 2004 'Tic Tac' Incident

The U.S. Government has known about the unconventional nature of the UFO phenomenon for decades and has chosen to hide and suppress that information from Congress and especially from the American people. The disinformation and media suppression regarding the reality of UFOs includes changes to accepted terminology. For instance, the U.S. Navy now refers to UFOs as 'Unidentified Aerial Phenomena' (UAP or 'Anomalous Aerial Vehicle' (AAV). The new definition states that these crafts definitely exist, but from a Black Project of an unknown origin, either here on Earth, or possibly from an Alien origin.

In November of 2004, The Nimitz Carrier Strike Group and its escorts were on a combat training exercise being conducted in the Pacific Ocean, about 100 miles off the coast of San Diego California, where they frequently observed a group of UAPs. The Ticonderoga-class guided missile cruiser USS Princeton had been tracking mysterious airborne craft intermittently for two weeks using advanced AN/SPY-1B passive scanning phased array radar. The UAPs were travelling southward from the Catalina Islands to Guadalupe Island in Baja California, Mexico. Near Campamento Militar Isla Guadalupe (a Mexican Military Base, the UAPs dropped off the radar screen and disappeared.

At 09:30 local time, on November 14, 2004 eight to ten objects traveled southwards in a loose, though fixed formation at 28,000 feet at 120 mph in the immediate vicinity of Catalina and the San Clemente Islands. Their presence was also picked up from radar operators on many other vessels.

The objects were faintly detected by an E-2C Hawkeye plane sent by the Princeton. An operations officer aboard Princeton contacted two airborne U.S. Navy Boeing F/A-18E/F Super Hornets from USS Nimitz, flying a combat exercise at the time. The aircraft were two-seat variants, and each pilot was accompanied by a Weapon Systems Officer (WSO). The lead Super Hornet was piloted by Commander David Fravor from Strike Fighter Squadron 41. The wingman was Lieutenant Commander Jim Slaight.

Princeton's radio operator instructed the pilots to change their course in order to investigate an unidentified radar return. When the jet fighters arrived on station, the crews saw nothing in the air, or on their radar. Princeton's radar however, showed that the object had now dropped from 28,000 feet to near sea level in less than one second. As the pilots looked down at the sea, they noticed a turbulent oval area of churning water with foam and frothy waves. The oval shaped object was described as the size of a Boeing 737 airplane, with a smoother area of lighter color at the center, as if the waves were breaking over something just under the surface. A few seconds later, they noticed an unusual object hovering with erratic movements about 50 feet above the churning water. Both Fravor and Slaight later described the object as a large bright white 'Tic Tac', 30 to 46 feet long, with no portholes, no wing nor empennage, and no visible engine or exhaust plume.

Fravor began a circular descent to approach the object. As Fravor descended, he reported that the object began ascending along a curved path, maintaining some distance from the F-18, mirroring its trajectory in opposite circles. Fravor then made a more aggressive maneuver, plunging his fighter to aim below the object, but at this point the UFO accelerated and went out of sight in less than two seconds.

The two fighter jets proceeded on a new course to the Combat Air Patrol (CAP) rendezvous point. Within seconds, Princeton radioed the jets that the radar target had reappeared 60 miles away. To get that far away in a matter of seconds, the UFOs would have required an air speed of at least 42,000 miles per hour. Two other jets went to investigate the new radar location, but by the time the Super Hornets arrived, the object had already disappeared. Both F-18s returned to Nimitz, where Commander Fravor reflected on his sighting: "I have no idea what I saw. It had no plumes, wings or rotors and outran our F-18s".

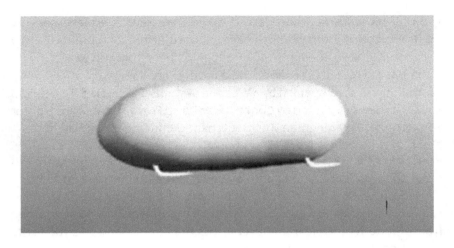

Artist's rendering of the 'Tic Tac' object

A second Nimitz team took off, this time equipped with an advanced Forward Looking Infra-Red (FLIR) camera. Lieutenant Commander Chad Underwood, the Navy pilot, recorded evasive maneuvers by the UAP, captured on video. When Commander Underwood was able to lock on the UFO with his on board radar his weapon system became inoperable. Strobe lines which are vertical lines on his onboard radar indicated his flight systems were being jammed.

The footage was publicly released by the Pentagon on 16 December 2017. The imagery is known as the 'Tic Tac" video or the 2004 USS Nimitz FLIR1 Video', which is a condensed version of the original footage which was much clearer and showed more detail, e.g. a 'black aura' surrounding the object.

A short while later, jet interceptors were launched from the Nimitz after Princeton radar noticed a large number of the unknown objects in their area of operations. Upon approach of the jets, the UAPs reacted by dropping from 28,000 feet to a mere 50 feet above the sea. Based on the SPY1 Bravo Radar returns, the objects descended at an astounding 24,000 miles per hour. Some of the UAPs dove into the sea, as confirmed by sonar technicians onboard the USS Louisville (SSN-724), a Los Angeles-class submarine that was participating in the exercises, saying that they had an active track on it under the water. They reported it was traveling about 575 miles per hour!

Navy Chief Petty Officer Kevin Day, stationed on Princeton said, "Clearly, the UAP was interested in, or following, another unknown submerged object. It is possible that this object and others like it are the reason that the UAPs were in the area." Day reported that the UAPs appeared to be avoiding the Nimitz Carrier Group and its aircraft." This area of the Pacific, off the coast of San Diego, south of Catalina Islands, has been a known testing ground for many Black Projects. Both the radar signatures and the pilots claim that over 100 UFOs/UAPs dove into the ocean waters off the coast of Guadalupe Island (28.91 °N 118.26 ° W) which they feel is one of the UFO bases.

Within a short time after the first interception by Navy pilot David Fravor a helicopter landed on the Nimitz, and a group of men in civilian suits quickly seized all hard drives and radar/sonar records, and ordered the crew to erase any picture, etc. relating to the incident.

There is little official information available, except for the 2004 USS Nimitz FLIR1 video, and a Navy Investigation Report Summary, as follows:

Executive Summary

During the period of approximately 10 thru 16 November 2004, the Nimitz Carrier Strike Group was operating off of the Western coast of the United States in preparation for deployment to the Arabian Sea. The USS Princeton, on several occasions, detected multiple anomalous aerial vehicles operating in and around the vicinity of the carrier strike group. The anomalous aerial vehicles would descend very rapidly from approximately 60,000 ft Mean Sea Level (MSL) altitude, down to approximately 50 feet in a matter of seconds. They hovered or stayed stationary, as shown on the radar, for a short time, then departed at high velocities and turn rates.

On 14 November, after again detecting the AAV, the Princeton took the opportunity of having a flight of two F/A-18Fs returning from a training mission to further investigate. The Princeton took control of the F/A-18Fs from the E-2C early warning and command aerial platform, and vectored the Navy jets to intercept. Visual contact was made approximately 1 mile away from the AAV, which was reported to be shaped like an elongated egg, or a "Tic Tac" shape, with a discernible midline horizontal axis. It was solid, white, smooth, with no edges. It was uniformly colored with no nacelles, pylons, or wings. It was approximately 46 ft in length, and although the F/A-18F's radar could not obtain a lock on the object, it could be tracked when stationary and at slower speeds using the FLIR.

The anomalous aerial vehicle took evasive actions upon intercept by the Navy jets, demonstrating an advanced acceleration, aerodynamic, and propulsion capability. The AAV did not take any offensive action against the carrier strike group, and demonstrated the potential to conduct undetected underwater reconnaissance, and left the Navy ships with limited abilities to detect, track, and/or engage.

Key Assessments

The AAV was no known aircraft or air vehicle currently in the inventory of the United States or any foreign nation.

The AAV exhibited advanced low observable characteristics at multiple radar bands, rendering US radar based engagement capabilities ineffective.

The AAV exhibited advanced aerodynamic performance, with no visible control surfaces and no visible means to generate lift.

The AAV exhibited advanced propulsion capability by demonstrating the ability to remain stationary with little to no variation in altitude, transitioning to horizontal and/or vertical velocities far greater than any known aerial vehicle, with little to no visible signature.

The AAV possibly demonstrated the ability to cloak or become invisible to the human eye or human observation.

The AAV possibly demonstrated a highly advanced capability to operate under sea, completely undetectable, by our most advanced sensors.

While the document does not characterize the "advanced aerodynamic performance", we can infer from radar and eyewitness accounts that they include instant acceleration; instant stop; vertical acceleration; near-instant reversal of direction and right angle turns - all in silence. It has been observed that multiple objects sometimes separate, then go back into each other. The accelerations exhibited by the craft during the observed maneuvers is estimated in the range of 100 to 1000 g-forces, with no observed air disturbance, no sonic booms, and no evidence of excessive heat that is commensurate with such energies. It should also be noted that at 28,000 feet, there is not nearly enough air in the atmosphere for any known powered craft to travel at a mere 120 MPH. A much higher airspeed would ordinarily be required in order to keep an 'air' craft from falling to the Earth.

With regard to his description of the "ocean turbulent oval" of churning water Navy pilot Fravor suggests that the pattern was due to the field associated with the craft above the water, since no underwater object was seen by the pilots. After the encounter, the churning stopped because the field stayed with the AAV, acting as a toroidal optical distortion.

The evidence allows one to infer that the optical distortion was due to a strong magnetic and/or gravitational field. A shock waves comes from objects (planes, some meteoroids, even a lightning bolt) which attain Mach speed (768 mph), thereby compressing the air around them. In hypersonic regimes, the rise of the temperature at the stagnation point is extreme. A Lorentz force (the force that is exerted by a magnetic field on a moving electric charge) may ensure a complete control of the Mach lines patterns, resulting in avoidance of Mach line compression, hence no shock waves. This could explain the common observation that UFOs don't produce shock waves, and appear to have some sort of ionized gas surrounding the structure.

Aguadilla Puerto Rico 2013 Incident

It was 17:20 on the evening of April 25, 2013 at the Rafael Hernandez Airport (BQN) in Aguadilla, Puerto Rico when a DHC-8 (Dash-8) Turboprop aircraft from U.S. Customs and Border Protection (CBP) took off on a routine flight. Soon after takeoff, they noticed "a pinkish to reddish light" over the ocean that was quickly approaching them from the south. The crew was concerned that the tower had neglected to inform them of the incoming traffic, so the crew let them know. The tower said that they also had a visual on the object, but they unsure of its identity and point of destination.

Once the object got close to land, its lights turned off, but at this time the DHC-8 was able to begin tracking and filming the object with their onboard thermal imaging system. The Dash-8 did not approach the object, but filmed it while circling the object. The flight crew did not pick up the object on radar, which was configured to look downward in order to track water craft on the ocean, not objects in the sky.

The object that had been captured by the thermal imager exhibited characteristics that cannot be explained by any known aircraft or natural phenomenon. It shows an object apparently moving very quickly over land and then into the ocean. It seems to be tumbling or changing shape. It moves over buildings, through trees, and eventually over the ocean. Then things get weird. The object appears to go in and out of the ocean without slowing down, and either joined by another object or breaks into two.

There were unknown objects that had been tracked on radar a few minutes prior to the DHC-8's take off, but it is not known for certain if one of them was the same object later captured on video. The unidentified radar returns indicated the UFOs were just off the shore to the north and northwest of the airport, and lasted about 16 minutes, ending at 21:14.

The length of the thermal video is just under 4 minutes, but the unknown object was tracked for a full 2 1/2 minutes. Although it was difficult to calculate the exact location of the object on the first half of its flight, authorities are confident of its position in the second half. They have determined that the object came onshore from the ocean, from the north or northwest of the airport's airstrip, and then flew over the airstrip, turning back to the north, and headed back out to sea, during this time, the Dash-8 that had been circling the airport, lost site of the object as they continued on their heading southward.

The object was described as between three to five feet in length, its speed varied between approximately 40 mph to 120 mph. Its median speed was roughly 80 mph. An interesting characteristic at the end of the flight was, when it apparently submerged into the ocean, traveled for over half a mile, and then flew back out. Its speed through the water reached a high of 95 mph and average 82.8 mph.

It was determined that the object was not a bird. Peregrine falcons do occasionally visit Puerto Rico, and have an average horizontal speed of 40 to 56 mph, and a maximum of 65 to 69 mph. The Navy had been working on a drone that would be able to fly through the air, then dive into the ocean and function as a submarine. The craft actually has a name, called a 'Flimmer.' Current Flimmer drones have not been tested underwater, but have an airspeed of 68 mph. It was also noted that the fastest known underwater battery-powered torpedo travels at 50 mph. It is doubtful that the U.S. Navy would be so irresponsible as to test it over a civilian airport runway.

In conclusion, there is no explanation for an object that is capable of traveling under water at over 90 mph with minimal impact as it enters the water, through the air at 120 mph at low altitude, through a residential area without navigational lights, and finally to be capable of splitting into two separate objects. No bird, no balloon, no aircraft, and no known drones have that capability.

On April 26th 2013 at a little after 06:00 two witnesses reported seeing an object matching the description of the Puerto Rico object diving into and out of the ocean, approximately 2 miles off the southeast tip of Florida. Through bearings taken from the observers' different positions, the location where the object dove into the water can be interpolated. Divers from the TV show, "Curse of the Bermuda Triangle" went to site, and found that the ocean was approximately 20 feet deep. A perfect 35 foot diameter circular crater was found that measured 8 feet deep. The crater was defined as a 'dead zone', with nothing living in it, including fish or ocean flora.

Samples of the sand were taken and analyzed by scientists who found the sand to have experienced extreme heat, melting the sand with no known cause. The crater was similar to 3 other craters at different locations off of Bermuda Island, where the divers investigated eyewitness reports of UFOs diving into the Atlantic waters.

The USS Roosevelt 2015 'GIMBAL' Incident

The nuclear aircraft carrier USS Theodore Roosevelt (CVN-71), cruising off the Florida coast, filmed a UFO encounter with a Navy fighter jet. Known as the 'GIMBAL' video, it was captured by a U.S. Navy F/A-18 Super Hornet using the Raytheon AN/ASQ-228 Advanced Targeting Forward-Looking Infrared (ATFLIR) imager. The ATFLIR utilizes state-of-the-art sensors and tracking lasers that are operated by a highly-trained Weapons Sensor Officer. ATFLIR captures extremely high resolution data, and uses it to locate and designate targets at distances exceeding 40 nautical miles.

GIMBAL footage records data from the pilot's heads-up display in the cockpit. Following are the major features of the device.

The video starts with what the pilots observe from inside their cockpit: The sensor is set to 'white-hot' mode, meaning white elements in the display are warmer than the dark, or cooler, areas. The UAP that was imaged appears as a white shape in the middle of the screen. The chasing aircraft is in a left-hand turn, flying Mach 0.58 at an altitude of 25,010 feet. The UAP is flying slightly below 2 degrees and 54 degrees to the left of the Super Hornet, traveling right to left. Looking closely, we see a dark or opaque field that appears to surround or encapsulate the object.

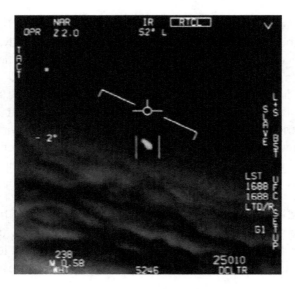

'GIMBAL' UFO as recorded by Navy pilots

The pilots aboard the Super Hornet are not only highly capable fighter pilots, but they are also trained observers, skilled at scrutinizing their observations and targets in order to ascertain 'friend or foe.' They are specifically trained to look for discreet changes in shape, size position, flight attitude (angles), and speed in order to determine the nature of the threat. They are able to discern nuanced details that few people would normally recognize. Paramount to their training is their ability to handle stress, and maintain radio discipline. In the audio track of the video, they are clearly struggling to understand and describe what they are witnessing.

Within 3 minutes of the first radio transmission, we hear one of the pilots state that it is "a drone" aircraft. At the 6-minute time stamp, upon further observation, another pilot calmly radios, "There is a whole fleet of them. Look on the ASA (radar display)." The first pilot responds with "My gosh!" It is important to note that the ATFLIR has only a single object in its display. The radar is simultaneously providing the pilots a picture of the larger air space, where they are tracking multiple targets.

At 11 minutes into the video, one of the pilots notes that, "They are all going against the wind. The wind is 120 knots (138 mph) out of the west." The speed and altitude of the object is unusual for any drone-type aircraft. On that information alone, the likelihood of an entire fleet of drones capable of operating under this scenario is highly improbable, and would require resources that few nations could afford.

In the midst of this exchange, the sensor is switched from 'white-hot' to 'black-hot'. The imaging of the object is now much clearer. It has a distinct shape: a distorted oval with small protrusions from the top and bottom. The object's opaque aura is now also very distinct: a "cool" glow that extends around the entire object. There appears to be no observable flight surfaces or exhaust plume, nor any typical components usually associated with conventional aircraft.

"Look at that thing, dude!" The pilot is clearly surprised at what he is witnessing. At 24 minutes into the video, the object makes a small, but very sharp altitude change, possibly indicating it may be operating in a vacuum environment. Its direction and speed remain unchanged despite the continuous 120-knot headwind it is encountering. At 27 minutes, the object begins a series of distinct rotations, then changes orientation by almost 100 degrees. It is now perpendicular to the horizontal plane, despite the headwinds. This maneuver is executed in a manner that is inconsistent with current principles of aerodynamics, and possibly indicative of a vacuum environment. As the video concludes, the object's orientation and performance seem to defy current principles of physics, including atmospheric resistance and normal aerodynamic forces. During the orientation change, it also slows to a near stop, but does not change altitude. One observer states "Look at that thing!" Another observer says, "It's rotating."

The fighter pilots struggled to determine the nature of object. Their key findings include: low observability in both electro-optical and electromagnetic spectrums; no distinguishable flight surfaces; lack of obvious propulsion system; never-before-seen flight capabilities; and a possible energy or resonance field of unknown nature.

With the chain-of-custody documentation that has been made available, GIMBAL can officially be designated as credible, authentic "evidence" of a UAP. Evidence shows a flying vehicle with a shape that is normally associated with science fiction. There are no known technologies that we can compare to what is being observed, in both performance and design. An unknown craft that demonstrates flight characteristics unlike anything we know, understand, or can duplicate. Because we cannot duplicate the flight characteristics of this type of object, we may conclude that the object employs technologies that are more advanced than those on Earth.

The USS Roosevelt 2015 'Go Fast' Incident

The U.S. Navy aircraft carrier USS Theodore Roosevelt (CVN-71) was conducting a training mission for a deployment to the Persian Gulf. The maneuvers took place in the Atlantic Ocean off the coasts of Virginia and Florida. From the summer of 2014 into March 2015, several pilots and other Navy personnel encountered strange objects, almost on a daily basis. The UAPs were noticed by the pilots after their outdated 1980s radar was upgraded to a more advanced system.

Lt. Graves, Lt. Accoin, and other pilots who had UAP encounters were part of the VFA-11 'Red Rippers' Squadron, based at Naval Air Station Oceana, Va. According to Lt. Graves, there are more than 50 witnesses of multiple UAP encounters. Graves and others report that the unknown objects had demonstrated outstanding flying capabilities, such as operating for 12 hours at extremely high rates of speed, and no visible engine or infrared exhaust plumes. Mid-air tilting, like a spinning top without losing altitude, as well as low visual observability are also mentioned. They appeared regularly, almost daily, high in the skies over the Eastern Seaboard.

In late 2014, a Navy fighter pilot had a near collision with one of the objects, and an official 'Mishap Report' was filed. The pilot told Lt. Graves that he and his wingman were flying in tandem about 100 feet apart when something flew between them. The pilot described the object as, "a sphere encasing a cube." The incident was captured on videos that were taken by F/A-18 ATFLIR systems, and became known as the 'Go Fast' video.

UFOs buzzing Navy warships off the coast of California in 2019

In the same general area were in 2004 Naval aviators encountered the Tic Tac UFO video the U.S.S Omaha and at least 8 other Navy ships were surrounded, sometimes swarmed, by as many 50 to 100 unknown objects over several day. The UFOs chased the destroyers for up to 100 nautical miles off the coast of California. Scores of similar UFO sightings in this area have been reported dating back to the 1960s, but most of the US military investigations into them remain classified.

USS Omaha in particular, was put under observation by these UFOs. At one time there were as many as 14 that surrounded the ship, The UFOs were picked on the forward looking infrared (FLIR) with, it's a thermal signature. It's used in a Sapphire system on that particular ship. The crew observed a large sphere that mirrored the ship's course for more than an hour the UFOs swarmed the ship at speeds of up to 160 mph. There were a few different colors of lights observed coming from the UFOs described as white, but also like a blue and a red. Video was shot onboard the revealed a small round object flying horizontal to the ocean and hovering over the USS Omaha then descended to the water and disappearing into the ocean.

The incidents began on the night of July 14 2019 just before 10pm were two UFOs were spotted. An onboard intelligence crew responsible for documenting and investigating contact with unknown vessels - known as the Ship Nautical or Otherwise Photographic Interpretation and Exploitation team - or SNOOPIE - was engaged to figure out who or what, the mystery flying objects were. Within a few minutes of the sighting, reports the USS Kidd moved into quiet mode, minimizing communications as it sought to work what the threat level was.

It contacted a nearby warship also on patrol, the USS Rafael Peralta, who also engaged their onboard photo intelligence team, or SNOOPIE. Several other US Navy destroyers on patrol nearby began noticing strange lights. The USS John Finn also reported UFO activity, and noticed a 'red flashing light' at 10.03pm, according to its logbook. Just over an hour later at 11.23pm, the USS Rafael Peralta spotted a white light hovering over the flight deck. The UFO was able to remain hovering above the destroyer's helicopter landing pad while traveling at speeds of 16 knots and in low visibility for nearly 90-minute.

The next night, the UFOs returned, this time as the warships were patrolling closer to the Californian mainland. They were first spotted by the USS Rafael Peralta and the ship's SNOOPIE team was engaged at 8.39pm. At 8.56pm, the USS Kidd had also come into contact with UFOs. The UFOs pursued the ships, even as they continued to maneuver throughout the incident,

The USS Russell reported pyramid-shaped UFOs were swarming all over it, dipping in elevation from 1,000 to 700 feet and seemingly able to move in any direction The USS Russell had nine separate incidents with the UFOs in less than an hour. Then at 9.20pm that night, the USS Kidd noticed 'multiple UFOs around the ship. The USS Rafael Peralta was also swarmed by as many as four UFOs. It was contacted by a passing cruise ship, the Carnival Imagination, to say they too had spotted up to six UFOs.

Most of the ships experienced one hovering directly above, still, stationary, with the others doing movements around the ships. The three-hour frenzy of activity continued until close to midnight, with none of the warships able to say with certainty where the UFOs had come from. The UFOs displayed abilities that exceed our own technologies, anything we know of, that is, and some of them appeared to be transmedium craft: They could fly in the air, they could enter the ocean, travel through water as easy as they travel through air.

Chapter 7

UFOs with Aliens Incidences

Aztec, New Mexico, 1948

The Aztec disc came to earth on March 25, 1948, having been detected by three separate radar units in the southwest, one of which was said to have disrupted the craft's control mechanism. The area of impact was calculated by triangulation, and this information was immediately relayed to Air Defense Command and Gen. George C. Marshall, then Secretary of State, who allegedly contacted the MJ-12 group.

A military convoy was sent using a route to the site that avoided main roads, and upon arrival, road blocks were established at strategic points within two miles of the recovery area. The owner of a ranch near the perimeter and his family were allegedly held incommunicado and told never to discuss the matter (as in the Roswell incident). Military trucks loaded with equipment were camouflaged to look like oil drilling rigs during the operation.

A team of scientists arrived at the site and began examining the disc. They entered the craft one by one, carefully entering through a fractured porthole. The portholes themselves looked metallic and only appeared translucent at a close proximity. Inside the craft they found two humanoids, about two feet in height, slumped over a charred instrument panel. Another 12 bodies lay sprawled on the floor in a chamber within the cabin, making a total of 14 bodies

The instrument panel had several pushbuttons and levers with hieroglyphic-type symbols, as well as symbols illuminated on small display screens. It was discovered that the control panel had drawers which rolled out, but no wiring could be detected. A book composed of parchment-like leaves with the texture of plastic also contained the strange hieroglyphs. This was given to General Marshall, who then passed it on to two leading cryptologists for analysis.

Three days later, segments of the UFO were loaded onto three trucks, together with the bodies, and transported under cover of a tarpaulin marked "Explosives". The convoy headed at night by the least conspicuous and often circuitous route to the restricted Naval Auxiliary Airfield Complex at Los Alamos, arriving one full week later. Here, they remained for over a year before being transported to another base.

According to a report of the incident, the bodies were described as averaging 42 inches in length. The facial features strongly resembled "Mongoloid Orientals" in appearance, with disproportionately large heads, large "slant" eyes, small noses and mouths. The average weight was about 40 pounds. The torsos were very small and thin, with very thin necks. The arms were long and slender, reaching the knees, with hands containing long and slender fingers with webbing between them. There was no digestive or gastrointestinal tract, no alimentary or intestinal canal, and no rectal point. No reproductive organs were apparent. Instead of blood, there was a colorless liquid with no red cells, and smelling similar to ozone. The saucer-shaped craft was 100 feet in diameter and 30 feet high, with one broken porthole which apparently caused suffocation to the five occupants - who had turned blue as a result. The metallic skin of the saucer was too hardened to penetrate, although as thin as newspaper.

A witness to the crash reported "That thing, or flying saucer, tried hard to clear a cliff jutting above the Animas River but it hit the very corner up there, shooting sparks and rocks in every direction," he claims. "Finally, it made a right-angle turn in midair and headed straight north in the direction of the alleged crash site at Hart Canyon. That's the last I saw of it. I ran into the house and called the military in Albuquerque. I never heard from them about it."

Papua New Guinea, 1959 Incident

Papua New Guinea was a hive of UFO sightings over the years of 1958-1959. During that period of time, there were over 60 UFO sightings, most of these being in the Mount Pudi region. On the 5th April 1959, Australian missionary Father William Booth Gill noticed there was a very bright and fast moving light travelling across the Mount Pudi area, which had contained a small village. Thinking not much of it, Father Gill went back to his normal routine.

On the 26th of June, at approximately 18:45 local time, Father Gill again noticed a bright light in the sky to the north-west of the village. Soon, the word had spread throughout the small community, as well as the surrounding areas, and the inhabitants had joined Father Gill in watching for the lights in the sky. In all, thirty-eight people verified for what was seen on that occasion. The witnesses described how, as the light got closer, they could make it out has being roughly the size of five full moons (not football fields) that were lined up against each other. It was in the shape of a disc, with a smaller round superstructure on the top, like the bridge of a ship. Underneath, it had four legs in pairs of two, and coming down in a diagonal manner. All of the witnesses that had gathered continued to watch the craft as it hovered in complete silence. They were astounded when they discerned four humanoid shaped figures on the top part of the craft. They all said that it had appeared as if these figures moved about as if carrying out duties, bending and reaching inside the craft. One of them would disappear and then come back into view. There was also a blue light that shined up from the craft at regular intervals. This went on for about forty-five minutes until about 19:30, when the craft rose high into the sky, becoming obscured by clouds, disappeared out of view.

An hour later at 20:30, a number of smaller objects returned to the skies over the mission. Twenty minutes later, the larger object from earlier in the night returned. This sequence continued for four hours, then at approximately 10:50 that night, the clouds rolled in, and obscured the large craft and the smaller ones, moving completely out of sight. That evening's events were not the only ones that occurred over the village. The next evening, at about 18:00, a number of smaller craft appeared along with the larger one that had been there the night before. As the crafts hovered silently about three to four hundred feet away, the beings were again visible in the top part of the craft. It appeared as if one of the beings leaned over a sort of rail and looked down toward the people on the ground.

On seeing this, Father Gill waved up to them and to his total amazement, the being waved back. Father Gill would later say that it was like a skipper on a boat waving back to someone who was on the wharf. Then all of the witness on the ground began waving to the beings. One witness waved a flashlight towards the craft, and as if in acknowledgement, the craft went into a movement like a swinging pendulum. The villager directed the light from the flashlight to the ground to see if it would encourage the craft to land, but the craft had no reaction. Throughout the encounter, many of the indigenous people had gestured to the craft to land, but they got no response.

The village resumed their normal routines, including its evening church service. At 19:45, the craft had silently gone from view. At 23:30 that night, while most of the community was in the mission, a loud bang was heard on the roof. The group ran outside and saw four of the craft high in the sky. The next morning the roof of the mission was inspected, but there was no apparent damage.

The Lonnie Zamora April 24, 1964 Incident

On April 24, 1964 at approximately 17:45 local time, Socorro, New Mexico police officer Lonnie Zamora began pursuing a speeding vehicle just south of town. He says he heard a "roar," and he broke off his pursuit to investigate. He knew of a nearby dynamite shack and decided to go take look, to see if it was the source of the noise. He noticed a flame in the sky, glowing bluish- orange, and appeared to be descending. He says that he could not focus on it because he was paying attention to navigating the steep, 2-track road. When he arrived at the crest of the hill, he noticed a white object on the ground, out in the desert, and two people who were clad in coveralls near the spot. He said the object looked oval and white. It also seemed to be on two legs. He thought it might be a car wreck, so he raced down the road to provide assistance. He called dispatch to let them know he would be assisting in a car wreck.

When he got closer to the object, he pulled his car around, stopped to radio that he was leaving his car, and got out. He fumbled with the radio handset, and just as he turned around, he heard a loud, "roar not exactly a blast." He said the object began to rise into the air, and it had a blue flame on the underside, and that the bottom of the flame looked orange. At this point he also noticed the object was smooth, with no windows, and it had an insignia on the side. He was afraid the thing was going to explode, so he ran. As he ran around his patrol car, his leg hit the fender and he fell down. He glanced back and saw the object was still rising, and the roar kept getting louder.

Zamora got up and kept running from the object, finally jumping to the other side of a hill for cover. At that point, the sound stopped abruptly. He had planned to continue running, but noticed that the object was moving away. It had been hovering only 10 to 15 feet from the ground. It flew over the dynamite shack, just clearing it by a few feet, and then it followed the contour of the ground, never higher than 20 feet or so, until it was out of Zamora's sight. Zamora went back to his car and asked the radio operator to look out the window to see if he could see the object. The dispatcher didn't see anything. Then New Mexico State police officer Sergeant Chavez arrived on the scene. Chavez asked what was wrong. He noticed Zamora looked out of breath and pale. Zamora told him the story, and they went to look at the area where the object had landed. When they got there, they noticed a burnt bush and impressions in the ground left by what appeared to be the two-legged landing gear.

Zamora's sighting made it into local newspapers, and caught the attention of some members of the USAF's Project BLUE BOOK, the official government investigation into UFOs. Investigators were impressed with Zamora's credibility, and with the physical evidence from the scene. A burnt branch from the bush and the soil at the site of the impressions were analyzed, but nothing unusual was found. They also tested for radiation, but levels were normal.

BLUE BOOK director, Hector Quintanilla said, "Zamora is puzzled by what he saw and frankly, so are we. This is the best-documented case on record, and still we have been unable, in spite of thorough investigation, to find the vehicle or other stimulus that scared Zamora to the point of panic." This case has continued to be important in UFO research, and occasionally finds itself back into the news. In 2009, a professor, along with some former students from New Mexico Tech, said they thought they might know who hoaxed it. They thought it was an elaborate trick played on Zamora. However, they did not produce anything definitive, and the story persists.

Over the years, the craft witnessed by Zamora has often been depicted with a red insignia that is based on a design that was released to the media in 1964. Recent findings indicate that the military had obtained Zamora's agreement not to divulge the real design of the red insignia that he saw on the observed craft. Instead, a modified symbol was submitted. The main reason behind this request was that, if other witnesses came forward, it would be a way to validate whether or not he was telling the truth.

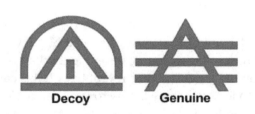

Decoy   **Genuine**

These are Zamora's sketches of the insignia (from the U.S. Air Force Project Blue Book

The 1974 UFO Crash in Coyame, Mexico

On August 25, 1974, at 20:07, U.S. Air Defense RADAR detected an unknown object approaching U.S. airspace from the Gulf of Mexico. Originally the object was tracked at 2,530 mph on a bearing of 325 degrees and at an altitude of 75,000 feet, a course that would intercept US territory about forty miles southwest of Corpus Christi, Texas. After sixty seconds of observation, at a position 155 miles southeast of Corpus Christi, the object decelerated to approximately 1,955 mph, turned to a heading of 290 degrees, and began a slow descent.

It entered Mexican airspace approximately forty miles south of Brownsville, Texas, traveling westward. Radar tracked it for 500 miles to a point near the town of Coyame, in the state of Chihuahua, not far from the U.S. border (Border XXI). There, the object suddenly disappeared from the radar screens. During the flight over Mexican airspace, the object leveled off at 45,000 feet, then descended to 20,000 feet. The descent was in level steps, not a smooth curve or straight line, and each level was maintained for approximately five minutes. The object was tracked by two separate military radar installations. It would have been within range of Brownsville civilian radar, but no civilian radar reported the event. The point of disappearance from the radar screens was over a barren and sparsely populated area of Northern Mexico. At first it was assumed that the object had descended below the radar's horizon, and an active watch was kept for any re-emergence of the object. None occurred.

Because of the high speed and descending flight path, some thought that it was a meteorite streaming through Earth's atmosphere, but meteors normally travel at higher speeds, and descend in a smooth arc, not in "steps." Additionally, meteorites do not make a thirty-five degree change in azimuth.

Shortly after detection, an U.S. Air Defense Alert was initiated. However, before any form of interception could be scrambled, the object turned to a course that would not immediately take it over U.S. territory. The alert was called off within twenty minutes after the object's disappearance from the radar screen.

Fifty-two minutes after the disappearance, civilian radio traffic indicated that a civilian aircraft had gone down in that area. It was clear that the missing aircraft had departed El Paso International Airport (ELP) with a destination of Mexico City, and could not, therefore, have been the object tracked over the Gulf of Mexico. It was noted, however, that they both disappeared in the same area and at the same time

A new day dawned, and Mexican authorities began a search for the missing plane. At approximately 10:35, there came a radio report that wreckage from the missing plane had been spotted from the air. Almost immediately, it was reported that a second plane was on the ground, a few miles from the first. Minutes later, the spotter reported that the second "plane" was circular shaped and apparently in one piece, although damaged. The Mexican military soon placed radio silence on all further search efforts.

With the U.S. Deep-Listening Station at Fort Huachuca less than 500 miles away, radio interceptions were reported through secure channels to the CIA. With great speed, the CIA began assembling a recovery team, whose specialized equipment and alacrity suggested that they were either well-rehearsed, or one that had deployed prior to this event. Requests were initiated at the highest levels between the United States and Mexican governments for the U.S. recovery team be allowed onto Mexican territory in order to "assist." These requests were met with ignorance, and a flat refusal of any cooperation between the two governments.

By 9 p.m. on August 26, 1974 the recovery team had been staged at Fort Bliss, Texas. Several helicopters were flown there from some unknown source, and assembled in a secured area of the base. The helicopters were painted a neutral sand color and bore no markings. Witnesses indicate that there were three smaller craft, very probably UHl Hueys, from their descriptions. There was also a larger helicopter, possibly a Sikorsky CH-53

Sea Stallion, which can carry up to 13,000 pounds of external cargo, and had been used in the Pacific to recover U.S. space capsules. Personnel from the flight teams remained with their aircraft and had no contact with other Ft. Bliss personnel.

Satellite and aircraft reconnaissance collected that day indicated that both the crashed disc and the civilian aircraft had been removed from the crash sites and loaded onto flatbed trucks. Later flights confirmed that the Mexican convoy had departed the area, heading south. At that point, the CIA had to make a choice: either allow the unknown craft to stay in the hands of the Mexican government; or launch the recovery team, supplemented by any required military support, to take over the debris. There occurred, however, an event that took the choice out of their hands. High altitude overflights indicated that the convoy had stopped before reaching any inhabited areas or major roads. Recon showed no activity, and radio contact between the Mexican recovery team and its headquarters had ceased. A low altitude, high speed overflight was ordered.

The photos returned by the reconnaissance aircraft showed that all trucks and jeeps had stopped, some with open doors, and two human bodies lying on the ground beside two of the vehicles. An immediate decision was made to launch the U.S. recovery team, but the actual launching was held up until the arrival of additional equipment and two additional personnel. It was not until 14:38 that the U.S. helicopters departed Ft. Bliss.

The four helicopters followed Border XXI towards Presidio, Texas, then turned and entered Mexican airspace north of Candelaria. They were over the Mexican convoy site at 16:53 All of the personnel were dead, most within the trucks. Some of the U.S. recovery team members, dressed in bio-protection suits, reconfigured the straps holding the object on the flatbed truck, attaching them to a cargo cable from the Sea Stallion. By 17:14, the recovered object was on its way to the U.S. Before leaving the convoy site, members of the recovery team gathered the Mexican vehicles and bodies, and then destroyed all with high explosives. This included the pieces of the civilian light plane which had been involved in the presumably mid-air collision.

The Hueys caught up with the Sea Stallion as it reentered U.S. airspace. The recovery team proceeded to a point in the Davis Mountains, approximately twenty-five miles northeast of Valentine, Texas. There, they landed and waited until 02:25 the next morning. At that time, they resumed the flight and rendezvoused with a small convoy on the road between Van Horn and Kent. The recovered disc was transferred to a truck large enough to handle it, and capable of being totally hidden from view. Some of the flight team and recovery team personnel transferred to the convoy. All of the helicopters then returned to their original bases in order to undergo decontamination procedures

The convoy continued non-stop, using back roads and smaller highways, and staying away from populated areas. The destination of the convoy reportedly was Atlanta, Georgia. Here is where the hard evidence thins out. One unconfirmed report says that the disc was eventually transferred to Wright-Patterson AFB.

The best reliable information about the disc was that it was sixteen feet, five inches in diameter, convex on both upper and lower surfaces to the same degree, and possessed no visible doors or windows. The thickness top to bottom was slightly less than five feet. The color was silver, much like polished steel. There were no visible lights, nor any identifiable means of propulsion. Two areas of the rim showed damage, one an irregular hole approximately twelve inches in diameter, dented on the perimeter of the hole. The other was described as a "dent" about two feet wide on the upper side. The weight of the object was estimated as approximately 1500 pounds, an easy haul for the Sea Stallion.

It seems plausible that the foot-long hole may have been caused by the collision with the civilian aircraft. Since the object was traveling approximately 1700 knots (1,955 mph), the UFO would have demolished the small private aircraft. No mention is made of the occupants of the civilian aircraft, and it is not known if anybody or bodies had been recovered. Considering the impact of the mid-air collision, bodies may not have fallen near the larger pieces.

Speculation about the demise of the Mexican recovery team includes chemicals that were emitted from the disc after impact; and unknown microbiological agents from its occupants. The U.S. recovery team reported no deleterious health effects associated with the crash site. It seems logical that the recovery team took at least one of the alien bodies back with them for analysis in the U.S., while keeping the potentially biologically contaminated being in quarantine.

Zimbabwe Ariel School 1994 UFO Event

On September 14, 1994, thousands of Zimbabweans had witnessed a UFO pass across the clear evening sky. Many felt that the object was a meteor, or perhaps some sort of space vehicle from the United States streaking across Earth's atmosphere. Some local students claimed to have watched a slow-moving light for 2-3 minutes, while others claimed it descended, levelling off at tree level.

Ariel School is a private elementary school located in Ruwa, Zimbabwe about 12 miles from Harare, the capitol. Two days later, at approximately 10:15 on the morning of September 16, the teachers were attending a mandatory weekly meeting inside the school, and the children outside on the school playground. One adult supervised the children.

It was a beautiful, clear morning, and then several children noticed three to five objects in the sky above the school. Described as round, silver, and saucer-shaped with lit portals around the perimeter, the objects seemed to move extraordinarily fast, disappearing in the blink of an eye, and then reappearing in another place in the sky. Eventually, one of the objects slowly, quietly landed on the ground about 300 feet from the schoolyard. The object settled in a brushy, wooded area that was uncleaned and ruled 'unsafe' for the children. Some of the students reported that it "hovered" inches above the ground.

The Elementary School students described a "small man" standing on top of the vessel. He was described as 3 feet tall, wearing a tight, shiny black and silver one-piece suit similar to a wetsuit, with a slender neck and very large black eyes. Some described the being as having long hair, or wearing a cape of some sort. He walked down from the craft and proceeded in the direction of the children. One of the older girls described him as a creature with a "small nose and a mouth that was a small, straight line," adding that, "the eyes were very big and slanting." Another described the ET as, "thin and skinny with a scrawny neck and eyes that were large and oval-shaped."

As the ET approached the children, it paused, and in an instant, disappeared. Almost at the same moment, another creature, or possibly the same one appeared behind the UFO craft, and once again disappeared. Within seconds, the craft lifted off and vanished into the sky over the school.

Hearing the children's stories, Colin Mackie, the Headmaster, had the children return to the classroom and sketch what they had seen. By the time authorities arrived the following day, they had 35 drawings waiting for them. All of the drawings were similar in their depiction of the UFO and its occupant, illustrating the same disc-shaped craft and diminutive, large-eyed creature.

The alien never spoke to the students directly, but a few of the older students said that they had communicated with the craft's occupant telepathically, and were informed that humans were destroying Earth by pollution, and unless we changed our ways, there would be dire consequences.

Chapter 8

Strange Incidences

Valentich Disappearance - 1978

Frederick Valentich was a 20 year old Australian pilot who disappeared while on a 125-nautical-mile training flight over Bass Strait in a Cessna 182L aircraft. It was the evening of Saturday, October 21, 1978. Described as a "flying saucer enthusiast", Valentich informed Melbourne air traffic control that he was being accompanied by an aircraft about 1,000 feet above him and that his engine had begun running roughly. Then he added, "It's not an aircraft!"

Valentich had about 150 total hours' flying time and held a class-four instrument rating, which authorized him to fly at night, but only "in visual meteorological conditions." He had twice applied to enlist in the Royal Australian Air Force (RAAF), but was rejected because of inadequate educational qualifications. He was a member of the RAAF Air Training Corps, determined to have a career in aviation. Valentich was studying part-time to become a commercial pilot but had a poor achievement record, having twice failed all five commercial license examination subjects, and as recently as the month before his disappearance, had failed three more commercial license subjects. He had been involved in flying incidents, like straying into a controlled zone in Sydney, for which he received a warning; and twice deliberately flying into a cloud, for which legal prosecution had been considered. According to his father, Guido, Valentich had an ardent believe in UFOs, and had been worried about being attacked by them.

The destination of Valentich's final flight was King Island. He filed a flight plan at Moorabbin Airport in Melbourne, but his motivation for the flight is unknown. He said that he was to fly to King Island in Bass Strait, via Cape Otway, to pick up passengers, and return to Moorabbin. However, he had told his family, girlfriend and acquaintances that he intended to pick up crayfish. During the accident investigations it was learned there were no passengers waiting to be picked up at King Island, he had not ordered crayfish, and could not have done so because crayfish were not available anyway. Valentich had also failed to inform King Island Airport of his intention to land there, going against "standard procedure".

The Cessna 182-L, with a cruising speed of around 160 mph, departed Moorabbin at 18:19 with good visibility with light winds. Valentich contacted the Melbourne Flight Service Unit to inform them of his presence, and reported reaching Cape Otway at 19:00.

At 19:06, Valentich asked Melbourne Flight Service Officer Steve Robey for information on other aircraft below 5000 feet altitude, and was told there was no known traffic at that level. Valentich said he could see a large unknown aircraft which appeared to be illuminated by four bright landing lights. He was unable to confirm its type, but said it had passed about 1,000 feet overhead and was moving at high speed. He then reported that the aircraft was approaching him from the east, and said the other pilot might be purposely "toying" with him.

Three minutes later Robe asked Valentich to confirm his altitude and that he was unable to identify the other aircraft. Valentich gave his altitude as 4500 feet and said the aircraft was "long", but it was traveling too fast for him to describe it in more detail. Valentich stopped transmitting for about 30 seconds, during which time Robey asked for an estimate of the aircraft's size. Valentich said the aircraft was "orbiting" above him and that it had a shiny metal surface and a green light on it. This was followed by 28 seconds silence before Valentich reported that the aircraft had vanished. There was a further 25-second break in communications before Valentich reported that it was now approaching from the southwest.

Twenty-nine seconds later, at 19:12 Valentich reported that he was experiencing engine problems and was going to proceed to King Island. There was brief silence until he said, "It is hovering and it's not an aircraft!" This was followed by 17 seconds unintelligible noise, described as being "metallic, scraping sounds", then all contact was lost.

A sea and air search was undertaken that included oceangoing ship traffic, a RAAF Lockheed P-3 Orion aircraft, plus eight civilian aircraft. The search encompassed over 1,000 square miles. Search efforts ceased four days later on 25 October 1978 without result.

An investigation into Valentich's disappearance by the Australian Department of Transport was unable to determine the cause of the presumed crash. Valentich was 'lost at sea.'

Five years after Valentich's aircraft went missing, an engine cowl flap was found washed ashore on Flinders Island. The Bureau of Air Safety Investigation asked the Royal Australian Navy Research Laboratory (RANRL) about the likelihood that the cowl flap might have "travelled" to its ultimate position from the region where Valentich's aircraft had gone down. The bureau noted, "The part has been identified as having come from a Cessna 182 aircraft between a certain range of serial numbers," which included Valentich's aircraft.

It has been proposed that Valentich staged his own disappearance. Even taking into account a trip of between 30 and 45 minutes to Cape Otway, the single-engine Cessna 182 still had enough fuel to fly another 500 miles. Despite ideal conditions, at no time was the aircraft plotted on radar, casting doubts as to whether it was ever near Cape Otway. Melbourne police received reports of a light aircraft making a mysterious landing not far from Cape Otway at the same time as Valentich's disappearance.

Valentich may have become disoriented over the water, which happens fairly often to new pilots who don't know to trust their onboard instrumentation. It may have seemed that he was flying upside down. The model Cessna that he was piloting, however, could not have flown inverted for long as it has gravity feed fuel system, meaning that its engine would have cut out very quickly. Another possibility is that he committed suicide, even though interviews with doctors and colleagues who knew him virtually eliminated this possibility.

A 2013 review of the radio transcripts and other data by astronomer and retired United States Air Force pilot James McGaha and author Joe Nickell proposes that the inexperienced Valentich was deceived by the illusion of a tilted horizon for which he attempted to compensate, and inadvertently put his aircraft into a downward, so-called "graveyard spiral." It was much the same case with John Kennedy, Jr., an inexperienced pilot who had upgraded from the Cessna 182 to the more complex Piper Saratoga, and spiraled into the Atlantic Ocean in 1999. According to the authors, the G-forces of a tightening spiral decreases fuel flow, resulting in the "rough idling" reported by Valentich. McGaha and Nickell also propose that the apparently stationary, overhead lights that Valentich reported were probably the planets Venus, Mars and Mercury, along with the bright star Antares, which would have behaved in a way consistent with Valentich's description.

The Dulce Underground Base

Dulce Base is the subject of a conspiracy theory claiming that a jointly-operated human and alien underground facility exists under Archuleta Mesa on the Colorado-New Mexico border near the town of Dulce, New Mexico. It is one of the most active areas in the U.S. for reporting UFOs, with almost everyone in the nearby town having reported seeing one.

In 1979 Albuquerque businessman Paul Bennewitz became convinced that he was intercepting electronic communications from alien spacecraft and their installations outside of Albuquerque. He was convinced that cattle mutilations were due to alien interaction. By the 1980s, he believed he had discovered a secret underground base near Dulce which was populated by grey aliens along with humans. He claimed that, "Diabolical invaders from another solar system have set up a secret underground base in the rugged mountains of northern New Mexico – so they can shanghai human guinea pigs for bizarre genetic experiments."

Thomas Edwin Castello claims he was a high level security officer at the base. He said the base at Dulce was a multi-level facility, and reported to have a central hub that is controlled by base security. The security level increases as one descends to the lower levels. He knew of seven sub-levels, but there may have been more. Most of the aliens supposedly are on levels 5, 6 and 7 with alien housing on level 5.

Phil Schneider, a geological engineer and structural engineer, was involved in a 1979 addition to the deep underground military base at Dulce, which is the deepest known black operations base. It goes down seven levels - over 2.5 miles deep. Schneider asserts that he was suspicious of the engineering operation while noticing the presence of Green Berets and Special Forces.

He had drilled four distinct holes in the desert, and was going to link them together and blow out large sections at a time. His dangerous job was to be lowered down the holes, checking the rock structure, and recommend the appropriate explosive. As he was lowered down one shaft, it opened to a large cavern, and he found himself face-to-face with a 7-foot tall, "stinky", gray alien. He said that he "freaked out," and grabbed his pistol fatally wounding two aliens. Another alien shot some "laser-plasma ball or whatever" at him, and blew off some of his fingers. He was saved by a Green Beret who allegedly gave his life for him. In all, 60 humans purportedly lost their lives that day, referred to as, "The Alien-Human Battle of Dulce." Schneider was one of three people who survived the 1979 Dulce firefight between the large Greys and U.S. personnel at the underground base.

Phil Schneider lost his life to what appeared to have been a military-style execution in January 1996. He was found dead in his apartment with piano wire still wrapped around his neck. According to some sources, he had been brutally tortured before being killed.

Lake Baikal 1982 Incident

Located in southeastern Siberia near Mongolia's border sits the planet's oldest and deepest lake. Astonishing depths of over five thousand feet have been measured. Nearly one-quarter of Earth's fresh water is contained within its 12,248 square miles. Lake Baikal has been home to many unexplained phenomena. Locals claim countless peculiar UFO encounters that frequently occur in this remote region of Russia. Some theorize that an extraterrestrial base is operating beneath the icy waters.

One of the most bizarre extraterrestrial reports occurred in 1982. During a routine Soviet submarine training dive, Russian Navy personnel noticed anomalous figures swimming nearby. Perplexed, they watched as several curious creatures approached them. Despite being stationed at a depth of over one hundred and sixty-four feet (5 atmospheres), these humanoids wore no breathing apparatus. Each wore tight-fitting metallic suits, complete with a helmet-which completely covered their heads. Upon further observation, the sailors noticed that the aliens were nearly ten feet tall. Then, just like that, they disappeared back into the dark abyss.

Following this eerie encounter, the intrigued sub commander ordered his sailors to capture one of the alien beings. Seven divers in deep-water SCUBA gear entered the glacial lake and began their descent. Soon after swimming in a downwelling of cold water, multiple beings emerged. One diver attempted to catch the unearthly specimen in a large net. At that moment, the nonhumans fought back by shooting intense sonar waves at the Russian divers. The powerful force rendered them unconscious, and rapidly propelled them to the surface.

Catapulting upwards from extreme depths has devastating effects on the human body, namely, the 'Bends.' Three were seriously injured, but lived to tell their stories. The remaining four divers needed immediate transfer to a decompression chamber. Unfortunately, there was only one chamber in the region, and it was designed for only two people at a time. Out of sheer desperation, all four men entered simultaneously in an attempt to save their lives. Tragically, this last-ditch effort did not go as planned. Three individuals perished as a result of their superior's hasty decision. Those who survived the terrifying ordeal would be left with life-altering disabilities. Following this harrowing incident, Russian Navy commanders ceased further attempts to interfere with the USO, but continued their extensive monitoring of the numerous underwater vessels.

Paintsville, Kentucky 2002 UFO and Train Collision

At exactly 02:47 in the early morning hours of January 14, 2002, a railroad worker who wishes to remain anonymous was rerouting a coal train from Russell, Kentucky to Shelbiana, Kentucky. "Our trailing unit and first two cars were severely damaged as we struck an unknown floating or hovering object. I know it was 2:47 because my watch froze, and to this day shows that time", he said.

"Along with my watch, the entire electrical systems on both locomotives went haywire. Approaching a bend near milepost 42, in an area referred to as the 'Wild Kingdom', for the many different types of animals spotted there, my conductor and I saw lights coming from around the way. This ordinarily means another train is coming and will pass on the other track. I killed our lights as not to blind the oncoming crew.

"As we rounded the corner, our onboard computer began to flash in and out, the speed recorder went nuts, and both locomotives died. Alarm bells began to ring and that's when we saw the objects. [It appeared that] they were scanning the river for something. At least three objects had several search lights trained there, the first object hovered about 10 to 12 feet above the track. It was metallic silver in color with multiple colored lights near the bottom and in the middle. There were no windows or openings of any kind that we could see. It was 18 to 20 feet in length and probably ten feet high.

"With both engines dead, as we rounded the corner we made little noise and the first object did not respond in time. I estimate that we hit the object at 30 mph with 16,000 trailing tons behind us. It clipped the top of our lead unit then skipped back slicing a chunk out of our trailing unit and first two coal cars. The other objects vanished.

"Our emergency brakes had engaged due to the loss of power, and we rolled to a stop approximately a mile and a half to two miles after impact. Our power restored after we were stopped, and we notified our dispatcher who was located in Jacksonville, Florida. We were told to inspect the cars to see if they'd hold the rail and try to limp into milepost 60 which used to be the Paintsville yard, but is no longer in full operation. We checked everything out, and the cab of the rear locomotive was demolished and smoking, the second two cars looked as if they had been hit with a giant hammer, but looked like they'd hold the rail.

"We pulled into Paintsville at approximately 05:15. The huge overhead lights lining the yard were noticeably dark, and the only lighting came from what we had assumed were railroad vehicles parked near the end of the track. We pulled to a stop and began unloading our grips off the wounded train. We could hear what sounded like an army of workers immediately tending to our train.

"Vehicle doors slamming, guys running by in weird outfits, and lights glaring from all directions. The one thing missing was railroad officials. A guy named Ferguson shook my hand and asked me to follow him into the old yard office. Once inside they and by 'they' I mean I have no idea who these people were, began to ask us hundreds of questions. They told us that for our own protection, we'd be medically tested before we could leave. I asked repeatedly to talk to my road foreman or trainmaster, and not only were these requests denied, but they confiscated my conductor's cellular phone.

"Hours later, we were led outside the yard office, and strange things continued to happen. The 2 locomotives and two cars were removed from the rest of the train we had brought in, and 4 tracks over, a huge tent structure was buzzing with activity.

"We were led off the property and told, due to national security, our silence on this matter would be appreciated. We were then put in a railroad vehicle and taken to Martin, Kentucky where we went through questioning again with railroad officials, and then drug tested. After all of this, we were sent on to Shelbiana, where we took rest for 8 hours and worked another train back to Russell. Working back we passed by Paintsville, no sign of the engines, cars, tent, people, nothing!"

Cessna 2002 Collision with Unknown object

Thomas J. Preziose was a 54 year old experienced veteran pilot who had worked for the New York City Police Department. He had been an instructor for the Cessna 208 at the Pan Am Flight Academy in Memphis, Tennessee. He had worked for several months for Mid-Atlantic Freight, the company contracting with DHL Worldwide Express, and had flown the same route numerous times.

On October 23, 2002 Preziose was flying in a single-engine Cessna 208B Cargomaster bound for Montgomery, Alabama with 420 pounds of business documents. Ten minutes after takeoff from Mobile Downtown Airport at Brookley, using the call sign 'Night Ship 282,' he was passed onto the FAA tower at Mobile Regional Airport, a standard procedure. Five minutes later, around 19:30, as Preziose climbed northeast through the overcast sky. Relying on instruments to take him to his cruising altitude of 3,000 feet, the Mobile Regional Controller alerted him to the presence of the DC-10 which was seven miles straight in front of him, flying at 4,000 feet and inbound for Brookley. Preziose acknowledged the DC-10 heavy, and a minute later, the controller told Preziose the DC-10, now just two miles from the Cessna, had crossed the smaller plane's path and remained at 4,000 feet. "Roger, I got him above me right now," Preziose replied, apparently confirming he saw the FedEx plane. A few seconds later, he came back on the air: "I need to deviate! I need to deviate! I need to deviate! I need --."

A commercial frog hunter in an airboat, who was assisting Alabama Marine Police and Coast Guard crews, found the wreckage around midnight, resting in shallow water, about 1 mile north of the Mobile Bay Causeway. Unidentified red marks on the severely damaged nose and front belly of the plane indicated that it had hit another object in the air. The wings were shattered, and most of the front of the plane was little more than fragments. The impact of that collision disintegrated the airplane before it hit the water. The Pratt & Whitney engine block was split in half, a strong indication that a violent impact had occurred.

The National Transportation Safety Board (NTSB) attempted to find the source of the red marks found on the Cessna. Investigators sent fragments with the markings to Wright Patterson Air Force Base in Ohio for testing. The markings were compared with other materials from the plane, including red paint and a red cargo bag. The tests also examined paint from an unmanned aerial vehicle, apparently to determine whether the Cessna had struck a military drone. "The main result from the investigation is that the material in the red streaks on the skin of the accident airplane was significantly different from the other materials that were examined for comparison," the NTSB report states.

Additionally, investigators were unable to identify the source of a small piece of what appeared to be black anodized aluminum, which was found embedded in the left wing near the fuselage. The report stated, "There's no chance that that particular incident involved a drone from the 53rd Wing, which operates unmanned airplanes out of Tyndall Air Force Base in the Florida Panhandle. Those drones do not fly as far west as the Mobile area, and definitely do not venture into airspace near Mobile."

The NTSB report said that the FedEx DC-10 doesn't appear to have been involved in the collision; investigators examined it the day after the crash and found it unscathed. The report said that malfunctioning radar recording equipment hampered efforts to determine the exact cause of the accident. Moreover, an air traffic controller at Mobile Regional Airport apparently gave incorrect positions to Preziose about the location of the DC-10 in the area. Based on the limited radar information they could find, investigators concluded that the Cessna never crossed paths with the DC-10, contrary to what the air traffic controller told Preziose. The Cessna 208 had passed a routine FAA inspection a few days earlier, the report states, and an autopsy revealed no drugs or alcohol in the pilot's system. The

Drug Enforcement Administration (DEA) office in Mobile said they could not rule out the possibility that a drug smuggling plane might have struck the Cessna, since there is a high volume of drug smuggling in Alabama, but no other wreckage was found.

The "Canneto di Caronia" Fires

In 2004 and 2005, there had been a series of unusual fires in Canneto di Caronia, Sicily, a village 60 miles east of Palermo. Events began on December 23, 2003, at Antonino Pezzino's home on Via Mare. Pezzino's television exploded, and similar malfunctions affected fuse boxes, air conditioners, kitchen appliances, computers, and electronic car door locks. Fires were also said to have struck boxes of wedding presents and some furniture. At least one person was said to have observed an unplugged electrical cable ignite.

On February 9, 2004, two houses on Via Mare burned. In response, Mayor Spinnato issued an order evacuating the 39 residents of Via Mare from their homes to the town's only hotel. The Italian utility company, ENEL, cut power to the town, but fires continued. From January through March, 92 fires were reported. On March 16, fires resumed, and investigators reportedly witnessed malfunctions in compasses, electronic car locks, and cell phones.

In April 2004, the government formed an interdisciplinary research group, coordinated by Francesco Venerando Mantegna from the Sicilian Protezione Civile. The team had widespread cooperation from the nation's armed forces, police, as well as ENEL. Venerando's team reported anomalous 'electromagnetic activity', and 'unexplained' lights. Scientists from the National Research Institute (CNR), with the support of NASA physicists, were also involved in investigating the mysterious events.

The Government found that they were "caused by a high power electromagnetic emissions which were not man made, and reached a power of between 12 and 15 gigawatts" coming from the nearby ocean. A helicopter operated by the Italian Government was chased by a UFO which shot off the rotors of the helicopter using some sort of ray gun. Fortunately no one was killed, and the entire incident was recorded on video which clearly showed an unidentified object in the presence of the helicopter. The Italian Government got the message, and is no longer sending aircraft into that area of the ocean. It says that UFOs are just one possibility, but they are also looking at the testing of top secret weapons by an unknown source, who are also capable of producing enormous amounts of energy.

Chapter 9

NASA and Space Agency Incidences

Astronaut Gordon Cooper

Before his selection as one of the original seven U.S. astronauts, Gordon Cooper was an Air Force test pilot and aeronautical engineer. While at Edwards Air Force Base in California, Cooper had reported that a high-resolution video of a flying saucer was recorded by two Edwards AFB range photographers on May 3, 1957. Cooper said that he had viewed the negatives of the object, which clearly showed a dish-like object with a dome on top and something like holes or ports in the dome. When later interviewed by James McDonald, the photographers and another witnesses confirmed the story. Cooper said military authorities had taken possession of the film, and neither he nor the photographers ever heard about it again. The incident was also reported in a few newspapers, such as the Los Angeles Times. The official explanation was that the photographers had filmed a weather balloon distorted by hot desert air.

Vandenberg Space Force Base UFOs

The Vandenberg Space Force Base, formally known as Vandenberg Air Force Base is located on the Pacific coast northwest of Lompoc, California. It launches manned and unmanned spacecraft from its Western Range, and also performs tests of a multitude of missiles. It is home to the U.S. Space Force's 30th Space Wing. In addition to its military space launch missions, it performs launches for civil and commercial space entities, such as NASA and SpaceX. The base has been a hot bed of UFO activity since the 1960s. Unsubstantiated reports claim that at least two missiles have been shot down by UFOs, the latest occurring on October 7, 2018, a SpaceX Falcon 9 rocket.

One of the earliest incidents transpired in April 1963 during a launch of a Scout missile that was fired down range into the mid Pacific area. The countdown was proceeding normally until 4 minutes to launch, when suddenly alarms sounded on the teletype machine, reading "Hold! Hold! Hold! UFO! UFO! UFO!" Another (closed circuit) teletype indicated that Vandenberg had scrambled two chase planes sent to investigate the UFO. Unconfirmed reports stated that the UFO was "huge" (no other dimensions given – no comparison with football fields), and was hovering over the mountains just south of the launch site. Upon approach from the jet interceptors, the UFO shot off at very high speed in a westerly direction. There were many cars driving north and south along U.S. Highway 101, which passes directly inland from the launch sites and a low mountain range between the two. Many vehicles had stopped on the freeway, and people got out and watched the UFO hovering over the mountains, leaving abruptly to the west at a high rate of speed.

From May 1963 to May 1966, Bob Jacobs, Ph. D., was the Officer-in-Charge of Photo-optical Instrumentation at the 1369th Photographic Squadron, Vandenberg. Kingston A. George "King" George was the Operations Analyst for Headquarters, 1st Strategic Aerospace Division. George said that the civilian and military engineers, whose job it was to evaluate the photographic instrumentation which was provided on every missile launch on the Western Test Range, were unhappy with the results of the imagery. Tracking footage from Vandenberg only provided a look up the "tailpipe" of the missile. George said that they wanted a side look at all stages of powered flight. This side-look was not possible from anyplace on the base. Because of the rugged California coastline, such a view was only possible from one spot, Big Sur, which is northwest of Vandenberg. Big Sur provided both a line-of-sight to the base, and well above the offshore fog bank which blankets the California shoreline much of the year.

Because of the 124 mile distance between Vandenberg and Big Sur, the use of a high powered lens with a very long focal length, a recording device that was capable of enhancing the image and a tracking system on which to mount the device was necessary. A telescope from Boston University, called "B.U." was utilized. The optical segment of the device was a folded Gregorian telescope with a 24-inch diameter objective lens, and a 240-inch focal length. The lens apparatus was sealed from the air and insulated against heat and cold. A set of Barlow lens extenders yields effective focal lengths of from 480 to 2,400 inches. (The normal focal length lens for a 35mm camera is about two inches). A light sensing element in the instrument used an Imaging Orthicon (I.O.) television tube. This enhanced the optical image, converted it to a series of electrical signals which displayed on a Kinescope, where it was photographed with 35 mm high-resolution motion picture film. The primary goal of the mission was to provide information on the detailed events following propellant depletion - at distance of from 300 to 800 nautical miles. The camera was placed in Big Sur near Anderson Peak on a Forest Service fire trail, 9 miles into the woods and uphill from Highway 1 at an elevation of 3,400 feet.

In early September of 1964, an Atlas-F, or possibly Atlas-D missile was launched, in support of the Nike-Zeus objectives. The Nike-Zeus was one of the United States' projects to develop an anti-missile missile. This particular mission was part of a test of an enemy radar-defeating system. "There it is!" Bob Jacobs shouted, as the Atlas soared through the snow-white coastal fog blanket, with both tracking mounts zoomed-in on the rocket in flight. The big Atlas could not have been cleaner, clearer, or more majestic. The magnification of the B.U. was truly impressive. The exhaust nozzles and lower third of the Atlas missile literally filled the frame at this distance of over 100 nautical miles. As the nose cone package approached T + 400 seconds, a sufficient angle of view had been established to include the whole inflight package centered in the frame.

A profile of the three stages of powered flight had been accomplished, and the photographic team was congratulating each other, letting the film run out in the 35 mm motion picture camera. The exposed film was quickly taken to Vandenberg's photographic laboratory. Processing of the film took all that night, and the results were ready for viewing the next day.

The image processing went smoothly, and Bob Jacobs was called by Major Florenz J. Mansmann Chief Science Officer at Vandenberg. Mansmann had asked Jacobs to come "right away" to his office at Headquarters. When he arrived, Jacobs found a movie projector had been set up in the office, and a large group of people waiting. Three men in plain gray suits spoke little, and watched him intently as the lights were dimmed in order to view the film. Bob Jacobs was delighted to see the recording from the Big Sur telescope, after all the months of planning and weeks of work. He was quite amazed and very pleased with the quality of the imagery, especially considering the distance involved, as they could make out quite clearly the separated nose cone, the radar experimentation, and the dummy warhead, all sailing along beautifully about 60 miles straight up from planet Earth, and some 300 to 500 nautical miles down range.

As they neared the end of the reel, Mansmann said, "Watch carefully now, Lieutenant Jacobs." At that point a most remarkable vision appeared on the screen. An object flew into the frame of the Atlas rocket profile, from left to right. It approached the warhead package, and then maneuvered around it. That is, this... "thing"...flew a relative polar orbit around the dummy warhead which was heading toward the South Pacific Ocean at 18 thousand miles an hour! The unidentified object emitted four distinct bright flashes of light from the 4 cardinal compass points of its orbit. These flashes were so intense that each "strike" caused the I.O. tube to form a lens aberration halo around the bright spot. Following this remarkable event, the unknown object departed the frame in the same direction from which it had come.

A still frame from the Big Sur footage

The shape of the object was that of a classic "Flying saucer." In the middle of the top half of the object was a dome. From that dome, or just beneath, it seemed to issue a beam of light which had caused the flashes as described. Subsequently the warhead component malfunctioned and tumbled out of its trajectory, hundreds of miles short of its target. This... unidentified flying... "thing" had apparently "shot down" a mock U.S. atomic warhead! Bob Jacobs was told, "What you just saw did not take place. It never happened."

Bob Jacobs' conclusions:

(1) What we photographed that September day in 1964 was a solid, three-dimensional, intelligently controlled "flying" device.

(2) It emitted a beam of energy, possibly a plasma beam, at our dummy warhead, and caused a malfunction.

(3) This "craft" was not anything of which our science and technology in 1964 was capable. The most probable explanation of the device, therefore, is that it was of extraterrestrial origin.

(4) The flashing strikes of light we recorded on film were not from laser tracking devices. Such devices did not exist then, aside from small scale laboratory models.

(5) Most probably the B.U. Telescope was brought out to California specifically to photograph this event which had been prearranged. That is, we had been set up to record an event which someone in our Government knew was going to happen in advance.

(6) What we photographed that day was the first terrestrial demonstration of what has come to be called S.D.I. or 'Star Wars.' The demonstration was put on for our benefit for some reason by extraterrestrials.

From 1965 through 1978, an employee of Convair Aerospace, MAB5, was involved with the Atlas-D & -F series' launch facilities at Vandenberg AFB in the early years of missile activity. He had witnessed several incidents while launching Atlas-D missiles from South Vandenberg (Point Arguello), LF04 & LF05. On many occasions, he was allowed to view the launches using the 'Big Eye', a 4400 mm telescope, and later, view the Range Camera data, at Bldg. 7000. The 'Big Eye' was used to receive immediate sight data in order to verify the flight profile for each missile launch. During the Thor launches, the much smaller BlueStreak missile was used for gathering exhaust data for analysis by Douglas Aircraft, in order to improve rocket main engine performance. While viewing some of the launch films, it was quite common to see UFO activity paralleling the flight. For many years, the Thor was considered the fastest ICBM that the U.S. had, on launch.

The BlueStreak was an, extremely fast, single stage missile used strictly for gathering various data about missile flight. It was fired T+10, into the exhaust trail of the mighty Thor, to within 1,000 yards of the rocket. On many occurrences, UFOs were seen to 'catch' the BlueStreak, track with it, then speed up and 'catch' the Thor, tracking with it for a brief time, then speed away at an extremely high speed. The launch radar units were capable of tracking at speeds of up to 10,500 m/h., but were unable to track the UFO's speed, which outran both U.S. rockets.

NASA Space Mission Encounters with UFOs

Given the training and acuity of the astronauts, their reports of UFOs should fall into the highest category of credibility. Almost all of the NASA Apollo missions to the Moon (11, 12, 13, 14, 15, 16, and 17) reported some type of UFO activity.

Gemini IV

Was the second manned spaceflight in NASA's Project Gemini, occurring in June 1965. It was the tenth crewed U.S. spaceflight. Astronauts James McDivitt and Ed White circled the Earth 66 times over a period of four days,. The highlight of the mission was the first space walk by an American, during which White floated free outside the spacecraft, tethered to it, for approximately 20 minutes. Astronaut McDivitt observed a cylindrical object with a protuberance as they passed over the Hawaiian Islands. They both reported a moving bright light at a level higher than their spacecraft.

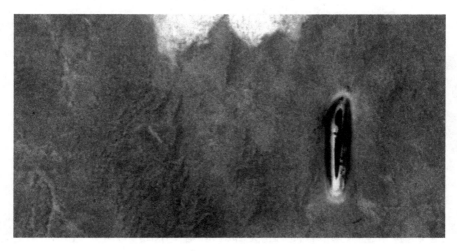

Astronaut McDivitt's photograph of an unidentified object

Gemini VII

Was the 1965 manned spaceflight of NASA's Gemini program. Frank Borman and Jim Lovell spent nearly 14 days in space, making a total of 206 orbits. It was always planned to be a long duration flight, investigating the effects of fourteen days in space on the human body. Lovell and Borman sighted a UFO during their second orbit, in December, 1965.

Astronaut Borman described what he referred to as a "bogey", flying in formation with the spacecraft. Gemini control told him he was seeing the final stage of their own Titan booster rocket. Borman confirmed that he could see the booster rocket, but that he was seeing something else, something completely different.

Apollo 8

Was the first manned spacecraft to leave Earth orbit, and also the first human flight to reach a non-Earth object, the Moon. The crew orbited the Moon without landing, and then departed safely back to Earth. The three astronauts aboard were Frank Borman, James Lovell, and William Anders. Lovell stated over his radio, "Please be informed that there is a Santa Claus," as he came around from the backside of the moon. 'Santa Claus' was the code word used by NASA for alien spacecraft.

Apollo 11

Was the first space flight to land humans on the Moon. Commander Neil Armstrong and lunar module pilot Buzz Aldrin landed the Apollo Lunar Module Eagle on July 20, 1969. An incident occurred on the last day of approach to the moon, which Aldrin, Armstrong, and Michael Collins have recounted. The two astronauts spotted what they, at first, assumed to be a stage of the Saturn V rocket which had boosted them into orbit, called the S-IVB. When they called to Houston to ask if that was the case, Houston told them that the S-IVB had been detached a while ago and was 6,000 miles away. Although Armstrong said it was just far enough away that he couldn't make out the object's shape, the other astronauts debated whether it was shaped like a cylinder or an L-shaped.

Apollo 12

Was the sixth manned flight in the NASA Apollo program, and the second to land on the Moon. It was launched on November 14, 1969, from the Kennedy Space Center, Florida. Commander Charles "Pete" Conrad and

Lunar Module Pilot Alan L. Bean performed just over one day and seven hours of lunar surface activity while Command Module Pilot Richard F. Gordon remained in lunar orbit.

On November 19, Conrad and Bean achieved a precise landing at their targeted location, within walking distance of the Surveyor 3 robotic probe, which had landed on April 20, 1967. The Lunar Module Intrepid lifted off from the Moon on November 20, docking with the command module which had just completed its 45th lunar orbit, and all three astronauts traveled back to Earth. The Apollo 12 mission ended on November 24 with a successful splashdown.

While on their mission the following exchange was captured:

APOLLO 12: We have company.

HOUSTON: Say again?

APOLLO 12: I say we have company. (Short period of silence).

HOUSTON: (Emphatically) You were told not to make transmissions such as that!

Put it on the flight recorder and we'll discuss it when you get back! (Long period of silence).

Apollo 17
Was the eleventh and final Moon landing mission of NASA's Apollo program. Its crew consisted of Commander Eugene Cernan, Lunar Module Pilot Harrison Schmitt, and Command Module Pilot Ronald Evans. Launched at 00:33 EST on December 7, 1972, the Apollo 17 mission included three days on the lunar surface, extending scientific capability, and used the third Lunar Roving Vehicle (LRV Cernan and Schmitt landed in the Taurus–Littrow valley, and subsequently completed three moonwalks, taking lunar samples and deploying scientific instrumentation. Evans remained in lunar orbit in the Command Service Module (CSM), taking scientific measurements and photography. When the CSM orbited the Moon, nearly half the time would be spent orbiting the far side (dark side), experiencing "loss of signal" to Mission Control in Houston. On day two, Evans came out from behind the Moon and reported to Mission Control saying, "I got

company." Everybody was just kind of taken aback. Mission Control's first reaction was, "Guys, are you joking?" Evans replied, "No, this is not a joke. There is an object flying in formation with me up here, circling the Moon."

When Evans reported that the object was leaving his orbit, he calculated that they had been orbiting in formation for approximately five-and-a-half orbits. He estimated the object was 40 to 45 feet long, and that it was cigar-shaped. Cernan, Evans and Schmitt returned to Earth on December 19, 1972.

Voyager 2

Was a space probe launched by NASA on August 20, 1977, on a mission to study the outer planets. As part of the Voyager program, it was launched 16 days before its twin, Voyager 1, on a trajectory that took longer to reach Jupiter and Saturn, but enabled close encounters with Uranus and Neptune. It had been the only spacecraft to have visited either of these two giant planets. Voyager 2 was carrying what NASA calls a 'Golden Record' on board. The record is, "... a kind of time capsule, intended to communicate a story of our Earth to other-worldly beings. The Voyager message is carried by a phonograph record-a 12-inch gold-plated copper disc containing sounds and images selected to portray the diversity of life and culture on Earth."

Voyager 2 sent mission control a bizarre message in an unknown language on April 22, 2010, thirty-three years after its launch. According to the journal, Physics Astronomy, NASA expert Kevin Baines said, "At a distance of about 9 billion miles from Earth, the probe suddenly started sending data in a language which they could not decipher. Something or someone changed the communications system of the space probe Voyager 2." Mr. Baines reportedly said subsequent analysis found that a component in a binary code system had been changed from 0 to 1. He added, "The Voyager team could not find any defect with any of the other systems. Only one specific system was changed."

It was argued that such a specific change to the computer system suggested that the probe had been tampered with. It is unlikely this change could have originated from Earth since it requires a large radio antenna for communication, of which only a few exist on Earth.

Chapter 10
Federal Aviation Administration
Incidences

Japan Airlines UFO Incident – Alaska 1986

On November 17, 1986, the crew of a Japan Airlines (JAL) Boeing 747-200F cargo plane was in route from De Gaulle airport (CDG) in Paris to Narita International Airport (NRT) near Tokyo, with a cargo of Beaujolais wine. On the Reykjavík to Anchorage section of the trip, the routine cargo flight entered Alaska on auto-pilot, cruising at 565 mph, altitude 35,000 ft.

At 17:09, the Anchorage Air Traffic Control (ATC) advised a new heading towards Talkeetna, Alaska. Two minutes later, Captain Kenju Terauchi, an ex-fighter pilot with more than 10,000 hours flight experience, noticed two craft to his far left, at 2,000 ft. below his altitude. The way that they were pacing his flight path and speed, he assumed they were military aircraft. At 17:18 the two objects abruptly veered to a position about 500 ft to 1,000 ft in front of the jumbo jet, and activated "... a kind of reverse thrust, and their lights became dazzlingly bright," according to Terauchi's statement. To match the speed of the aircraft from their sideways approach, the objects displayed what Terauchi described as a disregard for inertia: "The thing was flying as if there was no such thing as gravity. It sped up, then stopped, then flew at our speed, in our direction, so that to us it appeared to be standing still. The next instant it changed course.... In other words, the flying object had overcome gravity." The 'reverse thrust' caused a bright flare for three to seven seconds, to the extent that captain Terauchi could feel their warmth.

Air Traffic Control was notified of the encounter at 17:19, but ATC could not confirm any traffic in the area after three to five minutes, the objects positioned into a side-to-side configuration, which they maintained for another 10 minutes. They accompanied the aircraft with an undulating motion, and some back and forth rotation of the jet nozzles, which seemed to be under automatic control, causing them to flare with more, then less luminosity. Each object had a square shape, consisting of two rectangular arrays of what appeared to be glowing nozzles or thrusters, separated by a dark central section. Captain Terauchi speculated in his drawings, that the objects appeared cylindrical depending on the angle of view. The observed movement of the nozzles could be ascribed to the cylinders' rotation. The objects left abruptly, moving to a point below the horizon to the east in the vicinity of Mt. Denali.

At this time, Captain Terauchi noticed a pale band of light that mirrored the UFOs altitude, speed and direction. Setting their onboard radar scope to a 25 nautical miles range, he confirmed an object in the expected 10 o'clock direction at about 8 ½ miles distance, and informed ATC of its presence. Anchorage found nothing on their radar, but moments later, NORAD Regional Operations Control Center (ROCC) at Elmendorf AFB reported a "surge primary return" directly in JAL's flight path.

As the city lights of Fairbanks began to illuminate the object, Captain Terauchi observed the outline of a gigantic spaceship on his port side that was "twice the size of an aircraft carrier." The object followed in the same relative position as the JAL jet throughout its descent from 35,000 to 31,000 ft, and a 360 degree turn. The short-range radar at Fairbanks International Airport (FAI) failed to register the object.

Anchorage ATC offered military intervention, which was declined by the pilot, due to his familiarity with the Mantell incident. The object was not noted by either of two planes which approached JAL 1628 in order to verify a UFO presence, by which time JAL 1628 had also lost sight of it. JAL 1628 arrived safely in Anchorage at 18:20.

Chicago O'Hare 2006 UFO Incident

Sightings of an unidentified flying object at Chicago O'Hare International Airport (ORD) occurred on November 7, 2006, at 16:15 CST. A total of 12 United Airlines (UAL) employees reported seeing an object, and were certain that it was not an airplane, a jet, or any other kind of propeller-driven aircraft. The Federal Aviation Administration declined to investigate the incident because the UFO was not seen on radar, and called it a "weather phenomenon."

Authorities received a report that a group of twelve airport employees were witnessing a metallic, saucer-shaped craft hovering over Gate C-17.

The object was first spotted by a ramp employee, who was pushing back UAL Flight 446, departing ORD for Charlotte/Douglas International Airport (CLT) in North Carolina. The employee apprised Flight 446's crew of the object above their aircraft. The object was also witnessed by pilots, airline management and mechanics. No air traffic controllers saw the object, and it did not indicate on their radar displays.

Witnesses described the object as completely silent, 6 to 24 feet in diameter, and dark gray in color. One described a disc-shaped craft hovering over the airport, stating that it was "obviously not clouds." The witness said that the object hovered, and then shot through the clouds at high velocity, leaving a clear blue hole in the cloud layer which lasted for a minute or so.

According to the Chicago Tribune's Jon Hilkevitch, "The disc was visible for approximately five minutes and was seen by close to a dozen United Airlines employees, ranging from pilots to supervisors, who heard chatter on the radio and raced out to view it."

Both UAL and the FAA initially denied that they had any information on the O'Hare UFO sighting until the Chicago Tribune filed a Freedom of Information Act (FOIA) request. The FAA then ordered an internal review of air-traffic communications tapes to comply with the Chicago Tribune FOIA request. This action uncovered a call by the United supervisor to an FAA manager in the airport tower regarding the UFO sightings.

The FAA stance concluded that the sighting was caused by a "weather phenomenon", and that the agency would therefore not be investigating the incident. According to astronomer Mark Hammergren, weather conditions on the day of the sighting were right for a "hole-punch cloud", an unusual weather phenomenon.

UFO supporters have argued that the FAA's refusal to look into the incident contradicts the agency's mandate to investigate possible security breaches at American airports, such as in this case; an object witnessed by numerous airport employees, and officially reported on record by at least one of them, hovering in plain sight, over one of the busiest airports in the world. Some witnesses interviewed by the Chicago Tribune were apparently "upset" that federal officials declined to further investigate the matter.

Chapter 11

Miscellaneous UFO Incidences

Trans-en-Provence, France 1961

On January 8, 1981, outside the town of Trans-en-Provence, in the French department of Var, an unidentified flying object is claimed to have left physical evidence in an agricultural field in the form of burnt residue. It was described in Popular Mechanics as, "Perhaps the most completely and carefully documented [UFO] sighting of all time."

At 17:00, Renato Nicolai was at his home constructing a concrete shelter for an outside water pump. His home was on a raised area that overlooked the land. Nicolai noticed that it was becoming cold, and then he heard a "sort of faint whistling". He turned his attention toward the sound, and in front of him at tree-top height, at the very edge of his property was a "device in the air". He distinctly remembered the device "was not spinning". Furthermore, it was "coming lower to the ground". He made his way to a stone cabin, which was about 160 feet away from the object. He described the "device" as having the appearance of two plates, one inverted on top of the other, with the color like lead gray, and measuring about 5 feet in height and 8 feet in diameter. It had a "ridge" all the way around its circumference.

Nicolai continued, "Under the machine, I saw two kinds of pieces as it was lifting off. They could be reactors or feet. There were also two other circles which looked like trap doors. The two reactors, or feet, extended about 8 in below the body of the machine." He claimed that the object took off almost immediately, rising above the tree line and departing to the northeast. It left burn marks on the ground where it had set down. Nicolai had been a short distance away from where the craft landed, and waited a few moments until he was satisfied that it had gone.

The following day, Nicolai notified the local gendarmerie of the event, on the advice of his neighbor's wife, Mrs. Morin. The gendarmerie interviewed Nicolai at length, took photographs of the scene, and collected soil and plant samples from the field. The case was later sent for further review by Groupe d'Étude des Phénomènes Aérospatiaux Non-Identifiés (GEIPAN), as it was known at that time.

GEIPAN analyses indicated that the ground had been compressed by a mechanical pressure of about 4 or 5 tons, and heated to between 300 and 600° C (572 - 1,112° F). Trace amounts of phosphate and zinc were found in the sample material, and analysis of alfalfa grown near the landing site showed chlorophyll levels between 30% and 50% lower than expected.

Nicolai had initially believed that the object was an experimental military device, given the close proximity of the site to the Canjuers military base. However, GEIPAN's investigation focused on conventional explanations, such as atmospheric or natural terrestrial phenomena. Despite a joint investigation by GEIPAN and the gendarmerie, which lasted for two years, no plausible explanation has been established.

Some French scientists insist that the GEIPAN investigation was flawed, especially with the study of physical traces. The police report said that the traces, which appeared on an active road, looked like it had been made by the tire of a car. This explanation was dismissed by GEIPAN because of the sole witness saying otherwise. The physical traces shown on the photos are not perfect circles, in fact there are two more-or-less semicircles crossing over each other. Also, a circular shape does not coincide with the description of the UFO made by Nicolai. In an interview for French television, Nicolai confirmed that there were vehicles passing by on the road at the time of the sighting.

Shag Harbor Incident of 1967

The first indication of this mysterious occurrence came from local residents who noticed strange orange lights in the sky on the night of October 4, 1967. Most witnesses agreed that there were four orange lights in the skies above this small community in Nova Scotia. Five teenagers watched the lights flash in sequence, then suddenly dive at a 45 degree angle toward the ocean's surface. The witnesses were surprised that the lights did not dive into the water, but seemed to float on the water, approximately one-half mile from the shore.

At first, observers thought they were watching a tragic airplane crash, and quickly reported as much to the Royal Canadian Mounted Police (RCMP), who were located nearby at Barrington Passage. Coincidentally, Constable Ron Pound had already witnessed the strange lights himself as he drove Highway 3 in route to Shag Harbor. Pound felt that he was seeing 4 lights, all attached to one flying craft. He estimated the craft to be about 60 feet long.

Constable Pound made his way to the shore in order to get a closer look at the unusual sight. He was accompanied by Police Corporal Victor Werbieki, Constable Ron O'Brien, and a dozen or so local residents. Pound clearly saw a yellow light slowly moving on the water, leaving yellowish foam in its wake. All eyes were glued on the light as it slowly slipped into the icy waters. Canadian Coast Guard Cutter #101 and other local boats rushed to the spot of the sighting, but by the time they arrived, the light itself was gone. However, the crewmen could still see the yellow foam, indicating that something had possibly submerged. Nothing else could be found that night, and the search was called off at 03:00. The RCMP radioed the Rescue Coordination Center in Halifax, as well as The bi-national North American Aerospace Defense Command's (NORAD) radar station, located in Baccaro, on Nova Scotia's southern tip. They were told that there were no missing, or unusual aircraft reported that evening, either civilian, or military.

The following day, the Rescue Coordination Center filed a report with Canadian Forces Headquarters in Ottawa. This report stated that something had hit the water in Shag Harbor, but the object was of "unknown origin." The Her Majesty's Canadian Ship (HMCS) Granby was ordered to the location, where divers searched the bottom of the ocean for several days, but without positive results. The object that dove into the waters of the harbor had just as soon left the Shag Harbor area, ostensibly traveling underwater for 25 miles to the top-secret Canadian Forces Station at Shelburne, Nova Scotia. The Government Point submarine detection base was a shore terminus for the Sound Surveillance System from 1955 to 1994, and run cooperatively between the U.S. Navy and Canadian Forces. A Navy detachment was sent to Shelburne, where SONAR had picked up the object, and naval vessels positioned over the Unidentified Submerged Object (USO) After a couple of days, the military was planning a salvage operation, when a second USO joined the first. Common belief at the time was that the second craft had arrived to render aid to the first.

The Navy decided to wait and watch. After a week of monitoring the two USOs, some of the naval vessels were sent to investigate a Russian submarine which had entered Canadian waters. At this point, the two underwater craft made their move. They travelled to the Gulf of Maine, putting distance between them and the pursuing Navy vessels then broke the surface and sped away into the skies.

Southern California UFOs

A person would think that if UFOs had alien visitors onboard or that they were super-secret Black Ops crafts from Russia, China or the United States, that the number of sightings would be relatively small. Normally, UFO sightings are either by themselves, or in a group of less than a dozen.

On June 14, 1992 in Topanga Canyon, California large numbers of independent witnesses reported observing hundreds of mysterious strange metallic flying crafts, mysterious lights, and UFOs in the Santa Monica Mountains. According to witnesses in different parts of the canyon, over 200 craft were seen in one night. A husband and wife say that they each counted a little over 100 oval shaped objects with no windows, no wings or empennage, and no visible engine or exhaust plume.

The United State Military has about 3,000 known aircraft. The U.S. general aviation fleet in has 213,375 aircraft, and the commercial carrier fleet is 7,397. For a sample, a large carrier like Alaska Airlines has only 330 aircraft, of which about 200 are flying in the air at any given moment. The U.S. Navy Aircraft Carriers typically accommodate about 90 aircraft of different types, but typically number 64. So the UFOs seen over California that evening are comparable to the number of planes aboard two Aircraft Carriers, and approximately half of all the planes in Alaska Airlines fleet.

In November of 2004, the U.S. Navy's Nimitz Carrier Strike Group 11 (CSG-11) was conducting combat training exercises in the Pacific Ocean, about 100 miles off the coast of San Diego, California. Encounters with over 100 oval shaped unidentified objects were verified by official U.S. Navy reports, and released through the Freedom of Information Act (FOIA). Pilots from the other naval eyewitness descriptions matched the same descriptions as reported in the Topanga Canyon incident of 1992.

The first question that I always have when reading about UFOs is, where are they coming from or going to, and what are they looking for? Examples of three of the most famous UFO reports are: the Roswell New Mexico incident of July 1947; Shag Harbor Nova Scotia UFO/USO incident of October 1967; and the Rendlesham Forest Incident of December 1980.

- The Roswell UFO can be traced directly to the nearby White Sands Missile Range (Proving Ground) in New Mexico, where Dr. Wernher von Braun and his team were testing rockets powerful enough to escape Earth's gravity.
- The Shag Harbor UFO can be traced directly to the location of a top-secret U.S. military base, disguised as an oceanographic institute. The facility used underwater microphones and magnetic detection devices to track enemy submarines, but its true purpose wasn't revealed until the 1980s.

- In the Rendlesham Forest Incident is in the proximity to the British/ U.S. military bases at Royal Air Force Bentwaters, and Woodbridge. The bases had been used to store most of the nuclear weapons in Europe. The UFOs left their calling card by burning a hole through the hardened bunker that housed the nuclear arms.

A disproportionate number UFO reports came from the California coastline, from Santa Barbara on the central California coast to Long Beach in Los Angeles County in the south. The area has been known for many years as a test area for many United States 'Black Projects'.

One of the most active UFO areas in the world centers on the Catalina Channel, off the southern California coast. This body of water has for at least thirty years been the scene of myriad UFO reports. Witnesses have report sighting UFOs flying out to sea and others flying toward the shore from the sea. Surface sightings are reported of hazy craft which cruise leisurely in full view of military installations, aerial spheres bobbing in oscillating flight, gigantic cloud-cigars, and at least one report of an underwater USO with its occupants wearing uniforms. There are so many reports of UFOs in this area that Santa Catalina Island offers UFO tours. The California coast is heavily populated with covert development facilities, e.g. Vandenberg AFB, Lockheed-Martin Skunk Works, and Beale AFB.

Observers all over the Palos Verdes Peninsula reported UFOs coming out of the water from the San Pedro Channel. Many reported sighting squadrons of cigar-, orb-, and saucer-shaped UFOs performing complex maneuvers in broad daylight. One incident was witnessed by a crowd at Redondo Beach. Those present reported seeing a large glowing UFO that landed on the water and as the crowd looked on, it sank beneath the waves. Other onlookers told of seeing strange looking men coming out of a UFO, wearing black leather pants, white belts and light colored shirts. In the 1970s, many families were going down to the beach at Point Dume at night to watch the multi colored UFOs that would sink under the water at times.

Why Point Dume? There is a massive underwater anomaly, discovered in 2009, six miles off the coast of Point Dume (34° 1'23.31 N, 118° 59'45.64 W) that is referred to as, 'The Malibu Anomaly' or 'Sycamore Knoll'. The underwater feature, some believe an underwater base, is an oval shaped object with a large flat top, and what appears to be pillars or columns that seem to reveal an entrance. The anomaly is approximately 2,000 feet below the surface of the water, measuring nearly 3 miles wide. Geologists believe that it is a thrust fault, and since it is 2000 feet below the surface, they are reluctant to explore the depths. A TV documentary team working for the Science Channel sent divers for an exploratory look at the irregularity, and reported seeing lights below them, and hearing strange sounds.

Another TV documentary program shown on the Discovery Channel reported that there was a 50-story building in the Knoll that was a half a mile wide, but did not say how they obtained the information, which seems highly suspect.

A Ham radio operator, Emmet, had used the 12-meter band frequency to communicate with friends in New Zealand, and heard strange signals every 54 kilocycles. Emmett asked several of his colleagues from Catalina Island and Oxnard if they heard the sound, and was surprised to hear that they did not. Emmet's home is located adjacent to the Sycamore Knoll at Point Dume. At first, the broadcasts sound like data dumps or normal telemetry, but upon further observation, the electronic blips do not match with standard shortwave stations or data.

If the Sycamore Knoll is a base for a U.S. 'Black Project', foreign base, alien base, or a just a natural subsurface formation, we may never know. Most likely, the US Government knows, but they prefer to it a secret instead of releasing the information to the public.

Another point of interest is located at 28° 54' 36.0" N, 118° 15' 36.0" W, the coordinates which had been documented by the Ticonderoga-class guided missile cruiser USS Princeton, as part of the flotilla of CSG-11. Using the U.S.'s most advanced AN/SPY-1B passive scanning phased-array radar, Princeton reported that 100 UFOs dropped off the radar screen and disappeared. The event occurred near Guadalupe Island in Baja, Mexico, which is home to Campamento Militar Isla Guadalupe, a Mexican Military Base. The area is off limits to all civilians, but local fishermen have reported seeing strange lights coming from the ocean.

The Phoenix Lights of 1997

The 'Phoenix Lights' were a series of UFO sightings in the skies over Arizona, Nevada, and Sonora, Mexico on Thursday, March 13, 1997.

Lights of varying descriptions were seen and photographed by thousands of people between 19:30 and 22:30 local time. There were allegedly two distinct events: A triangular formation of lights seen to pass over the state, and a series of stationary lights seen only in the Phoenix area. The United States Air Force identified the second group of lights as flares dropped by A-10 Warthog aircraft that were on training exercises at the Barry Goldwater Range in southwest Arizona.

Witnesses claim to have observed a huge square-shaped UFO containing five spherical lights, possibly light-emitting engines. Fife Symington, the governor at the time, was one witness to the incident which he later referred to as, "otherworldly."

At about 19:55, a man reported seeing a V-shaped object above Henderson, Nevada. He said it was about the size of a Boeing 747, sounded like "rushing wind", and had six lights on its leading edge. The Triangular shaped object reportedly traversed in a northwest to southeast direction. A former police officer from Paulden, Arizona is claimed to have been the second person to report the object after leaving his house at about 20:15. Driving north, he allegedly saw a cluster of reddish or orange lights in the sky, comprising four lights together and a fifth light trailing them. Each of the individual lights in the formation appeared to the witness as two separate point sources of orange light. He returned home and peered through binoculars, watching the lights disappear to the south over the horizon.

Lights were also reportedly seen in the areas of Prescott and Prescott Valley. At approximately 20:17, callers began reporting the object as "definitely solid", because it blocked out much of the starry sky as it passed over. John Kaiser was standing outside with his wife and sons in Prescott Valley when they noticed a cluster of lights to the west-northwest of their position. The lights formed a triangular pattern, but all of them appeared to be red, except the light at the nose of the object, which was distinctly white. The object, or objects, which had been observed for approximately 2 to 3 minutes with binoculars, then passed directly overhead, and then bank to the right, disappearing into the night sky to the southeast. The craft's altitude could not be determined, but it was fairly low, and made no sound whatsoever.

The National UFO Reporting Center (NUFORC) received the following report from Prescott:

While doing astrophotography, I observed five yellow-white lights flying in a "V" formation, moving slowly from the northwest, across the sky to the northeast, then turn almost due south and continue until out of sight. The point of the V was in the direction of movement, and had three lights that were fairly close together. The two other lights were farther back on the object. During the NW-NE transit, one of the trailing lights moved up and joined with the front three, then dropped back to the previous position. I estimated that the three front lights covered about 0.5 degrees of sky, and the whole group of five lights covered about 1 full degree.

In the town of Dewey, 10 miles east of Prescott, six people saw a large cluster of lights while driving northbound on Highway 69. Tim Ley and his wife Bobbi, his son Hal and his grandson Damien first saw the lights when they were above Prescott Valley about 65 miles away. At first they appeared as five separate and distinct lights in an arc-shape, like on top of a balloon. They soon realized that the lights appeared to be moving towards them, and over the next ten or so minutes, as the craft approached, the distance between the lights increased and took on the shape of an inverted V. Eventually, when the lights appeared to be only a couple of miles away, the witnesses could make out a shape that looked like a 60-degree triangle, with five lights set into it - one at the front and two on each side.

The triangular-shaped object was now about 100 to 150 feet above them, traveling so slowly it appeared to hover, and was totally silent. It passed over their heads and went through a mountain pass near Squaw Peak in the direction of Phoenix Sky Harbor International Airport (PHX). Witnesses in Glendale, a suburb northwest of Phoenix, saw the object pass overhead at approximately 20:45 at an altitude high enough to become obscured by thin clouds.

The Phoenix 'Triangle'

When the Triangle entered the Phoenix area, Bill Greiner, a cement driver hauling a load from a mountain north of Phoenix, described the lights: "I'll never be the same. Before this, if anybody had told me they saw a UFO, I would've said, 'Yeah and I believe in the Tooth Fairy.' Now I've got a whole new viewpoint, and I may be just a dumb truck driver, but I've seen something that doesn't belong here." Greiner stated that the lights hovered over the area for more than two hours.

A report came from a young man in the Kingman area, traveling along dark Mojave Desert roads en route to Los Angeles, called from a public phone booth to report having seen a large and bizarre cluster of stars moving slowly in the northern sky.

A repeat of the Triangular aerial lights occurred February 6, 2007, and was recorded by the local Fox News television station. According to military officials as well as the Federal Aviation Administration (FAA), these lights were explained as flares, dropped by F-16 aircraft training at Luke Air Force Base.

On April 21, 2008, lights were again reported over North Phoenix by local residents. According to witnesses, the lights formed a vertical line, then spread apart and made a diamond shape. The lights also formed a U-shape at one time. Tony Toporek videotaped the lights. He was talking to neighbors at 8 p.m. when the lights appeared. He went and grabbed his camera to record the event. A valley resident reported that shortly after the lights appeared, three jets were seen heading west in the same direction as the objects. An official from Luke Air Force Base denied any United States Air Force activity in the area.

The most frequently seen sequence of events shows what appears to be an arc of lights appearing one by one, and then going out one by one. UFO advocates claim that these images show that the lights were some form of "running light" or other aircraft illumination along the leading edge of a large craft — estimated to be as large as a mile in diameter — hovering over the city of Phoenix., other similar sequences, taken over a half hour period, show differing numbers of lights in a V or arrowhead array. Thousands of witnesses throughout Arizona also reported a silent, mile-wide V or boomerang shaped craft. A significant number of witnesses reported that the craft was silently gliding overhead at low altitude. The first-hand witnesses consistently reported that the lights appeared as, "canisters of swimming light", while the underbelly of the craft was undulating, "like looking through water."

UFO skeptics claim that the video is evidence that surrounding mountains had partially obstructed the views from certain angles, thereby bolstering the claim that the lights were more distant than UFO enthusiasts claim.

Cognitech, an independent video laboratory, superimposed video imagery taken of the Phoenix Lights onto video that was taken during the daytime at the same location. In the composite image, the lights are seen to extinguish at the moment they reach the Estrella Mountain Range, which is visible in the daytime, but invisible in the footage shot at night.

Wind direction measured independently by several weather stations in the Phoenix area and archived by the National Climate Data Center (NCDC) is consistent with reports about the movement of the lights. During the events, wind direction was changing from blowing towards the east, then to the north, and changing again, blowing towards the south. This supports the hypothesis that the flying objects were wind driven, and could simply have been balloons or flares.

There is some controversy as to how best to classify the reports on the night in question. Some are of the opinion that the differing nature of the eyewitness reports indicates that several unidentified objects were in the area, each of which was its own separate 'event'. This is largely dismissed by skeptics as an over-extrapolation from the statistical deviation that is common in subjective eyewitness accounts. The media and most skeptical investigators have largely preferred to split the sightings into two distinct classes, a first and second event.

Two separate explanations are offered:

The first event, the "V" which appeared over northern Arizona and gradually traveled south over nearly the entire length of the state, was the "wedge-shaped" object reported by then-Governor Symington and many others. This event started at about 20:15 over the Prescott area, and was seen south of Tucson by 20:45.

The first event still has no provable explanation, but evidence exists that the lights were in fact airplanes. According to an article by reporter Janet Gonzales that appeared in the Phoenix New Times, videotape of the V shape shows the lights moving as separate entities, not as a single object; a phenomenon known as illusory contours can cause the human eye to see unconnected lines or dots as forming a single shape.

Mitch Stanley, an amateur astronomer, observed high altitude lights flying in formation using a Dobsonian telescope giving 43× magnification. After observing the lights, he told his mother, who was present at the time, that the lights were aircraft. According to Stanley, the lights were quite clearly individual airplanes; a companion who was with him recalled asking Stanley at the time what the lights were, he replied, "Planes".

The second event involved the set of nine lights appearing to "hover" over the city of Phoenix at around 20:00 local MST. The second event has been more thoroughly covered by the media, due in part to the numerous video images taken of the lights. This was also observed by numerous people who may have thought they were seeing the same lights as those reported earlier.

The U.S. Air Force explained the second event as slow-falling, long-burning LUU-2B/B illumination flares dropped by a flight of four A-10 Warthog aircraft on a training exercise at the Barry Goldwater Range at Luke Air Force Base. According to this explanation, the flares would have been visible in Phoenix and appeared to hover due to rising heat from the burning flares creating a "balloon" effect on their parachutes, specially designed to slow their descent. The lights then appeared to blink off, as they fell behind the Sierra Estrella, southwest of Phoenix.

A Maryland Air National Guard pilot, Lt. Col. Ed Jones, responding to a March 2007 media query, confirmed that he had flown one of the aircraft in the formation that dropped flares on the night in question. The squadron to which he belonged was based at Davis-Monthan AFB, conducting training sorties to the Barry Goldwater Range. A history of the Maryland Air National Guard that was published in 2000 asserted that the 104th Fighter Squadron was responsible for the incident. The first reports that members of the Maryland Air National Guard were responsible for the incident were published in The Arizona Republic newspaper in July 1997.

Military flares can be seen from hundreds of miles, especially in the wide-open, clear desert environment. Later comparisons of military flare drops were reported on local television stations, showing similarities between the known military flare drops and the Phoenix Lights. An analysis of the luminosity of LUU-2B/B illumination flares, the type which would have been in use by A-10 aircraft at the time, determined that the luminosity of such flares at a range of approximately 50–70 miles would fall well within the range of the lights, as viewed from Phoenix. Dr. Bruce Maccabee did an extensive triangulation of the four videotapes, determining that the objects were near or over the Goldwater Proving Grounds.

In March 2007, Arizona Governor Fife Symington publically admitted that he had witnessed one of the "crafts of unknown origin" in the 1997 event. In an interview with The Daily Courier in Prescott, Arizona, Symington said, "I'm a pilot and I know just about every machine that flies. It was bigger than anything that I've ever seen. It remains a great mystery. Other people saw it, responsible people. I don't know why people would ridicule it." Symington had earlier said, "It was enormous and inexplicable. Who knows where it came from? A lot of people saw it, and I saw it too. It was dramatic. And it couldn't have been flares because it was too symmetrical. It had a geometric outline, a constant shape."

Symington also noted that he had requested information from the Commander of Luke Air Force Base, the General of the National Guard, and the Chief of the Arizona Department of Public Safety. None of the officials he contacted had an answer for what had happened, and were also mystified. Later, he responded to an Air Force explanation that the lights were flares: "As a pilot and a former Air Force Officer, I can definitively say that this craft did not resemble any man made object I'd ever seen. And it was certainly not high-altitude flares because flares don't fly in formation."

Chapter 12

The Aliens

Extraterrestrial Species

Extraterrestrial life is hypothetical. It assumes that life occurs outside of the Earth, and did not originate on planet Earth. Such life might range from the most basic prokaryotes (bacteria or comparable life organisms), to intelligent beings who have established civilizations, quite possibly far more advanced than humanity.

The four most common Extraterrestrial Species (ETs) who are believed to be here on Earth are: Anunnaki, Greys, Nordics, and the Reptilians. The concept of extra-terrestrial life, particularly those with intelligence, has had major cultural impacts, most notably in works of Science Fiction. Over the years, science fiction has communicated scientific ideas, imagined a wide range of possibilities, and influenced public interest in, and perspectives of, life beyond Earthly existence.

Anunnaki Aliens

Various Mesopotamia cultures worship and regard as gods a group of aliens known as the Anunnaki. To the ancient Mesopotamians, their supreme God was known as "An". His children were called Anunna. The added -ki meaning "Earth which denotes that the Anunnaki are the "Children of Anu" which had come down to Earth. The "Children of Anu" (Mesopotamian) eventually translated to "Children of El " in Canaanite culture. The Israelites later adopted El, as God, to become Elohim אֱלֹהִים "sons of God" (ie. Gen 6:4).

The Anunnaki have often been related to the biblical Watchers (Books of Enoch), the "sons of God" in Genesis 6:4 who are the descent of the biblical race of giants or demigods known as "Nephilim".

The Anunnaki helped humans to develop the first human civilization known as "Sumer" in the historical region of southern Mesopotamia (now southern Iraq), emerging during the Chalcolithic and early Bronze Ages between the sixth and fifth millennium BC. and had taught them not only language but other advanced skill sets.

Anunnaki have the appearance resembling that of humans with a life span of over 150 years. They are believed to come from Aldebaran designated Alpha Tauri, a giant star measured to be about 65 light-years from the Sun in the zodiac constellation Taurus. It is believed to host a planet several times the mass of Jupiter, named Aldebaran b.

Anunnaki from ancient Mesopotamia art

Greys Aliens
The Grey alien is typically described as very thin with an oversized head (compared to its body size). They stand 3 ½ to 6 feet tall and weigh anywhere from 50 to 90 pounds. Those who have encountered this type of ET characterize their skin as having the texture of an ocean mammal, like a dolphin or a whale. There are no ears or indentations on the sides of the head. Some accounts have described them as having three or four

webbed fingers and similarly webbed feet. The Grey's primary method of communication seems to be through telepathy. They come from the third and fourth planets of the Zeta Reticuli star system.

It is believed that the small Grey aliens are soulless, biologically-engineered Cyborg races who were created by other aliens to do the "grunt work". The Greys are responsible for the cattle mutilations that have regularly occurred throughout the U.S. They have a genetic disorder in their digestive system that has atrophied and become non-functional. They sustain themselves by using an enzyme or hormonal secretion obtained from the tongues and throats of cows or humans. The secretion, extracted from cows blood, is mixed with other substances that are applied directly onto Grey skin, absorbing the mixture, then excreting the waste from their epidermal layer of skin. Calculations suggest that approximately 43% of all alien sightings in the United States are of the Greys. These beings were apparently responsible for the 1947 Roswell UFO crash, in which alien bodies were recovered. Descriptions and sightings of aliens like the Greys have occurred since the dawn of mankind. The majority of alien abduction cases are reports of Grey alien encounters.

There are two kinds of Greys: Tall Greys (Tall Whites), who are the authority figures; and Small Greys, who are Cyborg servants of the Tall Greys, and are said to come from a planet in the Zeta Reticuli star cluster, which is approximately 37 light years (11.3 parsecs) from Earth.

The Tall Whites are very large, anywhere from 6 to 9 feet tall. They are humanoid, very pale grey or white, and are hairless. They are believed to have originated from the Orion constellation. They oversee the role of the Small Greys. The Talls are understood to carry out 'diplomatic' missions, such as secretly negotiating treaties with Earth's governments. They have been known to intimidate humans in a variety of reported interactions, and behave in a clinical manner reminiscent of a medical physician conducting an experiment. The Talls are mostly involved in genetic experimentation and implantation of devices in humans for monitoring purposes.

Nordic (Pleiadian) Aliens
Ancient civilizations around the world have spoken of "Angelic" beings that descended from the sky, sent by God to assist humanity by sharing their spiritual and emotional wisdom with Earthlings. These mythological entities appear to continue their mission to this day. The Nordics are a

human-like species who first began appearing in the 1950s, claiming to be from the planet Venus, but then changed their story to have originated from the Pleiades star cluster. In either case, it is possible that they wish to keep their true home a secret for security reasons.

They are thought to be the "Angels" represented in many religions and ancient texts. Although generally considered a warmhearted species, Nordics are perhaps the most human in appearance of all ETs, and closely resemble people of Scandinavian descent (hence the name, "Nordic"). They tend to have blonde to reddish hair, blue/green eyes, and stand anywhere from 5-7 feet tall. They can easily pass as Earthlings, and those who have been in contact with this race state that their appearance allows them to freely explore our planet.

Nordics are generally observers, sometimes viewing events and contactees from within their craft, most of which have been described as spherical or cigar-shaped. Nordics often keep their distance from humanity, communicating telepathically and through dreams. Many contactees have claimed to receive channeled messages of peace and love from these beings, and much of the information available about the species is obtained in this manner. The Nordics are concerned with the spiritual evolution of humanity, and often remind contactees that we are closely related to them.

Notable abductees include: Travis Walton, a logger in Arizona, Billy Meier, a Swedish farmer, and George Adamski, an early Nordic contactee of the 1950s. It is also rumored that U.S. President Dwight Eisenhower had a secret meeting with a group of Nordic extraterrestrials who were attempting to convince the United States to disarm its nuclear missile program in exchange for advanced technology. The message that seems to follow each encounter with the Nordic species is the importance of spiritual awareness and the stewardship of our planet.

Reptilian Aliens

Reptilians are large, scaly beings that stand at almost 9 feet, and are extremely unpleasant. They are highly intelligent, and can communicate both verbally as well as telepathically. The Reptilians have been around since the beginning of mankind, and have been thought to have given the human race much of its early technology, including construction of the Egyptian, Mayan, and Asian pyramids. Apparently, they thought of themselves as gods, which assisted in the creation of human religions. Reptilians are the most dangerous to our existence as humans, and have very little respect for mankind.

Personally, I feel that there are only two types of Extra-terrestrials: the Greys who are considered to be a combination of a mechanical and living biologic (Cyborg), and the Nordics who have been well documented by human abductees, as well as having been recovered from crashed UFOs. I think the others on the list are from people with over-active imaginations.

The following is an alphabetical list of extraterrestrial species, as derived from the internet:

Alleged Extraterrestrial Species

Agharians (Aghartians)	Dragonworms	Insiders	Pleiadeans
Alpha-Draconians	Dwarfs	Janosian	Re-Brid
Altairians	Eva-Borgs	Korendian	Reptilian
Amphibians	Gizan (Gizahn)	Leviathans	Sasquatch
Anakim	Grails	Lyran	Serpents
Anunnaki	Greens, The	Martians	Sirians
Antarctican	Greys, The	Mib's	Solarians
Atlans	Gypsies	Moon-Eyes, The	Synthetics
Bernarians	Hav-Musuvs (Suvians)	Mothmen	Telosian
Burrowers	Hu-Brid	Nagas	Teros
Cetians (Tau Cetians)	Hyadeans	Nordic (Pleiadian)	Ulterrans
Chameleon	Hybrids	Orange, The	Ummites
Chupacabra	Iguanoids	Orions	Vegans
Draco-Borgs	Ikels (Satyrs)	Phoenians	Venusian

Alien Abduction

Sometimes also called Abduction Phenomenon, Alien Abduction Syndrome, or simply 'UFO abduction', the alleged 'abductee' describes "subjectively real experiences" of capture by non-human entities (ETs), and subjected to physical and psychological experimentation. Most scientists and mental health professionals explain these experiences as suggestibility, e.g. false memory syndrome, sleep paralysis, deception, and psychopathology.

Widespread publicity was generated by the Betty and Barney Hill abduction case of 1961, culminating in an eerie made-for-television film broadcast in 1975 (starring James Earl Jones and Estelle Parsons) dramatizing the events. The Hill incident was probably the prototypical abduction case and was perhaps the first in which the claimant described beings that later became widely known as the Greys, and in which the beings were said to explicitly identify an extraterrestrial origin.

The 1980s brought a major degree of mainstream attention to the subject of alien abduction as being within the realm of plausibility. Alien abductions were considered far more common than earlier suspected; it was estimate that tens of thousands (or more) North Americans had been taken by unexplained beings. The precise number of alleged abductees is uncertain. One of the earliest studies of abductions found 1,700 claimants, while contested surveys assert that more than 5 percent of the general population might have been abducted.

Investigations into the alleged abductions revealed that individual abductees averaged 40 years of age, some of whom were rejected by the aliens for what the humans inferred to be for medical reasons. One man reported being rejected because he had recently undergone a vasectomy. Alien rejections could also be due to the fact that people over the age of 40 are less likely to have the capacity to biologically reproduce.

Although abduction and other UFO-related reports are usually made by adults, sometimes young children report similar experiences. These child-reports often feature very specific details that are in common with reports made by adults, including the circumstances, narrative, entities and aftermaths of the alleged occurrences. Often, the young abductees have family members who have reported having similar experiences, especially families living in the proximity of a military base.

Abduction victims often join self-help communities of victims and may resort to questionable regression therapy, similarly to that of other victims of child abuse. The Center for Unidentified Flying Object Studies (CUFOS) defines an alien abductee as a person who has been taken against their will by apparent non-humans, who are taken to a special place which they perceive to be a spaceship. They experience physical examination, and are in some form of communication with the alien beings. Communication may be perceived as telepathic rather than verbal. The memory of the experience may be conscious or 'recovered' through means of hypnosis, such as was the case with Betty and Barney Hill.

The entire alien abduction event is precisely arranged. All of the procedures are predetermined. There is no standing around and deciding what to do next. The beings are task-oriented, and there is no indication that any aspect of alien lives is revealed outside of performing the abduction procedures.

Though not all abductions feature these events, the following sequence generally occurs:

Capture
The abductee is somehow rendered incapable of resisting and taken from terrestrial surroundings to an alien spacecraft.

Examination and Procedures
Invasive physiological and psychological procedures are performed on the abductee, and on occasion, simulated behavioral situations or sexual liaisons may occur.

Conference
The alien abductors communicate with the abductee directing them to interact with specific individuals for some purpose. Communication is typically telepathic, but sometimes the abductee's native language is vocalized.

Tour
The abductees are given a tour of their captors' vessel, though this is disputed by some researchers who consider this definition a confabulation in order to fill in the memory gaps.

Loss of Time
Abductees often rapidly forget the majority of their experience, either as a result of fear, medical/psychological intervention, or both.

Return
The abductees are returned to Earth, occasionally placed in a different location from where they were taken, sometimes having new injuries or disheveled clothing and appearance.

Theophany

Coinciding with their immediate return, abductees may have a profound sense of love, a 'high' similar to those induced by psychoactive drugs. Many feel that they have had a "mystical experience", often accompanied by a feeling of oneness with God and the universe, or a sense of sympathy for their abductors (Stockholm Syndrome).

Aftermath

The abductee must cope with the psychological, physical, and social effects of the experience.

Abduction claimants report "unusual feelings" preceding the onset of an abduction experience. These feelings manifest as a compulsive desire to be at a certain place at a certain time, or as expectations that something "familiar yet unknown," will soon occur. Abductees also report feeling severe, undirected anxiety, even though nothing unusual has actually occurred. This period of foreboding can last for up to several days before the abduction actually occurs, or it may be completely absent. Eventually, the experiencer will undergo an apparent "shift" into an Altered State of Consciousness (ASC).

British abduction researchers have called this change in consciousness "the Oz Factor." External sounds cease to have any significance to the experiencer and fall out of perception. They report feeling introspective and unusually calm. This stage marks a transition from normal activity to a state of "limited self-willed mobility." As consciousness shifts from 'real world' to ASC, one or more lights appear, either emanating from the alien space craft, but sometimes transforming into the alien figures themselves. Occasionally all of this is accompanied by a strange mist.

As the alleged abduction proceeds, claimants say they walked or were levitated into an alien craft. Many times, the person is transported through solid objects such as walls, ceilings or a closed window. Alternatively, they may experience rising through a tunnel or along a beam of light, with or without the abductors accompanying them, into the awaiting craft.

The examination phase of the so-called 'Abduction Narrative' is characterized by the performance of medical procedures and examinations by apparently alien beings against or irrespective of the will of the experiencer. Such procedures often focus on sex and reproductive biology.

However, the literature holds reports of a wide variety of procedures allegedly performed by the beings. The entity that appears to be in charge of the operation is often taller than the others involved, and is sometimes described as appearing to be of a different species.

There are differences between human medical practice, and the reported procedures conducted by the abductors. The purpose of the examination was routine human diagnosis and treatment, versus alien scientific examination of an unfamiliar species. The difference in the alien's level of technology may render certain kinds of manual procedures unnecessary.

The abductors' areas of interest appear to be the cranium, nervous system, skin, reproductive system, and to a lesser degree, the joints. Systems that are omitted almost entirely include the human cardiovascular system, the respiratory system below the pharynx, and the lymphatic system. The abductors also appear to ignore the upper region of the abdomen in favor of the lower one. The abductors do not appear to wear gloves during the "examination." Other constants of terrestrial medicine like pills and tablets are missing from abduction accounts, although sometimes abductees are asked to drink liquids. Injections also seem to be rare, and intravenous injections are almost completely absent, as are the common tongue depressors.

After the medical exam, the abductees often report other procedures being performed, such as those which abduction researchers refer to as Imaging, Envisioning, Staging, and Testing. Imaging procedures consist of an abductee made to view screens displaying images and scenes that appear to be specially chosen for that individual, with the intent to provoke emotional responses. Envisioning is a similar procedure, with the primary difference that the images being viewed seem to be projected into the experiencer's mind, rather than being displayed on a screen.

Staging procedures involve vivid, hallucinatory mental visualizations by the abductee who interacts with the illusion, much like a role player or an actor.

Testing marks something of a departure from the above procedures in that it lacks the emotional analysis feature. During testing, the experiencer is placed in front of a complicated electronic device and is instructed to operate it. The experiencer is often confused, saying that they do not know how to operate it. However, when they actually set about performing the task, the abductee will find that they do, in fact, operate the machine quite well.

Abductees of all ages and genders sometimes report being subjected to a "child presentation." As its name implies, the child presentation involves the abductee viewing the image of a child. It may appear to be neither human, nor the same species as the abductors. Instead, the child will almost always share characteristics of both species. These children are labeled by experiencers as hybrids between humans and their abductors, usually Greys.

Rare abduction episodes have been reported between the medical examination and the return. After displaying cold, callous disregard toward the abductees, sometimes the alien beings change drastically in behavior once the initial medical exam is completed. They become more relaxed and hospitable toward their captive, and lead him or her carefully away from the site of the examination. The entities then hold a conference with the experiencer, wherein they discuss things relevant to the abduction phenomenon. This usually includes five general categories: an Interrogation session, Explanatory segment, Task assignment, Warnings, and Prophecies.

Tours of the abductors' craft are a rare, but seemingly recurring feature of the abduction narrative. The tour seems to be given by the abductors as a courtesy, in response to the harshness and physical rigors of the forced medical examination. Sometimes abductees reported traveling in an orbit around Earth or to what appear to be other planets. Some abductees find that the experience is terrifying, particularly if the aliens are of a more fearsome species, or if the abductee was subjected to extensive probing and medical testing.

Eventually, the abductors will return the abductees, usually to exactly the same location and circumstances they were in before being taken. Usually, explicit memories of the abduction experience will not be present, and the abductee will only realize they have experienced "missing time" upon checking a timepiece. Sometimes the abductors appear to make mistakes when returning their captives. One type of common mistake is failing to return the experiencer to the same spot that they were taken from initially. This can be as simple as a different room in the same house, or abductees have even found themselves outside, with all the doors of the house locked from the inside like they never left home. Another common and amusing error is putting the abductee's clothes (pajamas) on backwards.

Abductees seek hypnotherapists to try to resolve issues such as missing time or unexplained physical symptoms such as muscle pain or headaches. This usually involves two phases, an information gathering stage, in which the hypnotherapist asks about unexplained illnesses or unusual phenomena followed by hypnosis and guided imagery to facilitate recall.

While some corroborated accounts seem to support the literal reality of the abduction experience, like the Hill case. Others seem to support a psychological explanation for the origin of the phenomenon.

Alien Implants

The most controversial aspect of the UFO phenomenon and by far the most bone-chilling have to be that of alien abduction. Typically, the day after their abduction, the Abductees notice marks — which may or may not feel sore — that they can't explain; they've no knowledge of how they were acquired. Bruises are typical, believed to have been left by restraints applied by the abductors to keep the humans in one place while undergoing the delicate procedures.

Also typical are puncture marks thought to be caused by needles, often in a triangular formation, but sometimes arranged in a grid or geometric pattern. These marks generally fade with time, but some experiencers report having a scar. Other marks are fluorescent and can only be seen under ultraviolet light.

The marks have been found in numerous locations — limbs, torso, face — appearing as both random splotches and deliberate designs. Some are superficial and can be wiped away, but others are not. The splotches are thought to be where the abductee had been bodily handled by their abductors. The red-pink fluorescence is common to abductees who've reported handling human/alien hybrid infants aboard the UFO during their abduction.

When X-rayed, some alien abductees were surprised to discover that their flesh was hosting a small anomalous object under the epidermis. Some of the objects were examined by pathologists before being shipped to independent laboratories for further detailed analyses. The labs included New Mexico Tech, and the National Institute of Discovery of Science (NIDS).

The results were far from conclusive, and were highly perplexing. Normally, when a foreign object penetrates flesh, it provokes an inflammatory response around it which may lead to fibrosis and the formation of a cyst. The embedded objects had caused no inflammation. It was as if the immune system had been 'persuaded' to accept the objects as an integral part of the body. The pathology analysis found that the objects were encased in a very resilient membrane, gray in color, made up of proteinaceous coagulum, hemosiderin, and keratin. In layman's terms, blood proteins and cells normally found on the outer surface of the skin. Most odd was that the membrane also contained nerve and pressure sensitive cells called proprioceptors that were of a different type to those that should have been present in that part of the anatomy.

Moreover, under UV illumination, the encasing membrane gave off a curious bright green fluorescent light. The lab analysis revealed the objects inside the membranes to have very unusual metallic properties. They were made up of at least 11 elements the closely correlated with the elements found in meteorites.

Over nineteen years, a total of 17 foreign objects were removed from sixteen alien abductees with an implant ranging in size between 6mm and 10mm in length, and about the thickness of a pencil lead. All were close to the bone and the skin's surface with none found in organs or other, deeper internal tissues. A Gauss meter (magnetometer) was passed over the site detected electromagnetic radiation that emitted waves at the 8 hertz, 14 megahertz and 19 gigahertz frequencies. The emissions ceased within 60 to 90 days once the objects were removed, suggesting that they drew energy from their host's body while in place. A scar was found which could have marked the entry point for the implants.

But something else had been observed. Two objects appeared to move under the skin during surgery as if they were trying to avoid extraction, and one object, when unintentionally broken during removal, actually reassembled itself. As incredible as it may seem, this suggests the presence of some sort of 'intelligence' within the implant material. Not all the anomalous objects were metallic. There were three broad categories: metallic, non-metallic and biological; seven fell into the metallic category. Highly significant is that all seven were virtually identical in shape and composition, which strongly suggests a common source of manufacture.

A metallurgical analysis found rare 'meteoritic' metals such as platinum, gallium, rhodium, iridium, germanium, and ruthenium were contained in the implants. Even more strange is the nickel that was found. Nickel is a somewhat common Earth metal, but this nickel possessed an isotopic ratio not known to exist on Earth! An evidence of built-in 'electronic circuitry' made of carbon nanotubes was also analyzed. These are one-atom-thick sheets of carbon rolled into tubes that, depending on the radius and 'chiral rolling angle', can be made to behave either as a metal or a semiconductor. Semiconductors are, of course, used in electronic circuitry. This discovery can only mean one thing: someone or some entity manufactured them using very advanced technology. Bear in mind that it wasn't until 1991 that carbon nanotubes were discovered by human science.

The evidence and its interpretation by experts strongly suggest that the objects have a technologically advanced, non-terrestrial origin, unearthly metal isotopes, seemingly 'intelligent' behavior, electromagnetic emissions, carbon nanotube 'circuitry', etc. Knowing all of this, it is still insufficient to support anything other than informed conjecture about their function and purpose. Much more research is needed to get to the bottom of this mystery.

Well Documented Alien Abductions

There are many skeptics who think that alien encounters are just made up by people who are desperate for attention, and it can't be denied that some of these phony abductions are well-documented and detailed.

Here are ten of the more convincing alien abduction stories:

Betty and Barney Hill (1961)
The alien abduction of Barney and Betty Hill is probably the most famous and well-documented case of its kind. Betty and Barney Hill were an

American couple who claimed to have been abducted by extraterrestrials in a rural portion of New Hampshire on September 19–20, 1961.

The Hills lived in Portsmouth, New Hampshire. Barney (1922–1969) was employed by the U.S. Postal Service, while Betty (1919–2004) was a social worker. Active in a Unitarian congregation, the Hills were also members of the NAACP and community leaders, and Barney sat on a local board of the U.S. Civil Rights Commission.

The alleged UFO sighting happened on September 19, 1961, at around 10:30 p.m. The Hills were driving back to Portsmouth from a vacation in Niagara Falls and Montreal, Quebec, Canada. There were only a few other cars on the road as they made their way home to New Hampshire's seacoast. Just south of Lancaster, New Hampshire, Betty claimed to have observed a bright point of light in the sky that moved erratically and grew bigger and brighter, Betty urged Barney to stop the car for a closer look.

Betty, through binoculars, observed an "odd shaped" craft flashing multicolored lights travel across the face of the moon. Because her sister had confided to her about having a flying saucer sighting several years earlier, Betty thought it might be what she was observing.

The object rapidly descended toward their vehicle causing Barney to stop directly in the middle of the highway. The huge, silent craft hovered approximately 80–100 feet above the Hills' 1957 Chevrolet Bel Air and filled the entire field of the windshield. Carrying his pistol in his pocket, he stepped away from the vehicle and moved closer to the object. Using the binoculars, Barney claimed to have seen about 8 to 11 humanoid figures who were peering out of the craft's windows, seeming to look at him.

Red lights on what appeared to be bat-wing fins began to telescope out of the sides of the craft and a long structure descended from the bottom of the craft. The silent craft approached to what Barney estimated was within 50–80 feet overhead and 300 feet away from him.

Almost immediately, the Hills heard a rhythmic series of beeping or buzzing sounds which they said seemed to bounce off the trunk of their vehicle. The car vibrated and a tingling sensation passed through the Hills' bodies. Betty touched the metal on the passenger door expecting to feel an electric shock, but felt only the vibration. The Hills said that at this point in time they experienced the onset of an altered state of consciousness that left their minds dulled. A second series of code like beeping or buzzing sounds returned the couple to full consciousness. They found that they had traveled nearly 35 miles south but had only vague, spotty memories of this section of road.

Aftermath arriving home at about dawn, the Hills were perplexed. After sleeping for a few hours, Betty awoke and placed the shoes and clothing she had worn during the drive into her closet, observing that the dress was torn at the hem, zipper and lining. Later, when she retrieved the items from her closet, she noted a pinkish powder on her dress. She hung the dress on her clothesline and the pink powder blew away. But the dress was irreparably damaged.

There were shiny, concentric circles on their car's trunk that had not been there the previous day. Betty and Barney experimented with a compass, noting that when they moved it close to the spots, the needle would whirl rapidly. But when they moved it a few inches away from the shiny spots, it would drop down.

Ten days after the UFO encounter, Betty began having a series of vivid dreams. They continued for five successive nights. Never in her memory had she recalled dreams in such detail and intensity. But they stopped abruptly after five nights and never returned again.

In one dream, she and Barney encountered a roadblock and men who surrounded their car. She lost consciousness but struggled to regain it. She then realized that she was being forced by two small men to walk in a forest in the nighttime, and of seeing Barney walking behind her, though when she called to him, he seemed to be in a trance or sleepwalking. The men stood about five feet to five feet four inches tall, and wore matching uniforms, with caps similar to those worn by military cadets. They appeared nearly human, but with bald heads, large wraparound eyes, small ears and almost absent noses. Their skin was a greyish color.

In the dreams, Betty, Barney, and the men walked up a ramp into a disc-shaped craft of metallic appearance. Once inside, Barney and Betty were separated. She protested, and was told by a man she called "the leader" that if she and Barney were examined together, it would take much longer to conduct the exams. She and Barney were then taken to separate rooms.

Betty then dreamt that a new man, similar to the others, entered to conduct her exam with the leader. Betty called this new man "the examiner" and said he had a pleasant, calm manner. Though the leader and the examiner spoke to her in English, the examiner's command of the language seemed imperfect and she had difficulty understanding him.

The examiner told Betty that he would conduct a few tests to note the differences between humans and the craft's occupants. He seated her on a chair, and a bright light was shone on her. The man cut off a lock of Betty's hair. He examined her eyes, ears, mouth, teeth, throat and hands. He saved trimmings from her fingernails. After examining her legs and feet, the man then used a dull knife, similar to a letter opener to scrape some of her skin onto what resembled cellophane. He then tested her nervous system and he thrust the needle into her navel, which caused Betty agonizing pain. But the leader waved his hand in front of her eyes and the pain vanished.

To put to rest Bettys dreams the subject of hypnosis came up. Perhaps hypnosis could unlock the missing memories. It was recommended that Dr. Simon's hypnosis sessions. Simon began hypnotizing the Hills on January 4, 1964. He hypnotized Betty and Barney several times each, and the sessions lasted until June 6, 1964. Simon conducted the sessions on Barney and Betty separately, so they could not overhear one another's recollections. At the end of each session he reinstated amnesia.

Barney was first to be hypnotized. Under hypnosis Barney recalled driving the car away from the UFO, but that afterwards he felt irresistibly compelled to pull off the road, and drive into the woods. He eventually sighted six men standing in the dirt road. The car stalled and three of the men approached the car. They told Barney to not fear them. Barney related that he and Betty were taken onto the disc-shaped craft, where they were separated. He was escorted to a room by three of the men and told to lie on a small rectangular exam table. Unlike Betty, Barney's narrative of the exam was fragmented, and he continued to keep his eyes closed for most of the exam. A cup-like device was placed over his genitals. He did not experience an orgasm or any pain but thought that a sperm sample had been taken. The men scraped his skin, and peered in his ears and mouth. A tube or cylinder was inserted in his anus. Someone felt his spine, and seemed to be counting his vertebrae.

While Betty reported extended conversations with the beings in English, Barney said that he heard them speaking in a mumbling language he did not understand. Betty also mentioned this detail. The few times they communicated with him, Barney said it seemed to be through telepathy. Both Betty and Barney stated that they hadn't observed the beings' mouths moving when they communicated in English with them. He recalled being escorted from the ship, and taken to his car, which was now near the road rather than in the woods. In a daze, he watched the ship leave.

Betty's a hypnosis account was very similar to the events of her five dreams about the UFO abduction, but there were also notable differences. Under hypnosis, her capture and release were different. The technology on the craft was different. Betty exhibited considerable emotional distress during her capture and examination. Barney's and Betty's memories in hypnotic regression were, however, consistent with one another.

Betty sketched a copy of the "star map" that she described as a three dimensional projection similar to a hologram. She hesitated, thinking she would be unable to accurately depict the three-dimensional quality of the map she says she saw on the ship. Eventually, however, she did what Simon suggested. Although she said the map had many stars, she drew only those that stood out in her memory. Her map consisted of twelve prominent stars connected by lines and three lesser ones that formed a distinctive triangle. She said she was told the stars connected by solid lines formed "trade routes", whereas dashed lines were to less-traveled stars.

Dr. Simon concluded after extensive hypnosis sessions that Barney's recall of the UFO encounter was a fantasy inspired by Betty's dreams.

In 1968, Marjorie Fish of Oak Harbor, Ohio was an elementary school teacher and amateur astronomer. Intrigued by the "star map", Fish wondered if it might be "deciphered" to determine which star system the UFO came from. Assuming that one of the fifteen stars on the map must represent the Earth's Sun; Fish constructed a three-dimensional model of nearby Sun-like stars using thread and beads, basing stellar distances on those published in the 1969 Gliese Star Catalogue. Studying thousands of vantage points over several years, the only one that seemed to match the Hill map was from the viewpoint of the double star system of Zeta Reticuli.

Carl Sagan and Steven Soter, argued that the seeming "star map" was little more than a random alignment of chance points. In contrast, those more favorable to the map, such as Dr. David Saunders, a statistician who had been on the Condon UFO study, argued that unusual alignment of key Sun-like stars in a plane centered around Zeta Reticuli described by Fish was statistically improbable to have happened by chance from a random group of stars in our immediate neighborhood.

Many of Betty Hill's notes, tapes, and other items were placed in a permanent collection at the University of New Hampshire, her alma mater. As of July 2011, the site of the alleged craft's first close approach is marked by a state historical marker.

Betty Andreasson (1967)
On the evening of January 25, 1967 a reddish-orange light suddenly shined in the kitchen window of Betty Andreasson's home. Andreasson rushed to the living room to comfort her frightened children while her father looked out the window. That's when he saw five, odd creatures "hopping" towards their house. Before anyone could react, the creatures made their way inside and placed the whole family in a state of suspended animation. Andreasson was brought inside a craft where she underwent a physical examination, and was given a bizarre test which she described as a painful, yet "religious" experience. When her captors brought her back home, they placed her family under some kind of mind control to put them to bed, then left.

An investigative team was assigned to Andreasson's case, including an Electronics Engineer, an Aerospace Engineer, a Telecommunications Specialist, a Solar Physicist, and a UFO Investigator. They studied the case for twelve months, and the results were presented in a 528-page review. The review stated that Andreasson was sane, and her claims were believable. Ray Fowler, founder of Mutual UFO Network (MUFON), concluded that Andreasson was "either the most accomplished liar and actress the world had ever seen, or else she really had [experienced] this ordeal."

Antonio Vilas Boas (1957)
At 23, Antonio Vilas Boas was working in the agricultural fields in the early evening of October 16, 1957. He saw a "bright red star" in the sky which he finally made out to be an egg-shaped spacecraft. Boas attempted to flee,

but was captured by a five-foot tall humanoid who dragged him inside the craft. Powerless, he was stripped of his clothes and covered with a strange gel.

Later, he was joined by a seemingly attractive female humanoid. The two had sexual intercourse, after which the female rubbed her belly and pointed towards the sky, gesturing that she will raise their child in space. Boas was taken on a tour around the ship, then escorted off the ship and realized that the abduction had lasted for four hours.

Dr. Olavo Fontes of the National School of Medicine of Brazil examined Boas and concluded that he had been exposed to a large dose of radiation from an unknown source. Boas continued to recall details of his experience, without hypnotic regression, and he stuck to his claims throughout his life.

Travis Walton (1975)

Travis Walton and six of his coworkers were riding in a truck when they suddenly encountered a saucer-shaped object hovering 110 feet away from the ground. Walton approached the mysterious object and was struck by a beam of light. Frightened, his coworkers hastily drove away from the scene on that early November evening in 1975. Walton woke up in what he thought was a hospital emergency room, but he found himself surrounded by three creatures.

Walton later turned up in Snowflake, Arizona after disappearing for nearly a week. He and the six coworkers who allegedly witnessed his abduction voluntary submitted to a series of tests, which they all passed, except for one whose results were inconclusive. Walton continued to tell his story throughout the years without any discrepancies in details. His coworkers also stood by their side of the story, even refusing bribes to contradict their narratives. Walton eventually wrote a book detailing his claims, and it became the basis for the 1993 film 'Fire in the Sky'

Pascagoula Abduction (1973)

On the night of October 11, 1973, Charles Hickson and his friend, Calvin Parker Jr., were fishing from an old pier in the Pascagoula River in Mississippi when they heard a "zipping sound" and spotted a glowing, elongated object hovering above the ground. Three humanoid creatures emerged and took Hickson and Parker aboard the spacecraft, where they were examined. They were returned to the fishing site after the examination, and they immediately reported the encounter to the sheriff.

After 30 minutes of questioning, Jackson Country Sheriff, Fred Diamond, left the two men alone in a room rigged with a hidden microphone to further attest the validity of their claims. The audio recording of Hickson and Parker's private conversation showed how distressed they were about what they've just experienced. UFO investigator Philip Mantle later published a book on this case, and calls it one of the "most unique close encounters on record".

John Salter Jr (1988)
John Salter Jr. and his son were driving on Central Wisconsin's Highway 14 on March 20, 1988, when suddenly, they realized they had been traveling in the opposite direction for an hour. Both men could account for the lost time, and they did not remember altering their intended route. Eventually, they decided to take a rest for the night and continue their journey in the morning.

During their drive the next morning, they saw a bright saucer-like form which immediately disappeared, traveling at an incredible speed. They began to feel some sort of familiarity upon seeing the mysterious saucer, but they would only start having detailed flashbacks months later.

They recalled getting forced off the highway by unknown creatures who communicated with them through telepathy. The creatures led them to a space craft, where they received painless injections in various parts of their bodies. After that, they were guided back to their truck, and Salter claimed that they parted with the creatures in a friendly manner.

These events take a bizarre turn when upon returning home, Salter noticed an improvement in his health. His immunity was heightened, cuts and scratches healed rapidly, age spots and wrinkles had faded, and he felt more energetic. Salter's son did not experience the same physical changes, but said that the encounter was the most extraordinary event in his life.

Whitley Strieber (1985)
Whitley Strieber is a well-known horror author who claimed that one of his books, 'Communion: A True Story' was actually based on an alien

encounter. It began in December 1985 when he was awakened by a strange noise, after which a "non-human creature" came rushing towards his bed. He woke up in the morning feeling disoriented, without knowing why. He recalled memories of his encounter months later through regressive hypnosis, claiming that he was abducted and assaulted by the creatures.

Strieber went on to write four additional narratives detailing his encounters with the creatures which he referred to as "Visitors". He theorized that these 'Visitors' might have more physical substance than what we normally assume, and that they're not even a little human, but they're clearly intelligent. At his own request, Strieber went through extensive tests for temporal lobe epilepsy and other brain abnormalities, only to find that his brain was functioning normally.

Jesse Long (1957)

Jesse Long claims that he was first abducted by aliens in 1957, when he was just five years old. The aliens conducted experiments on him, which became more painful and traumatic as time went on. He said that they placed a foreign object on his leg which remained with him for 34 years. It was eventually removed and sent for analysis at the Southwest Research Institute in Texas. The laboratory report stated that the object had unique characteristics which could not be explained.

According to Long, he was abducted multiple times over the years and was even forced to crossbreed with a female alien. He was driving to New Orleans in 1990 when a light appeared to bring him inside an alien craft. He was presented with a baby and was told "This is your child." Nine other children stood along the hallway and he knew right away that they were his children.

The Allagash Abductions (1976)

In August 1976, four artists were on a camping trip in the woods near Allagash, Maine when they suddenly spotted a glowing orb hovering over the tree canopies. Jim Weiner, Jack Weiner, Charles Foltz, and Charles Rak were night fishing in a canoe when they spotted the orb. As it slowly moved towards them, the four men panicked and paddled towards the bank as fast as they could. A blinding light suddenly beamed at them, and the next thing they knew, they were already standing on the bank, with no memory as to what happened.

Afterwards, they began to have nightmares which they believed to be recollections of their abduction. They dreamt of being examined by beings with long necks and large heads. The four of them went through regressive hypnosis and lie detector tests, which they all passed. Rak would later retract his recollections during the hypnosis saying, "The reason I supported the story at first was because I wanted to make money." He claimed, however, that they really did see strange lights during their camping trip.

Chapter 13

Sense of Humor

Aliens Sense of Humor

Is the Human Sense of Humor Truly Universal? There is good evidence that Aliens have a sense of humor. While this sounds crazy, I have the evidence that suggest this.

Someone Knocked on My Space Craft Door

On the nation's first manned space flight in 2003, China National Space Administration (CNSA) Astronaut Yang Liwei reported that someone knocked on the space craft door while in orbit. This was subsequently reported by other Chinese astronauts. China spent millions of yuan to try to resolve the cause, but were unable to come up with an explanation.

Space Angels

I have to admit I was somewhat puzzled about the "Space Angels," but it appears to be a factual story. The Russian Space craft Salyut 7 was a low Earth orbit space station that had been launched on April 19, 1982. The Salyut 7 would serve as the site of arguably the strangest close encounter in the relatively brief history of manned space exploration.

The first reported sighting occurred on July 12, 1984. Cosmonauts Leonid Kizim, Vladimir Solovyov and cardiologist Oleg Atkov were on their astonishing 155th day aboard the space vehicle conducting "medical experiments," when the trio noticed what they described as a "brilliant orange cloud" surrounding the station. The astronauts aboard the craft were understandably concerned that the glow might represent a life threatening fire. Fearing the worst, the cosmonauts rushed to the portholes only to find themselves blinded by an eerily intense luminescence the poured in through the circular apertures. After their vision adjusted to the light, the curious cosmonauts radioed ground control that the station was bathed in an anomalous, self-illuminated mist. The men returned to the portholes, shielding their eyes from the radiance, and that's when they spied something so incredible that it would forever alter their perception of reality.

According to reports published in newspapers across the globe — including, the Washington Post — the three Russian explorers saw colossal, winged, humanoid entities hovering just outside the station in the vacuum of space. The faces of these beings were said to resemble those of humans with "peaceful expressions" and the Soviet scientists even claimed that the creatures noticed them and offered distinctly beatific smiles. The Cosmonauts described seven giant figures in the form of humans, but with wings and mist-like halos, as in the classic depiction of angels. The men observed the soaring seraphim for approximately 10 minutes before they vanished, leaving the isolated and surely perplexed comrades to ponder what they had seen, and try to muster the courage to report it to their superiors below.

By their own admission, the cosmonauts were themselves reluctant to accept the existence of the oddly angelic beings which they had seen, and concluded that they were more likely suffering from some form of mass delusion brought on by their extended space travel, than an actual encounter with alien — perhaps even divine — beings.

Their self-induced denial would be put to the test 11-days later when additional cosmonauts arrived at the station and the celestial beings returned. On the evening of July 17, 1984, at 5:41 pm., the Soyuz T-12 spacecraft launched from the LC31 pad of the Baikonur Cosmodrome, in Kazakhstan. The Soyuz T-12 carried with it Crew Commander Vladimir Dzhanibekov, Flight Engineer Svetlana Savitskaya and Research Cosmonaut Igor Volk. Hours later the craft docked with the Salyut 7.

According to published reports, just days after the Soviet cosmonauts were safely nestled aboard the Salyut 7, the peculiar orange glow once again enveloped the station. This time, all six of the cosmonauts were said to have witnessed these gigantic, winged, and ghostly beings keeping pace with the station as it sped around the globe. As the cosmonauts stared out of the portholes, one can only imagine that they must have been overwhelmed by sensations of awe, wonder and perhaps a touch of fear. These men and woman were highly trained pilots, scientists and doctors who were now confronted with enormous, humanoid creatures soaring unprotected in the cold vacuum of space. The creatures seemed not merely alien, but supernatural in origin. According to news accounts, one of the cosmonauts was quoted as stating, "They were glowing, and we were truly overwhelmed. There was a great orange light, and through it, we could see the figures of seven angels. They were smiling as though they shared a glorious secret, but within a few minutes, they were gone, and we never saw them again."

After the space angels disappeared a second time, Kizim, Solovyov and Atkov could no longer dismiss the phenomenon as a communal hallucination brought on by the pressure of a long mission in orbit. They now shared this encounter with three new witnesses, all of whom were just as perplexed and frightened as they had been days earlier. Both the explorers and their mission control comrades on Earth had no explanation for the events.

Within days, Dzhanibekov, Savitskaya and Volk returned to Earth, but Kizim, Solovyov and Atkov remained in orbit aboard the Salyut 7 for a record setting 237 days. Upon their return, each of the cosmonauts were subjected to a battery of physical and psychological examinations to try to determine if there might have been a medical explanation for the heavenly phenomenon. According to all accounts, they passed all of the exams with flying colors.

If one is to believe the testimony of these professionals, then the medical diagnosis leaves only one of two viable conclusions:

First, were all six cosmonauts — in two separate instances —willing to seriously jeopardize their careers, reputations, and even their very lives (including their psychological health), all for the sake of a "prank?"

Second, one can only conclude that the cosmonauts had no hidden agendas, and quite simply, they saw what they had reluctantly described as, "angels." What they had described bears a distinct resemblance to what many of the followers of the Abrahamic traditions would consider to be divine messengers.

The evidence for mass hallucinations is dubious. While episodes of mass hysteria have been chronicled throughout the ages, there is very little to suggest that individuals share simultaneous hallucinations. Reports from individual cosmonauts and astronauts who have seen some decidedly surreal things from their spacecraft — a phenomenon which NASA researchers have attributed to pressure, temperature fluctuations and oxygen shortage — there's nothing in the medical record to suggest that these experiences are in any way contagious. In short, barring some kind of as yet undiagnosed psychic phenomenon, there's simply no known method to share a delusion as specific as the ones experienced by the cosmonauts in Salyut 7.

If for the sake of argument, we agree that we're not dealing with a figment of the cosmonauts' collective imaginations, then we must consider the possibility of encountering authentic entities, of either biological or spiritual origin. Perhaps we should cut to the chase and consider the most obvious, and most disturbing option: these creatures are the otherworldly embodiment referred in human mythology as, "angels."

From my limited knowledge of Angels, I believe that medieval artists portrayed them as having wings, and halos were used to distinguish them from mortal men. So what is going on here? Both of the above Chinese and Russian encounters are well documented, and to me, suggest that Aliens might be toying with us. One might even put crop circles in this category of, "Let's Have Fun With Humans." Someone out there has advanced knowledge of physics, and may be playing a joke on us. Humans can't be the only species who possess a sense of humor.

The fastest object ever launched into space ...
... was a manhole cover!

The very first underground nuclear tests were a bit of an experiment — nobody knew exactly what might happen. The very first underground test was nicknamed "Uncle." It exploded beneath the Nevada Test Site on November 29, 1951.

The more intriguing tests were nicknamed 'Pascal', part of Operation PLUMBBOB. Dr. Robert Brownlee designed the Pascal-Atomic Test, designed to contain nuclear fallout. The bomb was placed at the bottom of a hollow column — three feet wide and 485 feet deep — with a four-inch-thick iron cap. The test was conducted on the night of July 26, 1957. The explosion erupted out of the column, looking like a Roman Candle. Brownlee said the iron cap in Pascal-A exploded off the top of the tube "like a bat."

Brownlee wanted to measure how fast the iron cap flew off the column, so he designed a second experiment: Pascal-B. He replicated the first experiment, but the column in Pascal-B was deeper, 500 feet below the surface. They recorded the experiment with a camera that shot 1 frame per millisecond. On August 27, 1957, the "manhole cover" cap flew off the column with the force of the nuclear explosion. The iron cover was only partially visible in one frame, Brownlee said.

When he used this information to find out how fast the cap was going, Brownlee calculated it was traveling at five times the escape velocity of the Earth — or about 125,000 miles per hour. This dwarfs the 36,373 mph speed that NASA's New Horizons spacecraft — which people say is the fastest object launched by humankind — left Earth's gravity on its way toward Pluto.

Brownlee concluded that the cap was going too fast to burn up before reaching outer space. "After I was in the business and did my own missile launches," he said, "I realized that that piece of iron didn't have time to burn all the way up in the atmosphere."

On October 4, 1957, the Soviet Union launched Sputnik, the world's first artificial satellite.

While the USSR was the first to launch a man-made satellite, Sputnik, in 1957, Brownlee was the first to launch a man-made object into space a month and a half earlier. So the next time you look up at the stars, remember Brownlee's story. Somewhere out there, a manhole cover launched by a nuclear bomb is probably speeding away from Earth at about 125,000 mph.

Tesla Roadster Launched by SpaceX in 2018

Chapter 14

Crop Circles

Formation

I have always had great interest in things that don't seem to make sense, but are intriguing nonetheless. One of these fits into the category commonly referred to as, "Crop Circles." Although I had regarded them as inspired displays of human imagination, anyone who understands advanced mathematics and the Calculus can clearly see the relationship of mathematics and Crop Circles.

The phenomenon of Crop Circles began in the late 1970s when simple Crop Circles began to appear regularly in the fields of Wiltshire, Oxfordshire, Somerset, and Gloucestershire in southern England. They were basic circular shapes of different sizes, usually 20 or so feet in diameter, formed in the dark of night. The first circles took the form of a simple, yet elegant circle of pressed wheat – something that was truly out of the ordinary and unexplainable.

Now, in the 2020s with over 9000 known formations, Crop Circles have developed into complex mathematical fractals, with lengths up to three quarters of a mile and areas of 36,000 square feet. A Crop Circle, or 'agriglyph' – is a geoglyph that is constructed almost exclusively in agricultural fields, and can be found in most countries around the globe.

One of the issues in the argument regarding the origin of the circles is that no man-made Crop Circle that has been demonstrated has satisfactorily replicated the features associated with the real phenomenon. Worldwide, scientists and investigators are baffled by nearly 4000 Crop Circles that seem to have been created by a force that lies outside of human modern science.

Eighty-five percent of all Crop Circles appear in a concentrated area about twenty miles from Stonehenge, England. However, they do appear each year all over the world, sometimes near heavily populated cities. The first seasonal Crop Circles of 1996 were found in Laguna Beach, California. Many dramatic Crop Circles have appeared in Canada, Germany, Australia, Brazil, Japan, and the United States.

Designs
The more modern Crop Circle formations are absolutely stunning in their design, intricacy, and precise measurements. Many of them are huge, covering the space of ten football fields. Terrestrial surveys have calculated that the geometrical designs, some measuring over 1000 feet long, are accurate to within an eighth of an inch! For example, a hundred-foot circle will have an accurate and identical radius on all sides to within the thickness of a single stalk of wheat.

Pictograms
Some of the more complex designs are called pictograms, a graphic symbol that conveys its meaning through its pictorial resemblance to a physical object. Insect designs are sometimes characterized within the circle, although there is no apparent relationship of Crop Circles to the particular insect.

Cellular Changes
The grasses involved in Crop Circles all exhibit cellular changes. Using just the naked eye, one can clearly see the differences between Crop Circle stalks, and 'normal' healthy stalks. Crop-circle grass has expanded nodes, and stalks have been be bent up to a 90-degree angle with no breakage. The expansion and change of every cell of the Crop Circle grass becomes dramatic when looking through an even basic microscope. Although many have tried, no one has successfully managed to duplicate these cellular changes.

Magnetic Fields and Radioactivity
Crop Circles have a strong magnetic field in and around them. Many also exhibit strange patterns of radioactivity in which the level of radioactivity at a given spot will fluctuate significantly. Modern human physics considers

this to be impossible, because radioactivity is constant. That's why it is so important in carbon-dating techniques of ancient artifacts.

Grass Direction
True Crop Circles often have several layers of grass in the design. Often the bottom layers will flow in one direction, while the top layer flows in the opposite direction. Delicately braided grass has even been discovered.

Metallic disks
Often, thin metallic disks about the size of a U.S. Quarter are found within Crop Circles. Interestingly, the same type of disk has also been found near cattle mutilations. When these disks were analyzed by metallurgical laboratories at the University of Michigan and at MIT, they were found to be composed of a combination of titanium, silicone, and oxygen. Both labs concluded that no industrial match can be found on Earth.

It is fascinating to note that when the disks were touched by a metal object such as tweezers or a pen, they immediately changed from a solid into a clear liquid. Researchers have theorized that the disks had somehow been electrically charged, with the charge maintaining the molecular structure of the disk. When touched with metal, the charge was grounded and dissipated, which allowed the "metal" to return to its true liquid form.

Birds Fly Around Them
The Crop Circle is a slice of an invisible three dimensional form that surrounds it, like a, invisible cylinder that reaches vertically into the sky. In fact, it has been observed that when a flock of birds approaches a Crop Circle, they split ranks in order to avoid flying above the pattern, just as if a building or a solid object were there. The flocks then reform after passing the Crop Circle. Some people who stand inside a Crop Circle often experience a dramatic rush of emotions and increased perceptual abilities, as well as vertigo.

A number of eyewitnesses claim to have seen Crop Circles being created within a matter of seconds, with patterns so complex that it would have taken an army of people many hours to create it manually.

On July 8, 1996 three people witnessed the formation of an elaborate Crop Circle. A groundskeeper and a security officer had walked by a wheat field at about 5:30 p.m. The field looked uninteresting and completely normal.

At precisely the same time, a pilot flew his small plane over the field and indicated that everything seemed normal. Less than an hour later on his return trip, the pilot flew back over the field and discovered a huge Crop Circle. He was so excited by his discovery he radioed it in to the Thruxton Airport. The security officer and groundskeeper were also startled when they returned from supper an hour later and stumbled across the field with the Crop Circle.

The Crop Circle that the three witnesses found was the design of a very complicated mathematical equation which had been discovered by French mathematicians in the early 1900s, a calculation known as a Julia Set. The Crop Circle was comprised of 149 circles stretching over a square acre.

Julia Set Crop Circle

Recently, a videotape surfaced which purported to show the actual creation of a Crop Circle. The video shows a ball of light descend from the sky, rapidly go around a grain field, and instantly generate a Crop Circle, shooting off into space at high speed. The film looks pretty convincing, until it had been pointed out that the producer of the video is known to be a computer generated effects specialist.

Crop Circles are a challenging phenomenon. Their implications are dramatic, and they are studied very seriously by other countries in the world. In the United States, they are splashed over the front page of sensationalist tabloids, and shown on television shows like, "Unsolved Mysteries." All that the American public is likely to hear is that it's all a big hoax.

These circles appear to be literal responses to signals that we have sent out to the universe, searching for other life, for human understanding of the cosmos, and in the name of science. It may be that someone is returning our call.

Are Crop Circles really telling us how to construct our very own flying saucer? A former Air Force and commercial airline pilot for twenty-four years, Doug Ruby decided to take a simple approach in his investigation of Crop Circles: Why not treat them like engineering schematics?

Ruby approached each Crop Circle as if it were a flat, two-dimensional schematic of a three-dimensional item, just like a blueprint for a building a structure. At first, he started with the least complicated crop-circle designs, and then he simply constructed the items.

They didn't look like much- more like some partially-constructed Tinker-toy. Then Ruby had an intuitive thought: Why not spin the item, put it in motion? Voila! When the objects were spun, they literally took on a whole other dimension. For example, it became apparent that one part that merely looked like a ball stuck on a pole was representing an energy field that could only be seen when it was spun. Without spinning the model these energy fields would have remained invisible.

Along the way, Mr. Ruby discovered that each Crop Circle builds on the designs of the other ones. Fortunately, he started out with photos or diagrams of almost all the major Crop Circles that had ever been created, which provided him a full set of blueprints This allowed him to "see ahead" as he constructed each model, in the fashion of an architect or engineer.

Enthusiasts say that the scale models that are built from these blueprints actually tell us how flying saucers are constructed, how they operate, what powers them, and why they are shaped like saucers. The Crop Circles are an amazing representation of a technical puzzle, and Ruby's work is seen as sheer genius.

Perhaps most importantly, the Crop Circles diagram the saucer's power source, and tells how it works. The assembled models look exactly like the type of flying saucer commonly referred to as the "Adamski Beam Ships."

Ruby's description of how the crafts work confirms the statements of many people over the years about the rotating rings on the saucers, as well as the interference with electrical devices.

There is, however, one little problem having to do with the lack of Earthly materials. Our scientists are prohibited from building one of these craft to specs right now. The Crop Circles identify an atomic particle which has no charge, and it is the key particle in powering the ship. Our scientists say that is impossible. Of course, we now know that nothing is impossible, just unknown at this time.

In addition to Crop Circles appearing in grain fields, large sets of numbers have appeared as well. In one instance, the following equation appeared in a Kansas grain field in 1991:

$$E\ 97 +$$

It appears to refer to Element 97 on the periodic chart of atomic elements. Element 97 is Berkelium, with an atomic weight of 247. It is the element thought to be used to power flying saucers. Shortly after this equation appeared, it was eradicated by agents from people who said they were from "the government." At any rate, it was clear that someone doesn't want the Crop Circles to be deciphered.

Whether you appreciate the Crop Circles as art, or as an engineering marvel, there is no doubt that we are being communicated with by an amazing intelligence (human or otherwise). It is clear that these displays of information are given to all humanity in a benevolent manner.

The "Arecibo Message" Crop Circle

The so-called "Arecibo Message" was a radio message carrying basic information about humanity and Earth that was sent to the globular star cluster M13 in 1974. It was meant as a demonstration of human technological achievement, rather than a real attempt to enter into a conversation with extraterrestrials.

The content of the Arecibo message was designed by Frank Drake from Cornell University, who developed the 'Drake Equation', and collaborated with help from Carl Sagan and other scientists. The message traveled at near the speed of light, and should arrive at M13 in 25,000 years. By that time, the core of M13 will no longer be in precisely the same location because of the orbit of the star cluster around the galactic center. Even so, the proper motion of M13 is small, so the message will still arrive near the center of the cluster.

The message was broadcast into space only one time via frequency modulated (FM) radio waves as part of a ceremony to mark the remodeling of the Arecibo Radio Telescope in Puerto Rico in November of 1974. The carefully crafted message was aimed at the location of M13, a massive globular star cluster about 25,000 light years (7,665 parsecs) from Earth.

When correctly translated into graphics, characters, and spaces, the 1,679 bits of data form the image shown below. Color was added to highlight its separate parts. The binary transmission that was sent carried no color information.

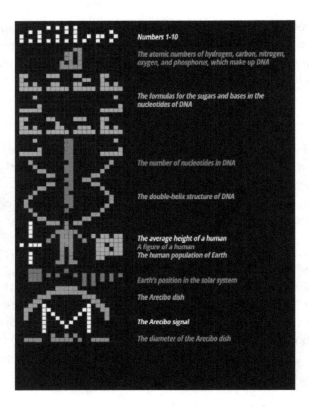

The message consists of seven parts that encode the following (from the top down in the image). Color was added to highlight its separate parts. The binary transmission sent carried no color information.

- The numbers one (1) to ten (10) (white)
- The atomic numbers of the elements hydrogen, carbon, nitrogen, oxygen, and phosphorus, which make up deoxyribonucleic acid (DNA) (purple)
- The formulas for the chemical compounds that make up the nucleotides of DNA (green)
- The estimated number of DNA nucleotides in the human genome, and a graphic of the double helix structure of DNA (white and blue, respectively)
- The dimension (physical height) of an average man (blue/white), a graphic figure of a human being (red), and the human population of Earth (white)

- A graphic of the Solar System, indicating which of the planets the message is coming from (yellow)
- A graphic of the Arecibo radio telescope and the dimension (the physical diameter) of the transmitting antenna dish (purple, white, and blue)

The entire message consisted of 1,679 binary digits, approximately 210 bytes, transmitted at a frequency of 2,380 MHz and modulated by shifting the frequency by 10 Hz, with a power of 450 kW. The "ones" and "zeros" were transmitted by frequency shifting at the rate of 10 bits per second. The total broadcast was less than three minutes.

The number 1,679 was chosen because it is a semiprime (the product of two prime numbers), to be arranged rectangularly as 73 rows by 23 columns. The alternative arrangement, 23 rows by 73 columns, produces an unintelligible set of characters.

```
1 2 3 4 5 6 7 8 9 10
----------------------
0 0 0 1 1 1 1 00 00 00
0 1 1 0 0 1 1 00 00 10
1 0 1 0 1 0 1 01 11 01
X X X X X X X X X X <-least-significant-digit marker
```

Numbers
The numbers from 1 to 10 appear in binary format, to be read from the top down. The bottom row contains markers which indicate the column from which the binary code for each number is intended to begin.

Even assuming that any extraterrestrial recipients would recognize binary, the encoding of the numbers may not be immediately obvious because of the way they have been written. To read the first seven digits, ignore the bottom row, and read them as three binary digits from top to bottom, with the top digit being the most significant. The readings for 8, 9, and 10 are a little different, as their binary code has been distributed across an additional column next to the first (to the right in the image). This is intended to show that numbers too large to fit in a single column can be written in several contiguous ones (a scheme which is used elsewhere in the message). The additional columns are not marked by the least-significant-digit marker.

DNA elements

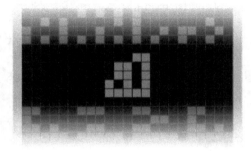

```
H C N O P
1 6 7 8 15
----------
0 0 0 1 1
0 1 1 0 1
0 1 1 0 1
1 0 1 0 1
X X X X X
```

The numbers 1, 6, 7, 8, and 15 appear, denoting the atomic numbers of hydrogen (H), carbon (C), nitrogen (N), oxygen (O), and phosphorus (P), the elements from which DNA is composed.

Nucleotides

| Deoxyribose (C_5H_7O) | Adenine $(C_5H_4N_5)$ | Thymine $(C_5H_5N_2O_2)$ | Deoxyribose (C_5H_7O) |

| Phosphate (PO_4) | | | Phosphate (PO_4) |

| Deoxyribose (C_5H_7O) | Cytosine $(C_4H_4N_3O)$ | Guanine $(C_5H_4N_5O)$ | Deoxyribose (C_5H_7O) |

| Phosphate (PO_4) | | | Phosphate (PO_4) |

The chemical groups from which the nucleotides of polymeric DNA sequences are built – the sugar deoxyribose, phosphate, and the four canonical nucleobases used in DNA – are then described as sequences of the five elements that appear on the preceding line. Each sequence represents the molecular formula of the chemical as it exists when incorporated into DNA (as opposed to the free form).

For example, the compound in the top left in the image is deoxyribose (C_5H_7O in DNA, $C_5H_{10}O_4$ when free), whose formula is read as:

```
11000
10000
11010
XXXXX
-----
75010
```

i.e., 7 atoms of hydrogen, 5 atoms of carbon, 0 atoms of nitrogen, 1 atom of oxygen, and 0 atoms of phosphorus.

It is displayed in this order because the DNA Elements in the previous section (Purple image as reference) describe hydrogen (H), carbon (C), nitrogen (N), oxygen (O), and phosphorus (P) in that order as well.

Double helix

11
11
11
11
11
01
11
11
01
11
01
11
10
11
11
01
X
11111111 11110111 11111011 01011110 (binary) [Using the double vertical columns above, read from top to bottom starting from the right column first, and then top to bottom from the left column.]
= 4,294,441,822 (decimal)

A graphic of the approximate shape of the double helix in which double-stranded DNA polymers naturally exist; the vertical bar in the middle is a binary representation of the number of nucleotide base pairs in the human genome. The value depicted is around 4.3 billion, which was believed to be the case when the message was transmitted in 1974; it is now known that there are only approximately 3.2 billion base pairs in the human genome.

Humanity

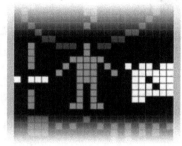

```
^        X011011
|        111111
|        110111
X0111    111011
|        111111
v        110000
```
1110 (binary) = 14 (decimal)
000011 111111 110111 111011 111111 110110 (binary)
= 4,292,853,750 (decimal)

Human form, the height and population of humans

The graphic in the center is a simple illustration of a human being. The element on the left (in the image) indicates the average height of an adult male in the US: 1.764 m (5 ft 9.4 in). This value is indicated by a horizontally written binary representation of the number 14, which is intended to be multiplied by the wavelength of the message (126 mm); 14 × 126 = 1,764 millimeters.

The element on the right of the image indicates the size of the global human population in 1974, approximately 4.3 billion (which, coincidentally, is within 0.1% of the number of DNA base pairs suggested for the size of the human genome earlier in the message). In this case, the number is oriented in the data horizontally rather than vertically. The least-significant-digit marker is in the upper left in the image, with bits going to the right and more significant digits below.

Planets

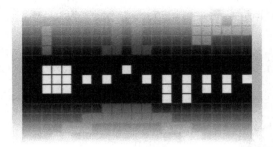

Earth

Sun Mercury Venus   Mars Jupiter Saturn Uranus Neptune Pluto

A graphic depicting the Solar System, showing the Sun and nine planets in the order of their distance from the Sun: Mercury, Venus, Earth, Mars, Jupiter, Saturn, Uranus, Neptune, and Pluto. (Pluto has since been reclassified as a dwarf planet by the International Astronomical Union, but it was considered a planet at the time the message was transmitted.) The Earth is the third planet from the Sun; its graphic is shifted up to identify it as the planet from which the signal was sent. Additionally, the human figure is shown just above the Earth graphic.

In addition to showing position, the graphic also provides a general, not-to-scale size reference of each planet and the Sun.

Telescope

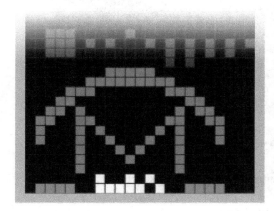

bottom middle two rows shown in White as reference in the image:
100101
<--- 111110X --->
100101 111110 (binary) = 2,430 (decimal)

The last part is a graphic representing the Arecibo radio telescope and indicating its diameter with a binary representation of the number 2,430; multiplying by the wavelength of 126 mm gives 306.18 m (1,004 ft 6 in). In this case, the number is oriented horizontally, with the least-significant-digit marker to the lower right in the image.

The part of the image that resembles a letter "M" is there to demonstrate that the curved line is a concave curved mirror.

The "Arecibo Message" Crop Circle

A crop circle appeared in the farmland next to the Chilbolton radio telescope in Hampshire, England, on August 19, 2001 appears to be a reply to the Arecibo message. It was 75 feet wide and 120 feet long. The crop circle is a near replica of the Arecibo message. The feature forms the same 23 × 73 grid because these numbers are primes and most of the chemical data remains the same with the exception that in the section detailing important chemical elements, the main focus is altered from carbon to silicon, and the diagram of DNA has been rewritten. At the bottom, the pictogram of a human is replaced with a shorter figure with a large, bulbous head, and the Arecibo telescope is replaced by a replica of a crop circle that appeared in the same field one year before.

The Crabwood Crop Circle

The Crabwood Crop Circle

A Crop Circle suddenly appeared overnight at Crabwood in England in August 2002. It displays three prominent features:

First, we see a humanoid figure, but one with facial features and a body habitus that would be very atypical for a human being. Note that the being's image very closely resembles what we have all heard in various physical descriptions of a "grey" alien (extraterrestrial) being. The image of this being is portrayed as inhumanly cold and unfriendly.

Second, this ET has a hand with fingers, and is holding a disc that resembles a CD or a DVD in its left hand.

Third, we see 3 points in alignment over the alien's right shoulder. These three points might represent the three bright stars Alnitak, Alnilam and Mintaka which comprise Orion's Belt.

The disc displays a message representing spiral-like bit sequences, starting from the center of the picture and proceeding counterclockwise. The message is coded using a 9-bit code separator with 8-bit portions in ASCII code. The binary number system represents values using two symbols, typically 0 and 1. Computers call these bits. A bit is either off (0) or on (1). When arranged in sets of 8 bits (1 byte) 256 values can be represented (0-255).Using an ASCII chart, these values can be mapped to characters and text can be stored.

Decoding the ASCII message, it reads:

"Beware the bearers of FALSE gifts & their BROKEN PROMISES. Much PAIN but still time. (Damaged word most likely is BELIEVE) There is GOOD out there. We OPpose DECEPTION. Conduit CLOSING\"

One thing is for certain: Whoever made this circle is extremely artistic, technologically adept, and mathematically advanced.

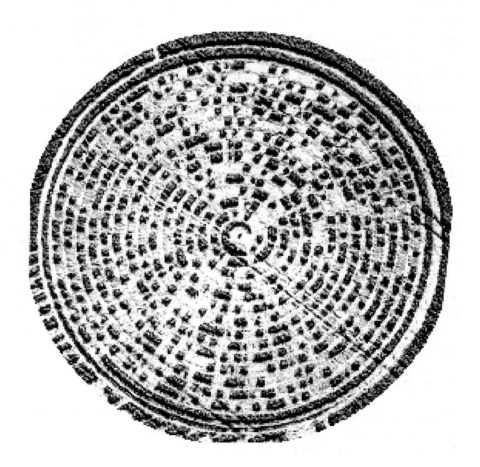

The Pi Crop Circle

This Crop Circle suddenly appeared on the 1st of June 2006 in a barley field near Barbury Castle in Wiltshire, England (51.488258 degrees north, 1.771964 west). It measured 150 feet in diameter, and correctly represented the first 10 digits of the irrational constant pi or 3.141592654.

The Pi Crop Circle

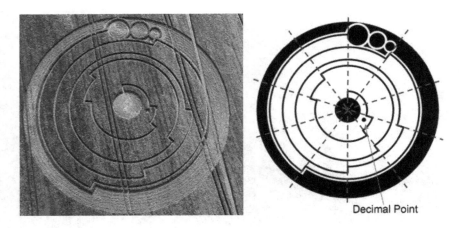

Decimal Point

Looking at the figure, one notices that the grooves in the circle spiral outward, with steps at various points along the way. These 'steps' occur at particular angles — the circle is divided into 10 equal segments of 36 degrees each. Starting at the center, the first section is 3 segments wide. Then there is a step, and underneath is a small circle. This is the decimal point. The next section is 1 segment wide and then there is another step. The following section is 4 segments wide, and so on until the final number encoded is 3.141592654. The three circles of different sizes in the outer upper right is believed to represent the three bright stars in Orion's Belt, possibly the home of the circle's creator.

Alnitak, Alnilam and Mintaka in Orion's Belt

In ancient Egyptian mythology, Orion and the bright star Sirius represent Osiris and Isis. Ancient Egyptians believed that the gods descended from Sirius and the Belt of Orion, and initiated the human race.

Chapter 15

Tours and Places to view UFO's

Area 51, Nevada

S4 Papoose Mountain Facility

This U.S. military installation is located almost 100 miles north of Las Vegas and is commonly known to UFO conspiracy theorists as a location the U.S. government refused to acknowledge. They believe that the area is a storage facility for the examination of a crashed alien spacecraft including its occupants both living and dead as well as materials recovered at Roswell. They also believe the area is used to manufacture aircraft based on alien technology.

Some are now claiming a secret underground facility has been discovered in the base of the Papoose Mountains, in Lincoln County, Nevada, where recovered alien space crafts and extraterrestrial beings are kept hidden away and no longer at Area 51.

Planet XV UFO Hunting Trip

This tour takes you to locations near the famed Area 51, departing from Las Vegas for nighttime explorations. Area 51 is a highly classified remote detachment of Edwards Air Force Base so visitors are limited on how close they can get. There are 3 tours available

Site 1: Close proximity to the Nuclear Testing Site, Area 51 and Area S4
Site 2: Dry Lake Bed observation post
Site 3: Mt. Charleston Lookout

You must wear pants or jeans (no shorts or skirts). You must bring a heavy jacket. The desert can be very cold at night, even during the summer. During the trip there are no restrooms, lighting or electricity. Price varies from $219 per person to $319 per person.

Hooper, Colorado

In a tiny town called Hooper in south central Colorado, there's a platform built for staring skyward. According to the National UFO Reporting Center the watchtower has actually yielded "results."

Because the San Luis Valley in Colorado has been hotbed for reported UFO activity, the watchtower was an inevitability. Getting into the watchtower won't cost you an arm and a leg. A single admission fee is $2, a whole car is $5, and you can camp for $10. Be careful camping, cattle mutilations have been also been reported in the area.

Joshua Tree, California

Joshua Tree is on 29 Palms Highway, about a three-hour drive from Los Angeles International Airport. The area is known to have many underground waterways all featuring a high mineral content. Joshua Tree National Park was once home to 300 mines and includes a unique white crystal quartz hill behind Giant Rock. Visitors often go searching for the hidden alien base that is rumored to be located somewhere beneath the expansive desert..

Dr. Steven Greer is a controversial UFOlogist who founded the Center for the Study of Extraterrestrial Intelligence (CSETI) and the Disclosure Project, which seeks the disclosure of allegedly suppressed UFO information. Each week-long expedition is limited to about 25 and includes an intensive training program with Dr. Greer. At night the group meets under the stars for 4-5 hours to make contact using Greer's CE-5 Contact Protocols. During the intensive training program, visitors learn how to make contact with ET civilizations and how to really become an Ambassador to the Universe. For the past five years, UFO researchers ranging from professionals to fans converge on the California High Desert for a long weekend of lectures and workshops on the unexplained. The Woodstock of UFOlogy is a weekend of education into the Science of UFOs & Extraterrestrial Life,

Ancient Aliens, Human Origins, Crop Circles, Government Disclosure, UFO Sightings and Interplanetary Living. Cost $2500 – $3500 per person.

Mt Adams, Washington

James Gilliland's ranch sits in an area that is a prime viewing spot for all these unusual sightings and occurrences. He "hosts" visitors to his ranch and lets them experience the nightly events.

If you check out the ECETI website you can learn more, ECETI is an acronym for "Enlightened Contact with Extra Terrestrial Intelligence". The website describes James as an "Author, minister, transpersonal intuitive, counselor, visionary and a contactee". He seems to have a devoted group of followers and sounds more like a cult, than an investigation into strange phenomena however many TV shows including Fox TV "Tucker Carlson Tonight" and Discover Channel "Expedition X" have filmed from here.

Popular Mechanics magazine did a country-wide study and issued a report of its findings in an article called "U.S. Map of the Top UFO Hotspots and How to Report a Sighting" in December 2009. Yakima County, WA ranked 4th in the nation for the most UFOs spotted in a "Less Populated County". The tally was counted for the years 1947 through 2005

Roswell, New Mexico

Roswell has been at the heart of the UFO scene since July 1947 when the military announced it had found the remains of a crashed UFO in the desert nearby. Ever since the legendary Roswell UFO crash of July 1947 alien conspiracy theorists have claimed the remains of a flying saucer, and even dead aliens, were secretly taken into storage. Visits to the crash sites are difficult to navigate deep in the desert; so many tourists visit the Roswell Spacewalk and the International UFO Museum and Research Center.

Roswell UFO Tours by local Researcher, Dennis Balthaser are offered twice daily Monday - Thursday (9AM & 1PM). All Tours are based on availability and require minimum 48 hour advance reservations - please visit our website for more information. Discover the 1947 UFO crash, retrieval, and cover-up at the actual locations where the events occurred in Roswell, New Mexico. See over 20 sites as you follow the fascinating story of the

Roswell UFO Incident. Explore Roswell Army Air Field, the former military base that was home to the 509th Bomb Group, the elite unit that was so closely involved with the UFO incident. Discover the infamous Hangar (Building 84) where the recovered spacecraft and alien bodies were kept, before being sent to other locations in the United States to be studied. Cost is $100 per person.

Santa Catalina Island, California

Santa Catalina Island is one of the best places to see UFOs. To the south of the island you have had numerous conformed UFOs reported observing our military ships. See chapter 6. To the north of the island is where most of the reported activity has been reported including the TV show "Expedition X" videotaping a UFO coming out of the water then going into outer space.

Catalina UFO Tours offered by Catalina resident Lili Dana a one-hour walking tour for $20

- • Discover why Catalina is a UFO hot spot and how we fit into the cosmos!
- • Find out why Catalina is a rare and unusual place on earth!
- • Learn about the amazing Catalina magnetic vortex energy that instantly relaxes visitors and residents!
- • Hear about the intriguing and sometimes frightening UFO sightings on and around Catalina Island that have fascinated islanders and visitors for many years!
- • Explore Catalina in a way never seen before on this one hour walking tour along the beautiful shores of Avalon, dress comfortably and have some fun!

For more info about the Catalina UFO Tours, and to schedule a tour, go to Catalinaufotours.com.

Sedona, Arizona

Sedona, Arizona is one of America's most popular destinations for spotting UFOs. Nightly tours go out with visitors equipped with night vision glasses, binoculars, and telescopes. The amount of activity recorded is staggering including reported sightings of; Orbs, portals, aliens, and even Bigfoots all within the high desert.

The mysterious Bradshaw Ranch also draws numerous tourists. Located deep within the national forest, it is reported to have been confiscated by the U.S. Government because it housed one of the most powerful inter-dimensional portals on the planet. Visitors are not allowed in the National Forest at night, but several tour operators will take you there and stay until dusk. According to accounts, it's in the last hour of twilight when many of these phenomena take place. There are even more outrageous reports of a top-secret underground base at the ranch as well as an elaborate tunnel system, possibly used by both extraterrestrials and the U.S. military.

Sedona UFO and Stargazing Night Tour

Experience anomalies in the night sky above Sedona's famous mesas this tour is truly unique from any other! See UFOs powering up in the sky; move in random and unusual formations, landing on far-off mountains, and more! You will be educated as to what you will see in the starry sky. Utilizing top of the line 3rd generation, custom military night vision goggles you will be amazed at what you see. Witness millions of stars and many constellations as well as occasional sightings of the Andromeda Galaxy. We entertain & educate at the same time. We offer zero gravity chairs, propane heaters during cold months, and beverages (hot during winter and cold during summer). When traveling to Sedona please book your UFO tour on the first couple of nights during your stay as sometimes we can have clouds come in that will impinge upon us being able to offer the tour with 50% or clearer skies. Offered by Sedona UFO Tours LLC – Price from $118.80 per person.

Chile

Chile is often mentioned as the country with the highest recorded number of UFO sightings. Due to its low humidity, high altitude ridges, and clear skies with little pollution, Chile has become a favorite among UFO-seekers from around the world.

Atacama Desert Observatory's
The following Observatory offer good views for watching the skys:

1) **Cerro Paranal Observatory in the Chilean Atacama Desert**

Located in the Atacama Desert of Chile, ESO's Paranal Observatory is one of the best astronomical observing sites in the world. In order to visit the observatory, it is a two-hour drive from Cerro Moreno airport and opens on weekends only with an advance reservation.

2) **ALMA Observatory**

ALMA Observatory is the most ambitious radio observatory on Earth.. It is open every Saturday and Sunday to members of the public who want to visit its facilities located in northern Chile (30 miles from San Pedro de Atacama).

San Clemente UFO Trail

San Clemente, Chile is considered to be the unofficial UFO capital of the world. Researchers say that hundreds of UFO sightings have been reported there, as much as one per week. So popular is the area that the Chilean tourism board established an official UFO trail in 2008. The 19-mile trail runs through the Andes Mountains covering sights where close encounters have been reported. Included in the experience is Colbún Lake, which has proved popular with UFOs because of its high mineral content, along with various areas highlighting historic sightings. But the trail's must-see location is El Enladrillado, a huge, bizarre flat area formed by 200 perfectly cut volcanic blocks that were reportedly laid by ancient civilizations. It takes four hours to get to the location on horseback and is believed by many to be a landing pad for extraterrestrials. You can reserve your spot on the UFO trail by calling Dontito Rodriguez at 985531402 at least a day before you plan to visit. From Talca take any of the buses headed to Viches or Viches Alto and ask the driver to let you off at the Parador Turistico, Donde Dontito. From here the route is just over four hours on horseback. Prices are approximately $ 30 per horse and $ 60 in total for a guide.

Elqui Domos Astronomical Hotel

Elqui Domos Astronomical Hotel is a small 10-year-old hotel located in the heart of the Elqui Valley, a narrow valley stretched in between the Andes Mountains. The hotel is equipped with a restaurant, an astronomical observatory, an outdoor pool and 11 air-conditioned and centrally-heated rooms. The rooms are divided into 7 geodesic domes and 4 observatory-style cabins. The domes have a private bathroom, a living room on the first floor and a bed on a mezzanine floor, from where you can uncover the roof of the domes and search the skies. The Elqui Valley is well known for its perfectly clear skies and nice weather, as well as for its great potential for UFO spotting and studying astronomy. Cost $157 per night.

Astronomic Horseback Ride

At dusk, go by horseback riding up to the observation site following a single trail. The excursion is also suitable for people with no experience in horseback riding. Also our horses are tame and we will give you all the necessary instructions at the beginning. At the observation site, around a campfire and with a Pisco Cocktail, our astronomical guide will explain the most important celestial phenomena and. After the talk you will have the chance to explore the cosmos yourself with a 20-inch telescope. The tour ends with a nocturnal photo with you and the very starry sky as a memorial gift. Duration of the tour is approximately 3 hours. Price is $52 per adult.

Wiltshire, England

Mysterious patterns have appeared in the fields of Wiltshire, just one mile from the equally bizarre Stonehenge. Many sightings have occurred here including a large disc-shaped object hovering above the site. The prehistoric monument includes a ring of massive stones dating back to around 3100 BC and is listed as a World Heritage site. Supporters of the theory that ancient aliens built the landmark also consider the area a landing pad for spaceships or a location marker for extraterrestrials. Why do weird and wonderful patterns suddenly appear in the corn fields of our countryside? Are they simply an elaborate hoax or are they caused by UFOs, earth energies or plasma vortexes? Whoever or whatever causes them they are striking features and are well worth checking out. Wiltshire is well known for its mysterious crop circles and much mystery still remains as to why they occur and the meanings behind their complex formations. Crop circles in Wiltshire often occur around the heart of the county in and around Stonehenge and Avebury, usually first appearing in April and continuing into the summer month - dozens of geometric symbols, mandalas and beautiful patterns appear in the farmers growing crop fields each and every year. This magical landscape includes not only the majority of crop circles, but also some of England's most remarkable ancient sacred sites including Stonehenge. You will visit them with an expert guide who will share their detailed knowledge of this area. You can expect to visit at least 5 recent crop circles on this day tour and see many more. This tour also visits the Crop Circle Exhibition & Information Centre. Book Stonehenge Tour - Weird Wiltshire Day Trip. Price: $170 per adult.

Fukushima, Japan

Japan's UFO Capital Fukushima is famously known for the 2011 Earthquake tragedy that struck Japan. However, reported UFO sightings have increased in the last several years. The UFO Interactive Hall was built in 1992 as a central facility. The museum has numerous exhibits on UFOs. For example, exhibits include their history, notable UFO incidents, photo panels, and a 3-D virtual theater. In addition, they have approximately 5,000 items related to UFOs on display. Many of the items come donated from the collection of Kinichi Arai. Mr. Arai was a pioneer in Japanese UFO research. His reputation remains one of the most prominent UFO researchers Japan has ever seen.

According to Japanese news outlet The Mainichi, the International UFO Laboratory located on UFO Interactive Hall will look into a number of sightings that have occurred near the district, which calls itself the 'hometown of UFOs. Iino Japan became host to a number of UFO sightings – including one "light-emitting cone-shaped object" spotted near the area's Mount Senganmori.

Wycliffe Well, Australia

UFOs are not an uncommon sight in Wycliffe Well. They are known to appear at the beginning of the dry season, from May to October. Wycliffe Well is located in the Northern Territory along the Stuart Highway between Alice Springs and Tennant Creek and considers itself the UFO capital of Australia. Wycliffe Well is said to be one of the top five UFO hotspots in the world and guarantees a sighting every couple of days. Visitors can stay in cabins at the Wycliffe Well Holiday Park located 236 miles from Alice Springs. Cost is $40 per night.

M Triangle, Russia

There are 2 major places that report of UFO sightings in Russia. The first is the M-triangle. Located at a distance of 600 miles from Moscow, the place is also known as Russia's Area 51. The second one is Sochi a resort area of

Krasnodar kray (territory), southwestern Russia where the 2014 Winter Olympics were held.

This famous Perm Anomalous Zone (Shutterstock) is located in a remote area near the Ural Mountains in Russia. The M Triangle is one of the most mysterious places in the world and was discovered in the 1980s. There are reports of watches that stop, and bright glowing and colored lightning appearing in the sky.

The village of Molyobka sits on the border of the Perm and Sverdlovsk regions. Opposite the village, on the left bank of the Sylva River, is the famous Molyobka Triangle. When Perm geologist Emil Bachurin found a circular, 206-foot impression in the snow in the 80's, the location quickly became a location for enthusiasts to explore Yetis, UFOs, shining spheres, and plasmoids.

The area is currently developing a UFO park, and local businesses are building hotels and observatories for tourists as well as installing gravity meters, infrared cameras, and magnetic-field sensors. UFO tourism is also popular in nearby Tolyatti, where visitors can see some of the world's largest crop circles

Bibliography

Chapter 1 – Ancient History of UFOs and Religion
    Early Egyptian and African Myths
        Wikipedia Encyclopedia Article "Pyramid Texts"
        Wikipedia Encyclopedia Article "Turin King List"
        Encyclopedia Britannica Article "Manetho"
    Paracas Skulls
        Gaia Article "What are the Paracas Skulls?"
        September 22, 2017
        "DNA Test reveal The Paracas Skulls are not
        Human" by Eva Knight 1/28/21
    Dogon mythology
        Gaia Article "Was the Sirius Star System Home to
        the Dogon African Tribe?" 10/ 13/ 19
    Religions and Aliens
        Wikipedia Encyclopedia Article "Bible"
    Who was Moses?
        "Moses and Akhenaten: The Secret History of
        Egypt at the Time of the Exodus" by Ahmed
        Osman October 1, 2002
    Ezekiel's Wheel within Wheel
        Bible History online "The Encampment"
    Where is haven?
        United Church of God "What Does the Bible Mean
        by The "Third Heaven"?" 1/25/2011
Chapter 2 – UFO History to 1947
    Brief UFO History
        "What Did the Ancients See? UFO's that Made an
        Impact on Early History" 4/11/17
        "10 Fascinating Early UFO Sightings" by Ronald
        Eayre March 28, 2017

*Educating Humanity Article "Earliest Know
Records of UFO and Alien Sightings" 8/30/ 11*

The Aurora UFO Crash of 1897

*Wikipedia Encyclopedia Article "Aurora, Texas,
UFO incident"*

The Battle of Los Angeles

*Wikipedia Encyclopedia Article "Battle of Los Angeles"
UFO Casebook "The Battle of Los Angeles" by BJ Booth
UFO Insight "The Battle of Los Angeles" First
Published: November 4, 2018*

Maury Island Incident of 1947

Website Weird U.S. "The Maury Island Incident"

Kenneth Arnold 1947 UFO Sighting

*Wikipedia Encyclopedia article "Kenneth Arnold
UFO sighting"*

Roswell UFO Crash

*Wikipedia Encyclopedia Article "Roswell UFO incident"
UFO Casebook Article "The Roswell UFO Crash (1,
2, 3)" January 12, 1991
"Roswell UFO Crash: There Were 2 Crashes, Not 1,
Says Ex-Air Force Official"
"Richard French, UFOs and Roswell" August 15, 2013
"EBE The Alien – The Sole Survivor" September 28, 2020*

FBI Director J. Edgar Hoover UFO Memo's

*UFO Explorations Article "J. Edgar Hoover's Saucer
Crash Secrets" published April 2011 by Anthony Bragalia
Popular Mechanics Article "Why So Many People
Are Reading This Old FBI Memo About UFOs" By
John Wenz January 7, 2016*

Chapter 3 – The UFO Conspiracy

The Extraterrestrial Accord

*"Eisenhower's 1954 Meeting with
Extraterrestrials" by Michael E. Salla, PhD 2/ 12/ 04
Exopolitics Article "1954 Greada Treaty"
"President Eisenhower at Holloman AFB?" by Art Campbell
"Deathbed Confession by former CIA agent on
UFOs" Feb 28, 2019
"Emenegger/Sandler/UFO Landing Film - Holloman
AFB" UFO Casebook Magazine 493.*

Majestic-12 and Special Projects

Aliens UFO Sightings Article "Extraterrestrial UFO
Are Rea: Ben Rich Lockheed Skunk Works Director
Admitted in his Deathbed Confession" May 8, 2012
Mufon UFO Journal May 2010 issue written by Tom Keller
Wikipedia Encyclopedia Article "Gary McKinnon"
"Solar Warden – The Secret Space Program" by
James Rink 8/12/ 20

Black triangle

Wikipedia Encyclopedia Article "Black triangle (UFO)"
"The TR-3B – A Real Life UFO" by Claudio Zorrospín 9/ 22/11

Antigravity Vehicles

Wikipedia Encyclopedia Article "Philip J. Corso"
UFO Digest Article "12 Kinds of Antigravity and
Reduced-Gravity" by Richard Boylan

Chapter 5 - Nuclear Facility's and UFOs

The Hanford Site

http://www.project1947.com/fig/hendershot.htm
http://www.nicap.org/reports/hanford.htm
Article by KOMO News "194 UFO sightings
reported in Washington State last year" January 7th 2020

UFOs over Chernobyl Nuclear Plant

Pravda Article "UFO Prevents Blast at Chernobyl
Nuclear Plant" 9/16/2002

UFOs over Fukushima Power Plant

Survival Article "UFOs over Fukushima Power
Plant" September 9, 2019

Chapter 6 - UFOs and Military Encounters

Malmstrom Air Force Base Incident of 1967

"Malmstrom Air Force Base Incident of 1967" by
Jim Klotz and Robert Salas 11/27/ 1996

Chilean Air Force 1978 Incident with Huge UFO

Inexplicata, Scott Corrales, editor / Ovnivisión
(Chile) / Revista TOC / Terra Chile

Rendlesham Forest UFO Incident of 1980

"The Decoded Binary Code" by Joe Luciano
"Vet says government has acknowledged he was
injured by UFO while on duty" 3/3/15
"Encounter in Rendlesham Forest" September 22nd, 2019
UFO Digest Article "THE RENDLESHAM MATRIX" by
Steve Erdmann 8/ 7/ 14

Index

fundamental forces 23

G

Gamma-ray band X-rays from a UFO 126

Gary McKinnon (Scottish systems administrator and hacker) 151

gaseous matter target 144

Gaza (ancient Egyptian City now located in the Palestinian territory) 14

GEIPAN (Groupe d'Étude des Phénomènes Aérospatiaux Non-Identifiés) 230, 231

Gemini IV 221

Gemini VII 222

Gen.32\
1-2 22

gendarmerie (France) 230, 231

General of the National Guard 242

General Relativity 23, 25

genetic disorder 56

genetic experimentation 58

genetic makeup of alien DNA 56

George Adamski (alien abductee) 246

George C. Marshall, General 61

George N. Raines, Captain (chief psychologist at the U.S. Naval Hospital at Bethesda) 98, 99

George Schulgen, Brigadier General 51

Georgetown University, Washington, D.C. 99

George Wilcox (Sheriff) 42

Gerald Anderson (Roswell UFO witness) 45

German Scientists 40

German technology 40

Germany 40

gigantic spaceship 226

gigantic, winged, and ghostly beings 266

GIMBAL video 187

Glendale, Arizona 237

Glenn Dennis (Roswell, New Mexico mortician) 46

Gliese Star Catalogue 259

globular star cluster M13 277

Gloucestershire, England Crop Circles 271

glow surrounding UFO's 125

gods 243, 247

Go Fast video 191

Golden Globe award 61

Golden Record 224

Gordon Cooper (Astronaut) 216

Gordon Gray (Secretary of the Army) 62

Government had no jurisdiction over Area 51) 59

gradiometer 158

Grady L. \ 45

Graves, Lieutenant 190

graveyard spiral 207

gravitational time dilation 139

gravitation Force 23

gravity 23, 24

gravity amplifiers 0 to 90° Phase Shifts = Lift or Repulsion 146

gravity amplifiers 90 to 180° Phase Shifts = Amount of Attraction 146

gravity as the propulsion medium 118

Gravity-controlled propulsion 142

Gravity Generators 143, 144, 145, 146

gravity wave generator for UFOs 143

gravity wave on the dimension of time 118

gravity wave vectors 147

Greada Treaty 58

Great Los Angeles Air Raid 30

Green Berets and Special Forces 208

Grey alien hormonal secretion 245

Grey aliens a genetic disorder 245

Grey alien skin 56, 245

Greys Aliens 26, 56, 57, 58, 119, 121, 208, 209, 243, 244, 245, 247,

CPSIA information can be obtained
at www.ICGtesting.com
Printed in the USA
BVHW091740251021
619847BV00016B/457/J

9 781649 617781